Integrating Europe
through Cooperation among Universities

Other volumes in the Higher Education Policy series

Study Abroad and Early Career
Experiences of Former ERASMUS Students
Friedhelm Maiworm and Ulrich Teichler
ISBN 1 85302 378 7
Higher Education Policy Series 35

Transition to Work
The Experiences of the ERASMUS Students
Ulrich Teichler and Friedhelm Maiworm
ISBN 1 85302 543 7
Higher Education Policy Series 28

Learning in Europe
The ERASMUS Experience
A Survey of the 1988–89 ERASMUS Students
Friedhelm Maiworm, Wolfgang Steube and Ulrich Teichler
ISBN 1 85302 543 7
Higher Education Policy Series 14

Higher Education and Work
John Brennan, Maurice Kogan and Ulrich Teichler
ISBN 1 85302 537 2
Higher Education Policy Series 23

Impacts of Study Abroad Programmes on Students and Graduates
Susan Cooper, Ulrich Teichler and Jerry Carlson
ISBN 1 85302 532 2
Higher Education Policy Series 11, Volume II

Higher Education in a Post-Binary Era
National Reforms and Institutional Responses
Edited by David Teather
ISBN 1 85302 425 2
Higher Education Policy Series 38

European Dimensions
Education, Training and the European Union
John Field
ISBN 1 85302 432 5
Higher Education Policy Series 39

Higher Education Policy Series 43

Integrating Europe through Cooperation among Universities

The Experiences of the TEMPUS Programme

Barbara Kehm

Friedhelm Maiworm

Albert Over

Robert D. Reisz

Wolfgang Steube

Ulrich Teichler

Jessica Kingsley Publishers
London and Philadelphia

The right of Barbara Kehm, Friedhelm Maiworm, Albert Over, Robert D. Reisz, Wolfgang Steube and Ulrich Teichler to be identified as author of this work has been asserted by them in accordance with the Copyright, Designs and Patents Act 1988.

First published in the United Kingdom in 1997 by
Jessica Kingsley Publishers Ltd
116 Pentonville Road
London N1 9JB, England
and
1900 Frost Road, Suite 101
Bristol, PA 19007, U S A

The information contained in the present study does not necessarily reflect either the position or views of the European Commission

Library of Congress Cataloging in Publication Data
A CIP catalogue record for this book is available from the Library of Congress

British Library Cataloguing in Publication Data
A CIP catalogue record for this book is available from the British Library

ISBN 1 85302 495 3

Printed and Bound in Great Britain by
Athenæum Press, Gateshead, Tyne and Wear

Contents

Acknowledgments

The authors of this study would like to express their gratitude to:

- the European Commission for permission to publish the findings of the evaluation studies
- Ms Christelle Leman in DG XXII for intensive reading and helpful comments on various versions of the manuscripts
- the Association for Empirical Studies in Kassel and the Centre for Research on Higher Education and Work, University of Kassel, for providing institutional support and backing
- the European Training Foundation in Torino for supplying huge amounts of data, copies and valuable documents and material
- the directors and staff of the TEMPUS offices in all TEMPUS partner countries in Central and Eastern Europe for their support, their patience in the face of our many questions and their information
- the many other individuals in the ministries and universities of the TEMPUS partner countries who were willing to give interviews and provided us with information
- Kristin Gagelmann, who turned our manuscripts into a proper text.

Chapter 1

The Rationale and Approach of the Study

1.1 International Cooperation in Europe

For more than a decade the European Commission has encouraged institutional cooperation and individual mobility in the field of education. The ERASMUS Programme, supporting cooperation and mobility in the field of higher education, has undoubtedly been one of the most successful programmes in this framework. Many higher education institutions all over Europe are actively developing strategies of internationalisation, thus integrating cooperation and mobility into an overall mission aimed at a renewal of teaching, learning and research with a view not only to European integration but to global economic and scientific activity as well.

The fall of the 'iron curtain' and the 'velvet revolutions' in Central and Eastern Europe, in 1989, opened the borders to the East for the first time after the Second World War. Many of the Central and Eastern European countries started immediately to rebuild their national and cultural identities on those values and norms prevalent up to the First World War and strongly oriented towards Western Europe. Democracy, market economy and reforms of their systems of education became large, looming projects. Help was needed especially for economic and social restructuring and renewal. Many countries all over the world tried to give support in the form of various programmes, expertise and advice, funds for special purposes channelled through foundations, etc.

The European Communities quickly decided about a support programme (Phare) to help with economic and social restructuring in Central and Eastern Europe. One of its elements became the TEMPUS Programme which is the subject of this study. TEMPUS is modelled on the ERASMUS Programme, supporting international cooperation of higher education institutions in the framework of joint projects and mobility. Since education plays an important role for economic and social renewal, TEMPUS was and still is intended to help the process of transformation in

1

a number of direct and indirect ways. In the meantime ten CEEC countries (all expect for Albania among those supported in the mid-1990s) have signed an association agreement and are in the process of pre-accession. Also Bosnia and the former Yugoslav Republic of Macedonia became eligible for TEMPUS support.

1.2   Context of the Study

The TEMPUS Programme was launched by the Council of the European Communities on 7 May 1990.[1] The legal basis for this decision was the EC Decision from 18 December 1989 referring to 'economic aid for Hungary and Poland', the so-called Phare Programme.[2] The number of countries eligible for economic aid under Phare was quickly extended to include also other Central and Eastern European countries which thus became TEMPUS partner countries as well. In April 1993, the Council of the European Communities decided to continue the TEMPUS Programme for a second period of four years (TEMPUS II). TEMPUS II ran from the academic year 1994/95 until 1998. A new Council Decision on November 21, 1996 extended the duration of TEMPUS II from 1998 to 2003.

The TEMPUS Programme is financed by the Phare Programme and intended to promote reforms of the higher education systems in the Central and Eastern European (CEE) partner countries eligible for Phare[4] and to support the adjustment of these countries to the needs of a market economy. The framework in which activities can be supported under TEMPUS requires a collaboration of higher education institutions from the CEE partner countries and the EU Member States. Enterprises and other organisations from both groups of countries can participate in TEMPUS as well. Higher education institutions, enterprises and organisations from the other G24 countries that are not EU Member States[5] also

---

1   Council Decision 90/233/EEC of 7 May 1990; OJL 131/21 of 23 May 1990.

2   Council Decision 89/3906/EEC of 18 December 1989; OJL 375 of 23 December 1989.

3   Council Decision 96/663/EC of 21 November 1996; OJL 306/36 of 28 November 1996.

4   In 1995, there were altogether eleven CEE countries receiving Phare aid that are TEMPUS partner countries: Albania, Bulgaria, the Czech Republic, Estonia, Hungary, Latvia, Lithuania, Poland, Romania, the Slovak Republic, and Slovenia.

5   Namely, Australia, Canada, Iceland, Japan, Liechtenstein, New Zealand, Nor-

have the opportunity to join in TEMPUS activities.[6] The collaboration takes place in the framework of project consortia and is based on cooperation, knowledge transfer, equipment aid, structural and curricular development, student and staff exchange.

In order to acquire information about the results of the TEMPUS Programme in terms of its implementation, administration and activities, the Council Decisions for each of the two phases of the programme required evaluations to be undertaken after the first half and at the end of each phase.[7] The results of these evaluations were supposed to serve as a basis for necessary adjustments within the next phase of the programme. Following the call for tender in July 1994, the European Commission awarded a contract to the Association for Empirical Studies (GES) in Kassel, Germany in cooperation with the Centre for Research on Higher Education and Work at the University of Kassel to carry out the evaluation of the first phase of TEMPUS (TEMPUS I) lasting from 1990 until 1994. The assignment was extended to include the evaluation of the first two years of TEMPUS II (1994/95 – 1995/96) as well.

Two separate reports[8] were submitted to the European Commission – one containing the findings and results of the evaluation of TEMPUS I, the other those of the evaluation of the first two years of TEMPUS II.

The study presented here is an integrated version of these two reports. By using similar methods for both evaluation exercises the opportunity was provided to take into account the transition between the programme's

---

way, Switzerland, Turkey, and the USA. Since the beginning of TEMPUS II, Cyprus and Malta also are part of this group.

6 Cf. Art. 9 of the Council Decision 90/233/EEC.

7 Council Decision 90/233/EEC, Art. 11 from 7 May 1990; OJL 131/21 from 23 May 1990. Council Decision 93/246/EEC, Art. 11 from 29 April 1993; OJL 112/37 from 6 May 1993.

8 Both reports were published by the European Commission in a mimeographed version as Working Documents. The evaluation of TEMPUS I caries the title 'Evaluation of the First Phase of TEMPUS 1990 – 1994' and the number XXII/1182/96-EN. The evaluation of the first half of TEMPUS II carries the title 'Evaluation of the First Two Years of TEMPUS II 1994 – 1996' and the number XXII/183/96-EN. In addition, the summary of the evaluation of TEMPUS I was published by the European Commission as an official document in all official languages of the EU. The English version carries the title 'Evaluation of the First Phase of TEMPUS. 1990/91 – 1993/94. Report from the Commission to the Council, the European Parliaments, the Economic and Social Committee and the Committee of the Regions'. Brussels, 20.09.1996 COM (96) 428 final (Office for Official Publications of the European Communities).

two periods, the changes and differences and the eventual adjustments of the programme in the face of a rapid pace of transition. The study was carried out between July 1995 and February 1996.

1.3 Aims and Objectives

The object of this study is to provide evidence of the programme's intentions and actual achievements, that is, to support renewal and reforms in the field of higher education in the CEE partner countries and to contribute to economic restructuring.

To achieve the goals of providing a comprehensive evaluation and an accurate overview, a description and analysis of the programme activities is necessary according to their structure, their administrative support and their actual realisation in the higher education institutions. Additional emphasis is put on the relationship of TEMPUS activities to the structural changes within the higher education institutions and on the role of various national authorities and key actors involved in policy formation for TEMPUS. The study focuses on the following lines of inquiry:

* *The policy framework of the TEMPUS Programme*: What are the general procedures of policy formation and decision-making for the TEMPUS Programme? Who are the major actors in policy formation on the national and the supra-national level? What role do they actually play? How are the national priorities in the CEE partner countries established and how do they function? Has the growing importance of national priorities strengthened the coherence between TEMPUS activities, national education policies and the overall Phare objectives?

* *The administration of the TEMPUS Programme on the national and the supra-national level*: Are the procedures established for TEMPUS administration functioning well? What are the major tasks of the EC TEMPUS Office and − since 1995 − the TEMPUS Department at the European Training Foundation (ETF) in Torino and the National TEMPUS Offices in the CEE partner countries? In which way are tasks and responsibilities divided between them? What is the quantity and quality of information about TEMPUS-related issues? What is the quality of advice and support for applicants? Are the results of TEMPUS activities disseminated in an organised way?

* *The participating institutions and institutional settings*: What kind of institutions participate in TEMPUS? In which countries are the institutions located? Which role is played by size and type of higher education institutions from CEE partner countries for participation in

TEMPUS? Which is the role of the central level of higher education institutions in fostering TEMPUS activities? What kind of support is provided to TEMPUS Joint European Projects by the institutions? Have TEMPUS activities fostered managerial and administrative reforms in the institutions?

- *The financial conditions of TEMPUS Joint European Projects (JEPs)*: What is the proportion of the TEMPUS budget spent on JEPs? How is the overall budget assessed by partners in the JEPs? What are the major financial problems JEP partners and the central level of institutions have experienced? Can serious changes be observed in the amount of the TEMPUS budget at the national level?

- *The cooperation within the JEPs*: What is the role played by partners from Western and CEE countries in initiating the establishment of JEPs? What kind of prior contacts did the JEP partners have among each other? What are the reasons for participation in JEPs? How many partners participate in JEPs? In which language(s) do the partners communicate? From whom do the partners receive information about the TEMPUS Programme?

- *The administration of the JEPs*: In which countries are the JEP management functions, coordinator and contractor, located? How many hours per week do the partners spend on administrative work related to TEMPUS? What kind of information related to the overall administration of the JEP is available to the partners? On what basis is the JEP grant administered?

- *The educational and infrastructural activities*: What kind of educational activities (e.g., cooperative measures in the field of teaching and education, structural development, staff and student mobility) are undertaken within the JEPs? What are the objectives of the individual activities? Are there preferences for individual activities? Can changes be noted in these preferences? With which subject areas are the JEPs concerned? What major difficulties were encountered? What use is made of newly introduced measures of the TEMPUS Programme?

- *Outcomes and impacts of TEMPUS*: To what extent are the envisaged goals of TEMPUS realised? How do the JEP partners assess the impact on the targeted department or institution? Are there synergetic effects among the various educational activities? Are there spin-off activities from the activities of the JEPs? Do the JEP partners continue their cooperation after the end of TEMPUS support for their JEP? Was the cooperation between universities and industry strengthened? Was a relationship established between Phare and TEMPUS?

1.4 Project Design

In order to ensure a high validity of results a combination of various methods and approaches was chosen. The findings of the two surveys are based on representative samples, and a complete coverage of all eleven CEE partner countries involved in TEMPUS was achieved through site-visits and interviews. In addition, extensive analyses of available documents and data bases were made. The following approaches and methods were applied in the framework of our study:

- A wide-ranging analysis of the TEMPUS data bases existing at the European Training Foundation (ETF) in Torino responsible for administering TEMPUS was carried out to provide a quantitative description of the various institutions and measures involved in TEMPUS.

- Team members travelled to Albania, Bulgaria, the Czech Republic, Estonia, Hungary, Latvia, Lithuania, Poland, Romania, Slovenia, and the Slovak Republic. In each of these countries intensive interviews were conducted with the director of the National TEMPUS Office (NTO), a representative of the Ministry of Education responsible for TEMPUS, the national Phare Coordinator, a representative of the EU Delegation responsible for Phare (in some countries) and academic experts involved in the national assessment of TEMPUS applications. In addition, between four and six higher education institutions were visited in each of the CEE countries interviewing the rector or vice-rector responsible for international relations, in some cases the director of the international relations office, academic staff members acting as JEP partners, contractors and/or coordinators, and staff members and students having been abroad and supported by TEMPUS mobility grants. Higher education institutions were selected according to the following criteria: large and small institutions, institutions located in the capital and located in the province, state and private institutions, universities with a full range of subjects and specialised higher education institutions, institutions with a high, a medium and a small number of JEPs.

- Telephone interviews were conducted with the National TEMPUS Contact Points in all EU Member States responsible for advice and information of Western partner institutions participating in TEMPUS.

- A standardised written survey was carried out of all JEP contractors, co-ordinators and partners from CEE countries, from EU Member States as well as from G24 countries within the TEMPUS I period.

- A second standardised written survey was addressed to the central level (rectors and administrators) of all higher education institutions in

the CEE partner countries which were involved in TEMPUS I and
TEMPUS II.

• A wide range and variety of existing TEMPUS documents published
either by the European Commission or provided by the key actors for
TEMPUS who were interviewed in the framework of our visits to all
CEE partner countries was taken into account for context information
on TEMPUS.

1.5 Structure and Content of the Study

Work on the evaluation study was resumed in July 1995 and originally
intended to cover the first phase of the TEMPUS Programme (TEMPUS
I). The assignment was subsequently extended to include an evaluation of
programme activities during the first half of TEMPUS II.[9] The next eight
chapters of this study present our findings in the following sequence:

• Chapter 2 is a description of the TEMPUS Programme providing *basic
information* about its aims and objectives, its structure and activities,
its regulations and criteria for support, its administrative procedures,
and changes in the measures and activities eligible for support. This
chapter takes a large number and variety of official TEMPUS documents into account.

• A *statistical overview* of the TEMPUS Programme is presented in
chapter 3. The overview is primarily based on our analysis of the ETF
data bases and complemented by additional empirical information.
Taken into account are the following features of the structural and
quantitative development of the Joint European Projects: the institutional recipients of TEMPUS support, the quantitative expansion of
TEMPUS activities, the profile of networks and participating organisations as well as the composition by country, the subject areas and
activities supported by TEMPUS, student and staff mobility, the financial support for Joint European Projects and some figures on Complementary Measures and Youth Exchange activities.

• The *policy formation and administration* of the TEMPUS Programme
are analysed in chapter 4. It is based on our interviews with key TEM-
PUS actors carried out in the CEE partner countries but also considers
a variety of TEMPUS documents provided by these actors. An empha-

---

9 Parallel evaluation of the first two years of TEMPUS II using the same meth-
odological instruments and approaches as for the evaluation of TEMPUS I.

sis is put on the administrative and decision-making processes which have been established for TEMPUS policy formation and operation on the national level and the role played by the various actors in these areas, including also the tasks and responsibilities of the national TEMPUS Contact Points in the EU Member States. The chapter concludes with an assessment of policy developments and the functioning of the operational system during TEMPUS I.

- An *analysis of the Joint European Projects* (JEPs) is presented in chapter 5. The findings are based on a survey addressed to all JEP partners involved in activities supported under TEMPUS I (JEP questionnaire). After a reminder letter, altogether 1,710 valid questionnaires were returned – a response rate of 44.7 per cent. The analysis includes 1,696 JEP questionnaires, among them 694 from Central and Eastern European countries and 1,002 from Western countries. A number of issues are addressed in this chapter concerning the persons in charge of TEMPUS activities, the profile of participating institutions, departments and networks, the quality of information about TEMPUS, the application and award procedures, the quality of cooperation among partners within the JEPs, the objectives of JEP activities and the actual activities which were carried out. The chapter concludes with an overall assessment of TEMPUS activities by the JEP partners and a discussion of problems and achievements.

- In chapter 6 we analyse the TEMPUS involvement and the perception of TEMPUS by the *higher education institutions from CEE partner countries* participating in TEMPUS. The findings are based on a survey addressing the central level (rectors, vice-rectors, top administrators) of these institutions (institutional questionnaire). In addition, results of our interviews carried out at CEE higher education institutions are taken into consideration as well. After a reminder letter, altogether 113 valid questionnaires were returned - a response rate of 44 per cent. Our analysis covers the following issues: a profile of the participating institutions, changes and reforms which were introduced, the degree of involvement in TEMPUS and the perceived contributions of TEMPUS to innovation and change, the role of the central institutional level with respect to TEMPUS activities, perceptions of the supra-institutional setting and a general assessment of outcomes and impacts of TEMPUS activities.

- Chapter 7 will discuss the most important *changes of activities* in the six years of programme operations covered by this study and address patterns of policy formation and administration, the development of national priorities and their role for the TEMPUS activities, as well as impacts of priorities and actual activities for strengthening the central level of higher education institutions. The chapter combines the results of our site-visits with some findings of the institutional questionnaire and the document analyses.

- Chapter 8 presents a comprehensive discussion and assessment of the *major achievements and problems* of TEMPUS activities as they have been perceived by respondents to the JEP questionnaire as well as to the institutional questionnaire. The chapter includes the views of respondents as regards TEMPUS outcomes and impacts.

- Chapter 9 concludes with a *final assessment* of what can be regarded as the most important issues for further consideration concerning the future of the TEMPUS Programme by the authors of the study.

Chapter 2

Basic Information on the TEMPUS Programme

2.1 History of Key Decisions

In the aftermath of the political changes of 1989 in Central and Eastern Europe, the Council of Europe agreed to launch a comprehensive programme of practical assistance and expertise to help the Central and Eastern European countries concerned in the restructuring of their economies and political systems. Thus, the Phare Programme was inaugurated in December 1989, providing a framework for European Community assistance to support the economic and social reform processes in Central and Eastern Europe. Phare operations began in 1990.

Phare consists of a number of sub-programmes which are divided into four groups: national programmes, multi-country programmes, cross-border programmes and the democracy programme. Reforms in nine economic and social priority areas are supported in the framework of these four groups of programmes:

- private sector development and enterprise support
- education, health, training and research
- humanitarian and food aid
- agricultural restructuring
- environment and nuclear safety
- infrastructure (energy, transport and telecommunications)
- social development and employment
- public institutions and administrative reforms
- others.

The field of higher education and training had already been identified by the Central and Eastern European countries as a priority area when the Council of Ministers asked the European Commission in December 1989 to present a proposal for appropriate measures in this field to be effected within the Phare framework. The proposal became known as the TEM-

PUS Programme, which constitutes a class of its own among the Phare sub-programmes.

In January 1990, the Commission submitted two proposals to the Council and the Parliament: the TEMPUS scheme and the establishment of a European Training Foundation. TEMPUS stood for Trans-European Mobility Programme for University Studies and was adopted by the Council of Ministers on 7 May 1990, within a perspective of five years for an initial pilot phase of three years beginning on 1 July 1990. A later Council decision extended the pilot phase for one year, until the end of June 1994. The Council also adopted the regulation to set up a European Training Foundation to assist in the areas of vocational training, continuing education and management training. The European Training Foundation (ETF) took up its work at the beginning of 1995 in Torino. At the same time the EC TEMPUS Office in Brussels was dissolved. Instead a special unit was established as the TEMPUS Department within the ETF, which took over its tasks and responsibilities.

Initially, only Poland and Hungary were eligible for aid under the Phare Programme and, accordingly, under TEMPUS. However, the Phare Programme quickly expanded, thus also making more and more Central and Eastern European countries eligible for TEMPUS support. In September 1990, Bulgaria, Czechoslovakia, Yugoslavia and East-Germany joined Phare. Aid to East-Germany ceased after unification. In 1991, Albania and Romania were added and aid to Yugoslavia was suspended. In 1992, the three Baltic States, Estonia, Latvia and Lithuania, joined the Phare Programme as well as Slovenia. Finally, in 1993, former Czechoslovakia was replaced by two countries being eligible for Phare aid, the Czech and the Slovak Republic, thus bringing up the number of CEE partner countries in TEMPUS to eleven.

The Council Decision of 29 April 1993 established a second phase of TEMPUS (TEMPUS II), now being called 'Trans-European Cooperation Scheme for Higher Education'. Starting from the academic year 1994/95, TEMPUS II was expected to be in operation until 1998 and was eventually extended in 1996 to be in operation until 2000. In addition to TEMPUS–Phare addressing the Central and Eastern European partner countries, a similar scheme was set up for the republics of the former Soviet Union eligible for Tacis aid, namely Belarus, the Russian Federation and the Ukraine. Like Phare, Tacis is an aid programme to give technical assistance to the countries of the former Soviet Union according to the specific social and economic needs of these countries. TEMPUS–Tacis also addresses the needs of higher education reforms in the countries eligible under Tacis. TEMPUS–Tacis is not part of the evaluation presented here.

In November 1992, the Commission and the national Phare coordinators of all CEE partner countries agreed on two issues concerning the last year of the TEMPUS I pilot phase:

- Funds allocated to TEMPUS for the 1993/94 activities would have to be used primarily to pay off the remaining financial liabilities for JEPs operating in their second and third year of funding in order to start TEMPUS II in 1994/95 with a clean slate
- Funding for JEPs on the basis of annual renewal applications up to the maximum duration of three years was substituted by a provision of the full three-year support for all JEPs being selected to start in 1993/94.

The 'financial overhang' of second and third year JEPs and the decision to make provisions for the full three-year support for all JEPs newly accepted in 1993/94 had two important consequences:

- The total budget for TEMPUS in 1993/94 increased by almost one third as compared to 1992/93 (cf. Table 2.1)
- The 1993/94 call for JEP applications was cancelled completely in Bulgaria, the Czech Republic, Slovakia, Poland and Romania, and in the remaining CEE countries the number of newly accepted JEPs starting in the academic year 1993/94 was exceptionally low.

For a country like Romania, for example, this decision and its consequences meant that during the four-year pilot phase of TEMPUS I there were only two rounds JEP applications and selections.

2.2 Aims and Objectives

The TEMPUS objectives are based on the objectives of the Phare Programme. This causes a certain ambiguity in the objectives of TEMPUS, which was critically discussed in the first TEMPUS evaluation done by Coopers & Lybrand: TEMPUS is expected to achieve positive impacts in the fields of economic restructuring as well as higher education reform.

The main objectives of TEMPUS I as laid down in Article 4 of the Council Decision from May 1990 are the following:

- to facilitate the coordination of the provision of assistance to the CEE partner countries in the field of exchange and mobility, particularly for university students and teachers, whether such assistance is provided by the Community, its Member States or the third countries of the G24 group
- to contribute to the improvement of training in the CEE partner countries and to encourage their cooperation with partners in the European

Community, taking into account the need to ensure the widest possible participation of all the regions of the Community in such actions
- to increase opportunities for the teaching and learning in the CEE partner countries of those languages used in the Community and covered by the LINGUA Programme, and vice-versa
- to enable students from the CEE partner countries to spend a specific period of study at university or to undertake industry placements within the Member States of the Community, while ensuring equality of opportunity for male and female students as regards participation in such mobility
- to enable students from the Community to spend a similar type of period of study or placement in a CEE partner country
- to promote increased exchanges and mobility of teaching staff and trainers as part of the cooperation process.[1]

The major aims of the TEMPUS Programme, namely to contribute to higher education reform and renewal in the CEE partner countries and to support economic restructuring as promoted in the framework of Phare, have remained the same for TEMPUS II.

Article 4 of the Council Decision specifies as an essential objective of TEMPUS II 'the promotion of the development of the higher education systems in the eligible countries through a cooperation with partners from all Member States of the Community, as part of the overall objectives and guidelines of the Phare Programme in the context of economic and social reform'. Within the framework of this overall objective the following areas are specified for which TEMPUS support may be awarded:
- issues of curriculum development and overhaul in priority areas;
- the reform of higher education structures and institutions and their management;
- the development of skill-related training to address specific higher and advanced level skill shortages during economic reform, in particular, through improved and extended links with industry.

Overall aims and objectives of TEMPUS II as well as the description of measures and eligible activities in the annex to the Council decision point at a shift in emphasis with regard to the following aspects of the programme:
- The reform aims to be supported by means of the TEMPUS Programme are adjusted to the prevailing needs of the individual CEE countries.

---

1   OJL 131/22 from 23 May 1990, Article 4.

- Under TEMPUS II, structural reform projects on the level of higher education institutions and in the context of reform policies for the national higher education systems are more clearly emphasised than under TEMPUS I.

- The overall aims of the programme as well as the framework within which TEMPUS support is awarded are specified and legally documented to a higher degree than in TEMPUS I.

- The implementation and realisation of the TEMPUS Programme on the national level in the CEE partner countries is supposed to take social and economic reform requirements more strongly into account.

2.3 Funding of TEMPUS

TEMPUS is funded by the CEE countries from within the allocation they receive under the Phare Programme. The Phare budget for each of the CEE partner countries is determined annually by the European Commission on the basis of fixed criteria and after consultation with the national authorities of the partner countries. The disposition of funds within the national Phare budget is determined by the national authorities on the basis of national indicative programmes which are developed according to the framework of objectives and aims to be achieved with the help of Phare. A certain proportion of the Phare budget is allocated to TEMPUS on an annual basis by the national authorities in consultation with the European Commission. The national authorities of the CEE partner countries involved in this process are the Education Ministries, the national Phare coordinators, other Ministries involved in Phare activities and as a rule − to decide about the final version of the proposed allocations − the Council of Ministers.

Between 1990 and 1994, the European Union made available from its budget 4,283 million ECU to finance the Phare Programme. The Phare country shares are determined on the basis of population, gross domestic product and qualitative criteria. Poland, Hungary and Romania receive the largest share of Phare aid.

In 1990, an initial TEMPUS budget of 20 MECU was earmarked for Poland and Hungary. When Czechoslovakia and East-Germany joined TEMPUS in October 1990 this budget was increased by a further 5 MECU. For 1991/92, when three additional countries joined TEMPUS, a budget of 55.5 MECU was made available and additionally increased by the inclusion of 15 MECU from the Phare Regional Fund. The Phare Regional Fund mainly served to finance a small number of 'regional' JEPs, involving more than one partner country from Central and Eastern Europe.

The TEMPUS budget of the initial four years, i.e. between 1990/91 and 1993/94, for each eligible country is shown in Table 2.1. It also indicates the percentage for TEMPUS of the respective country's Phare budget.[2]

The decision-making process to determine the TEMPUS budget involves a complex and decentralised procedure of negotiation and consultation (cf. Chart 2.1). As a rule, the Education Ministers of the CEE partner countries propose a draft budget for TEMPUS based on an estimate of necessary funds to finance running TEMPUS projects and an envisaged number of new projects to be accepted. This draft proposal is submitted to the national Phare coordinator in the CEE country, who is either a member of a ministry or part of a unit in the Council of Ministers. Following the decisions on the national level, there is a process of consultation with the Phare Operational Service of the Directorate General I (External Relations) of the European Commission. A further step in this decision-making process involves consultation with the Phare Management Committee in which all EU Member States are represented.

In 1994/95, the first year of TEMPUS II, a shift from annual to multi-annual funding for Joint European Projects (JEPs) was introduced. Once a JEP application was selected for TEMPUS support the full three-year grant was provided, although paid out on an annual basis and depending on the approval of the annual activity report and the submission and approval of a revised budget plan. In order to make appropriate provisions for the financial means necessary for this shift, the call for applications had been cancelled in the majority of CEE partner countries in the last year of TEMPUS I. This created the opportunity for TEMPUS II to start with a clean slate, that is with no 'debts' resulting from financial obligations for JEPs having been accepted in the period of TEMPUS I. The shift to multi-annual funding was thus organised in such a way that it did not influence the number of newly established JEPs or the amount of financial support awarded to them in TEMPUS II.

---

2   A similar budget breakdown for the first two years of TEMPUS II was not available at the time this survey was conducted.

Table 2.1
Development of the TEMPUS Budget (in MECU and as percentage of the national Phare budget)

	1990/91		1991/92		1992/93		1993/94	
	TEMPUS Budget in MECU	TEMPUS Budget in % of Phare Budget	TEMPUS Budget in MECU	TEMPUS Budget in % of Phare Budget	TEMPUS Budget in MECU	TEMPUS Budget in % of Phare Budget	TEMPUS Budget in MECU	TEMPUS Budget in % of Phare Budget
Albania	–	–	–	–	1.2	16.7	2.5	8.3
Bulgaria	–	–	5.0	3.1	8.0	9.9	15.0	16.7
Czechoslovakia	3.7	10.9	9.0	7.5	13.0	13.0	–	–
Czech Republic	–	–	–	–	–	–	8.0	13.3
Estonia	–	–	–	–	1.0	10.0	1.5	12.5
GDR	0.9	2.7	–	–	–	–	–	–
Hungary	6.2	6.9	12.0	10.0	16.0	16.0	16.0	16.0
Latvia	–	–	–	–	1.5	10.0	2.0	11.0
Lithuania	–	–	–	–	1.5	7.5	2.5	10.0
Poland	12.4	6.2	13.5	6.1	26.0	13.0	35.0	15.6
Romania	–	–	10.0	11.1	13.0	14.3	18.0	13.8
Slovak Republic	–	–	–	–	–	–	5.0	12.5
Slovenia	–	–	–	–	2.3	25.0	2.5	25.0
Yugoslavia	–	–	6.0	–	–	–	–	–
Phare Regional Funds	–	–	15.0	–	12.5	–	10.3	–

Chart 2.1
The Co-Decision-Making Process on the TEMPUS Budget

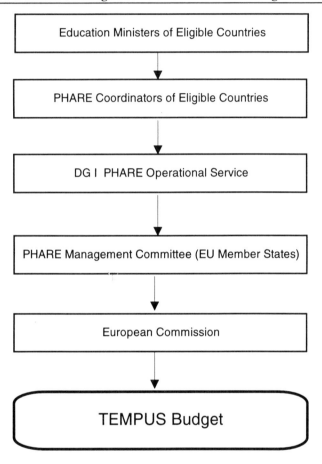

2.4 Modes of Administration

The administration of the TEMPUS Programme is a decentralised activity involving key actors on various levels. It remained basically the same in TEMPUS I and TEMPUS II. Overall responsibility for the TEMPUS Programme was given to the European Commission's Task Force Human

Resources, Education, Training and Youth, which is now the Directorate General XXII (DG XXII). TEMPUS is managed on the basis of the guidelines adopted annually. There is a close liaison between the Task Force/DG XXII and the Phare Operational Service of DG I with regard to TEMPUS.

On the Community level the implementation of the TEMPUS Programme and all relevant programme decisions are assisted by the TEMPUS Management Committee consisting of two representatives of each EU Member State and chaired by the TEMPUS representative of the European Commission. The Committee also assists the Commission in establishing the general guidelines governing TEMPUS, including the financial guidelines, all questions relating to the geographical and content related balance of TEMPUS activities and arrangements for monitoring and evaluation of the programme.

For technical assistance in the management of the programme an EC TEMPUS Office was established, first in Brussels. Since 1995 a department of the European Training Foundation (ETF) in Torino has taken over the technical assistance for the programme. The ETF TEMPUS Department took up its work shortly after the beginning of TEMPUS II. The EC TEMPUS Office/ETF TEMPUS Department provides technical assistance and advice to the Commission in the overall implementation of the TEMPUS Programme. In particular, the Office/Department is responsible for the design, preparation and distribution of official documentation, for providing support to the Commission throughout the selection process as well as for the issue and follow-up of contracts and grant payments. General monitoring and day to day advice and help for the programme as well as project management in the CEE partner countries is provided by the so-called 'country responsibles' in the EC TEMPUS Office/ETF TEMPUS Department.

In each Member State of the European Union a National Contact Point was established. It is expected to provide assistance, information and advice to all institutions and organisations interested in participating in the programme.

In each of the CEE partner countries a National TEMPUS Office (NTO) was established, responsible for the implementation of TEMPUS in the country and providing all necessary help and support to participating institutions. The NTOs have also gradually become involved in some aspects of the assessment of applications and in the monitoring of running projects. All NTOs work in close cooperation with the Education Ministry of their country on the one hand and the 'country responsibles' of the ETF TEMPUS Department on the other. They have gradually acquired an increasingly influential role for the steering of the TEMPUS Programme at the national level of the CEE countries. The legal status of the NTOs varies from country to country, the most common frameworks being either a semi-autonomous foundation with a board consisting of all political key actors involved in TEMPUS (e.g. national Phare coordinator, representative of the Ministry of Education, representatives of the universities, sometimes representatives of other ministries, etc.) or a department or unit of the respective Ministry of Education.

The ETF TEMPUS Department regularly organises meetings of the directors of all NTOs to coordinate management, information flows, selection processes, and exchange of information on specific TEMPUS projects. These meetings also aim at a progressive development of common procedures in all CEE countries, including transfer of comparable data on applicants and projects and the establishment of a common data base and assessment procedure. All NTOs have been supplied with comparable hardware and software for standardisation of data processing and most of their staff have been trained for short periods in the EC TEMPUS Office in Brussels or in the ETF TEMPUS Department in Torino.

2.5   Measures of the Support Scheme and Their Development

The TEMPUS Programme consists of three actions, each of which covers a number of activities. Action 1 provides support for Joint European Projects (JEPs), Action 2 provides support for Individual Mobility Grants (IMGs), and Action 3 provides support for Complementary Activities or Measures (CMEs). In addition, there is some funding for other activities like monitoring and external evaluations.

2.5.1   Joint European Projects (Action 1)

Joint European Projects (JEPs) are consortia of at least one institution of higher education from a CEE partner country and partner organisations from at least two different EU Member States, one of which must be a higher education institution. JEP grants are designed to promote the development and reform of higher education in the CEE countries and to encourage cooperation between higher education institutions of the CEE countries and higher education institutions, enterprises and other organisations of the EU Member States. Institutions, organisations and enterprises from G24 countries may participate as partners in a JEP consortium. Between 1990/91 and 1993/94 the range of activities supported in the framework of JEPs gradually broadened.

In 1990/91 JEP activities eligible for support were divided into three groups:

(1) Cooperative education/training actions: these included (a) the development and organisation of mobility programmes for students, teachers or staff of enterprises from CEE countries to undertake a period of study, a placement in industry, or a teaching or training assignment in the European Community and vice versa; (b) curriculum development activities involving the transfer of education/training knowledge between partners on a trans-European basis, including review and restructuring of complete curricula, development of teaching material, and development of multi-media education and training; (c) continuing education and retraining schemes for higher education teachers and other trainers in priority subject areas identified by the CEE countries and for secondary education teachers in the form of short intensive courses with participants from the CEE countries as well as from EU Member States and the development of open and distance learning schemes in the CEE partner countries.

(2) Structural development of higher education: this included (a) the creation of new or the restructuring of existing higher education centres or institutions; (b) the upgrading of facilities such as university libraries, teaching laboratories, teacher centres, documentation centres, etc. through the provision of equipment, materials and advice; (c) the development of universities' capacities to cooperate with industry through the establishment of technology transfer units, education/ training and consultancy advice.

(3) Sector-specific actions: these included (a) the development of education/training capacities at higher education levels in priority areas identified by the CEE partner countries through development of teaching material, exchange and training/retraining programmes; (b) the creation of new teaching and training posts in priority areas.

In 1993/94, the last year of TEMPUS I, there were two types of JEPs, one called Structural JEP (S-JEP) and the other called Mobility JEP (M-JEP). JEP activities eligible for support were divided into five groups:

(1) Cooperative education and training actions: (a) continuing education and retraining schemes for higher education teachers; (b) short intensive courses; (c) development of open and distance learning capability.

(2) Structural development of higher education: (a) creation of new or restructuring of existing higher education centres or institutions; (b) curriculum development activities; (c) upgrading of facilities including the provision of equipment.

(3) Development of universities' capacities to cooperate with industry: (a) curriculum development activities in cooperation with enterprises, including the creation of courses in priority areas relevant for the process of economic restructuring, substantial periods of student placement and exchange of university/industry personnel; (b) industrial placements for undergraduate students and young graduates; (c) exchange of staff between universities and enterprises; (d) establishment of appropriate service structures to encourage cooperation with industry and cooperative ventures in training and research; (e) provision of consultative advice to enterprises through university-based small business centres.

(4) Student and teacher mobility (M-JEP): (a) student mobility for a period of study abroad as an integral part of their degree course; (b) university staff (teachers and administrators) mobility for a period of teaching, studying or retraining abroad. M-JEPs were introduced in 1993/94.

(5) Regional activities: these included two or more CEE countries from Central or Eastern Europe cooperating in the framework of one JEP; (a) development of cooperative education/training actions, in particular curriculum development in common priority areas (e.g. environmental problems, agricultural practices); (b) development of capacities at higher education level, designed to deal with common regional problems. Regional activities were introduced in 1992/93.

TEMPUS II only distinguishes between Structural JEPs and Mobility JEPs. Eligible activities under these two types of JEPs were redefined and some new emphases were identified. Additionally, a special type of JEP, called JEP+, was introduced in the first year of TEMPUS II but discontinued one year later. JEP+ projects were proposed and their objectives defined by the national authorities of the CEE partner countries to support in a concrete way the development of national policies and strategies for the higher education system as a whole.

In 1994/95, the first year of TEMPUS II, the eligible activities supported in the framework of Structural JEPs can be divided into three groups:

(1) Cooperative education and training activities including notably: (a) curricular development and reform; (b) the development of universities' capacities to provide continuing education and retraining; (c) the provision of short, intensive courses; and (d) the development of multimedia education.

(2) Structural activities related to the reform and development of higher education including: (a) the restructuring of the management of higher education institutions and systems; and (b) the upgrading of facilities.

(3) Promotion of university/industry relations, supported by activities for: (a) the development of universities' capacities to cooperate with industry; and (b) cooperative university/industry training actions.

Within all Structural JEPs grants can be awarded for equipment necessary to carry out the project activities.

Regional activities which were supported in TEMPUS I were undertaken in the framework of Structural JEPs in which institutions from more than one CEE country cooperated together with Western partners. As they had to comply with the national priorities of two CEE countries and pass their respective assessment procedures, the success of applications for JEPs with regional activities had always been difficult to achieve. Regional activities were supported by a special Phare regional fund. When this fund was dissolved the number of regional JEPs diminished gradually until they constituted less than one per cent of all JEPs awarded TEMPUS support. Regional activities were no longer eligible for JEP support since the end of TEMPUS I. They were re-introduced in 1996/97.

For the academic years 1995/96 and 1996/97, JEP activities have been strengthened and refined by the introduction of overall objectives with a number of eligible activities subordinated to them. New emphasis is put on the objective to review and improve university management. In general, TEMPUS support is more strongly related to structural reforms addressing the central institutional level. In 1995/96 four overall objectives for Structural JEPs were introduced on top of the national priorities; a fifth one was addressed at Mobility JEPs. Each application clearly has to fit one of these objectives:

- introduction of new degree courses or restructuring of existing degree courses and their contents
- review and improvement of university management
- creation of new institutions or faculties or restructuring of existing institutions or faculties
- development of universities' structural capacities to cooperate with enterprises and other local bodies; in particular, to introduce or improve universities' delivery of continuing education.

The overall objective introduced by the EU and addressed to Mobility JEPs is the creation of a network for the organisation of student mobility. Within Mobility Joint European Projects support can be awarded for students spending a period of study abroad. Contents of studies abroad are supposed to be closely related to the students' degree programme. Eligible activities in the framework of Mobility JEPs are:

- the creation of a network for the organisation of student mobility in order to facilitate the practical arrangements
- student mobility grants as an integral part of the student's degree, including study periods abroad as well as practical placements in enterprises
- staff mobility for the purpose of (a) retraining of academic staff from CEE countries to provide better support for the organisation of student mobility; (b) teaching/training assignments for partners from CEE countries as well as for partners from EU Member States in their respective partner institutions; (c) participation in intensive courses.

Mobility JEPs also provide the possibility to apply for TEMPUS support regarding the development of teaching material based on an assessment of the needs of students involved in such JEPs.

In the first year of TEMPUS II projects were supported in the framework of a special JEP-type called JEP+. JEP+ projects provided national authorities of the CEE partner countries with a means to achieve practical aims in accordance with their national higher education policy. They had to pre-define the objectives as well as identify the local partners for such JEPs. As eligible activities in the framework of these JEP+ projects were defined nationally, their scope was relatively broad although clearly directed at the institutional level of higher education. Standing out were activities related to internationalisation and to the creation of computerised information networks. Other projects were concerned with managerial and administrative issues of the central institutional level.

2.5.2 Mobility Grants for Staff and Students (Action 2)

Mobility grants served to support mobility of university staff, staff of enterprises and students in both directions, that is, from East to West and from West to East. In the second year of TEMPUS I the Individual Mobility Grants (IMGs) for students were discontinued. From that time on student mobility was only supported within the framework of a JEP. Individual Mobility Grants in the first year of TEMPUS I distinguished between staff and students:

(1) Grants for teaching and administrative staff from universities and for trainers from enterprises: (a) for teaching and training activities in a host organisation abroad for periods from one week up to one academic year; (b) for practical placements abroad undertaken by university teachers or administrators for periods from one up to six months;

(c) visit grants for periods from one week up to one month in order to prepare JEPs, collect and prepare teaching material, participate in short language courses, congresses, scientific symposia and seminars in priority areas, exchange expert advice on teaching or higher education management.

In 1993/94, the last year of TEMPUS I, IMGs for practical placements were replaced by a more general category of IMGs for retraining and updating of knowledge of university staff from CEE countries for periods from one week up to one year. These IMGs were awarded to follow doctorate-level post-graduate courses, short language courses or training in enterprises in an EU Member State.

(2) Grants for undergraduate and postgraduate students: (a) for a study period at a higher education institution abroad for periods from three months up to one academic year and longer periods for CEE students seeking a further qualification in an EU Member State; (b) for a practical placement in an enterprise abroad, particularly where the placement is an integral part of the study programme.

Individual Mobility Grants (IMGs) in TEMPUS II can be awarded to academic and administrative staff of higher education institutions, to senior officials from the Ministries of Education and to educational planners. With the exception of the academic year 1995/96 in which IMGs were only available for staff from CEE countries, grants have been and are now again available for respective staff from both EU Member States and CEE partner countries.

Eligible activities and purposes of mobility have been clearly defined and restructured in TEMPUS II. Most CEE partner countries have also introduced pre-selection criteria and preferences for IMG applications. In TEMPUS II three types of eligible activities have been defined for IMGs:
- course and teaching material development (including case studies)
- staff development (including practical placements)
- activities to support the development of higher education (participation in conferences and exchange of expert advice).

2.5.3 *Complementary Measures (Action 3)*

Complementary measures under TEMPUS I provided support for four – and in the last year of TEMPUS I for five – groups of activities. Complementary measures projects in the first three groups are called CMEs, activities in the fourth group are called Youth Exchange Projects (YEX), and projects in the fifth group (which was introduced in 1993/94) are called Joint European Networks (JENs).

(1) Grants to associations: these included grants to associations or consortia of universities, of recognised associations of students, teachers or administrators to facilitate the participation of organisations or associations within the CEE partner countries in the activities of European associations.

(2) Support for publications and other information activities: this provided funds for organisations or individuals for publications and other information activities of particular importance for the TEMPUS objectives.

(3) Support for surveys and studies: this provided funds awarded to organisations to conduct surveys and studies designed to analyse the development of the higher education/training systems in the CEE countries and their interaction with the European Community and other Western countries.

(4) Grants for youth exchange activities: two categories of grants were established in order to provide (a) funds for short preparatory visits (up to two weeks) of small groups of youth organisers of the Community visiting CEE countries or vice versa for purposes of learning about the structures in the host country, establishing contacts with potential exchange partners, and participating in workshops concerning the development of youth organisations and exchange models; (b) funds for the organisation of reciprocal exchanges of groups of young people and language summer camps bringing together young people and language teachers from EU Member States and from the CEE countries. Youth exchange activities were not anymore administered under TEMPUS II but rather by the European Commission directly.

(5) Grants for Joint European Networks (JENs): in 1993/94 grants were provided to enable the most successful JEPs – having been completed after three years of funding – to maintain their networks, wrap up project activities, arrange for dissemination of their results as examples of good practice, stabilise achievements, and possibly make arrangements for continuing cooperation without TEMPUS funding. The following activities were eligible for grants: (a) maintenance of results through continuation of teaching of new courses developed in the JEP; (b) maintenance of international networks through the organisation of workshops and seminars; (c) maintenance of new equipment; (d) dissemination of results through staff mobility, meetings, seminars, workshops and conferences; (e) publication of course material and other teaching and curriculum related material having been developed in the framework of the JEP. JENs were introduced in the last year of TEMPUS I as a pilot scheme and officially introduced

in the first year of TEMPUS II. JEN grants are awarded for a maximum of two years and funding is considerably lower than it is for JEPs.

Activities under Action 3 of the TEMPUS Programme were completely restructured in TEMPUS II and have been more intensively analysed by the authors of this study. Support for youth exchange activities as provided under TEMPUS I was no longer a part of the TEMPUS II Programme. However, in the first year of TEMPUS II, Complementary Measures (CMEs) provided support for activities in three areas still bearing a relatively close resemblance to TEMPUS I:

- participation of CEE institutions and higher education associations in the activities of European (university) associations
- facilitation of publications and information activities important for the reform of higher education
- assistance for reforms of higher education in the CEE countries, in particular by the dissemination of results and experiences of JEPs.

In the second year of TEMPUS II CMEs were completely redefined and provided support in the framework of three new strands of activities:

- the development and strengthening of capacities for strategic planning and institutional restructuring and development (including faculties)
- support for the dissemination of TEMPUS results including the dissemination of comparable results achieved in programmes other than TEMPUS
- support for the formulation of national higher education policies.

A number of CEE partner countries introduced additional preferences for CME project applications alongside their national priorities.

In the first year of TEMPUS II a new type of CME project was introduced, called CME+ project. Regulations for CME+ projects were similar to those of JEP+ projects, that is, objectives, scope and possible partners had to be identified by the national authorities of the CEE partner countries. Applications could only be submitted by the national authorities as well. Just like JEP+ projects, CME+ projects were designed to give national authorities a means by which to reach practical objectives in accordance with their policy for the development of higher education in the country. CME+ projects were clearly directed at the systems level.

Most CME+ projects which were awarded support for one year were feasibility studies. Some of them were concerned with the introduction of assessment, accreditation and quality assurance systems; others looked into possibilities for the establishment of short-cycle higher education, for the integration of research into universities or for a restructuring of postgraduate studies.

2.6 Eligibility

There are three groups of countries eligible for participation in the TEM-PUS/Phare Programme:

- eleven Central and Eastern European Countries supported in the framework of Phare
- originally twelve, now fifteen EU Member States
- the remaining G24 countries that are not members of the European Union, namely Australia, Canada, Iceland, Japan, Liechtenstein, New Zealand, Norway, Switzerland, Turkey and the USA.

There are three groups of institutions or organisations which can participate in the TEMPUS/Phare Programme:

- 'universities': universities and other higher education institutions accredited in their respective countries as well as consortia of higher education institutions, such as ERASMUS ICPs or COMETT UETPs
- enterprises: enterprises or companies in the strict sense
- organisations: other kinds of organisations, such as professional or scientific organisations, industrial federations, trade unions, employers' organisations, chambers of commerce, etc.

Finally, there are six groups of individuals who can participate in the TEMPUS/Phare Programme:

- academic staff from universities and other higher education institutions involved in teaching (in some cases also members of the Academies of Sciences who are at least involved in part-time teaching activities)
- administrative staff from universities and other higher education institutions
- undergraduate and postgraduate students
- personnel from enterprises and companies acting as trainers
- youth organisers and (organised) groups of young people (only in youth exchange activities under Action 3 of TEMPUS I)
- consultants and researchers (individuals and teams) conducting surveys and studies or preparing other informative publications relating to TEMPUS (only in complementary measures activities under Action 3).

Another form of eligibility, that of a contracting and/or coordinating institution for a JEP, underwent a certain degree of change and development during TEMPUS I. The contracting institution or the JEP contractor is the institution signing the JEP contract with the European Commission on behalf of all institutions involved in the JEP. The contractor is responsible for all legal and financial matters concerning the contract and receives the yearly grant from the European Commission to be distributed among the

JEP partners. The coordinating institution or JEP coordinator is the institution responsible for communication and cooperation of all partners involved in the JEP and for the distribution of tasks and activities as well as for the reports about achievements according to the JEP objectives.

In the first year of TEMPUS I, 1990/91, contracting and coordinating institutions were identical and had to be located in a Member State of the EU. In 1991/92, the two functions could be separated for the first time: the JEP contractor still had to be an EU institution while the JEP coordinator could also be located in one of the CEE partner countries or in one of the G24 countries. In 1992/93, Czechoslovakian and Hungarian institutions could become contractors and in 1993/94, the last year of TEMPUS I, contractors could also be institutions located in Slovenia. The eligibility for the management functions of CEE countries during TEMPUS II is shown in Table 2.2. Coordinators and/or contractors can come from the following CEE countries:

Table 2.2
Eligibility of CEE countries for Management Functions in Joint European Projects During TEMPUS II

	Management functions	
Academic year	Coordinator	Contractor
1994/95	any CEE country	Czech Republic, Hungary, Poland, Slovak Republic, Slovenia
1995/96	any CEE country	Czech Republic, Hungary, Poland, Romania, Slovak Republic, Slovenia
1996/97	any CEE country	Bulgaria, Czech Republic, Hungary, Poland, Romania, Slovak Republic, Slovenia

2.7 Development of National Priorities

Since the start of the TEMPUS Programme preference was given to project applications planning to develop and establish activities in so-called priority areas which were identified by the Central and Eastern European countries. Priority areas were supposed to be closely linked to the Phare priorities and then translated into subject areas of university studies.

The regulations in TEMPUS I relating to contents and objectives of activities were rather general. In contrast to this, the Council Decision for TEMPUS II explicitly stated the requirement for TEMPUS activities to fit into the strategic framework for higher education development within each country and to facilitate structural changes in the institutions of higher education. Thus, it was not only intended to create stronger synergy effects between TEMPUS activities and other developments supported within the Phare scheme but also to achieve a higher degree of structural impact in the field of higher education.

Already during TEMPUS I the process of establishing national priorities did not only become more and more complex, involving a consultative process with a number of policy makers in the CEE partner countries as well as in the European Commission, but also the priorities themselves frequently became increasingly detailed and were given a greater importance for the selection of applications. Each year the focus of the national priorities shifted to a certain extent in each of the CEE countries, thus also making additional efforts necessary for proper and targeted information of potential applicants. Since the beginning of TEMPUS II, national priorities thus provide an important framework for the selection of applications.

In the first round of application and selection in TEMPUS I, Poland and Hungary had put a specific emphasis on the following priorities:

- management and business administration
- applied economics
- applied sciences, technologies and engineering
- modern European languages
- agriculture and agro business
- environmental protection
- social and economic sciences related to the process of economic and social change in the CEE partner countries, including European Studies.

National TEMPUS priorities for Poland in the last year of TEMPUS I covered ten different areas with a total of 44 sub-specifications including political sciences and public administration, medical sciences, social welfare and modernisation of the educational system. The priorities also stated specifications concerning eligibility of certain institutions for JEPs and eligibility of individuals for IMGs (i.e. age limits). In contrast, Hungary's national TEMPUS priorities for 1993/94 were more general, specifying only that preference will be given to projects in which the contractor and/or coordinator is a Hungarian higher education institution, to projects encouraging active participation of enterprises, industry and banks, to projects promoting the cooperation of several Hungarian higher education institutions, and to projects developing the capacities of Hungarian higher education institutions to provide continuing education, retraining and distance education. In addition, some objectives were specified.

The national TEMPUS priorities of most of the other CEE partner countries specified university subjects and disciplines, sometimes mixed with more structural preferences, such as development of short-term higher education or development of university-enterprise cooperation. Also humanities and social sciences are represented more strongly among the priority subject areas often connected to the promotion and support of the general democratisation processes.

Concerning the focus on certain subject areas in TEMPUS I, there was a relative decline in the initially strong emphasis on projects in applied sciences and technology. The proportion of projects in business and management studies remained the same, while that in applied social sciences, medicine and environmental studies increased.

Towards the end of TEMPUS I, and more widespread at the beginning of TEMPUS II, CEE partner countries began to introduce preferential criteria for the selection of applications in addition to the national priorities in order to promote those projects which were coordinated and/or contracted by partners from CEE countries. Meanwhile another preference introduced by many CEE countries is directed at TEMPUS projects in which several institutions from the same country cooperate with Western partners.

Since the beginning of TEMPUS II, full compliance of project applications with national priorities is required in order for the projects to become eligible for support. Comparing the development of the national priorities in the CEE partner countries, considerable differences can be observed with regard to the scope and the details of definition. The following examples may serve as an illustration.

In Slovenia, priorities in 1994/95 were defined in great detail and specified not only disciplines but also subject areas and field of expertise (e.g. 'management and economics in the areas of: a) banking and public finance, b) the establishment of short cycle courses in tourism in coastal areas').

In Estonia, the priorities only defined structural areas without specifying particular subject areas (e.g. 'promotion of interdisciplinary studies; introduction of new types of management and structures in Estonian higher education institutions').

Hungary's national TEMPUS priorities for 1994/95 stated that preference would be given to projects having objectives such as the 'development of new curricula leading to the creation of new academic and professional profiles in higher education institutions' or 'significant contributions to current Phare projects'. Other TEMPUS priorities were even more general, such as 'development of teaching methods that can be used with greater numbers of students, development of university-industry (enterprise) cooperation', etc. By and large, the same priorities appeared again one year later, this time including additional specifications, for example, with regard to the subject areas in which the priorities would be especially relevant.

In contrast, Lithuania shifted the focus of its priorities from defining study areas and disciplines in 1994/95 ('environmental studies in the areas of: energy saving, material saving technologies', etc.) to more structural aspects in 1995/96 ('development of information structures, networks and technologies within higher education; for example, modernisation of libraries and access to databases').

Although national priorities reflect the differences existing in the development and various stages of transition among the CEE countries, each year a number of foci also overlap or are similar so that cooperation among CEE countries in the framework or regional activities would suggest itself in a few areas.

2.8 Requirements and Selection Criteria

Requirements for successful applications have become more and more specified and selection criteria more and more detailed. During the first two years of TEMPUS I, the National TEMPUS Offices (NTOs) in all CEE partner countries were established and equipped and their staff was trained in order to provide for comparable procedures and achieve a certain routine in the organisation of application and selection rounds. General requirements have been explained in the section on eligibility (see pp. 28 – 29). This section refers to the various assessment exercises and their respective selection criteria.

The selection procedure of JEP applications is a co-determination process involving the European Commission and the CEE partner countries in several stages (cf. Chart 2.2). JEP applications are sent to the EC TEMPUS Office/ETF TEMPUS Department which in turn sends a receipt and acknowledgement of the proposal to the applicant. The application is checked for completeness and correctness of necessary forms and receives an eligibility status and an identification number.

Chart 2.2
Stages of the Selection Process for TEMPUS Projects

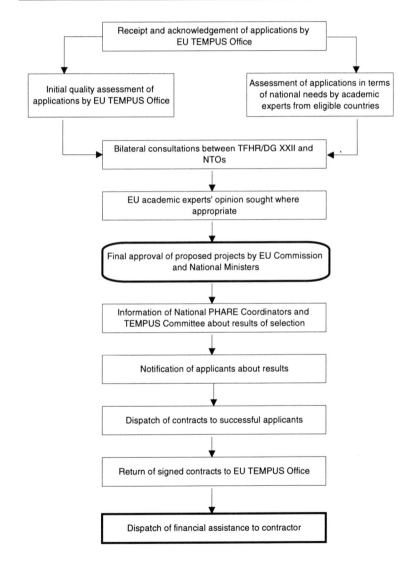

Subsequently, two parallel assessment procedures take place. The ETF TEMPUS Department undertakes an initial quality grading of applications. Copies of all applications involving the country concerned are sent to the respective National TEMPUS Office where a technical assessment and a check are carried out to determine whether they comply with national priorities. NTOs then determine a provisional eligibility status according to the degree of compliance, that is, full compliance, partial compliance, no compliance. Academic experts from the CEE countries make a further assessment of applications, predominantly concerned with their academic quality but also taking into account again their compliance with the national priorities and the national needs. Each application is assessed independently by two academic experts. The quality grading of the ETF TEMPUS Department and information on the available budget are sent to the NTOs for comparison with their own and the experts' assessments and for preparation of the bilateral meetings. ETF TEMPUS Department assessments, NTO assessments and academic experts' assessments are combined into a first draft list of applications being recommended for TEMPUS support in the framework of bilateral consultations between Directorate General XXII – formerly the Task Force Human Resources, Education, Training and Youth – and the National TEMPUS Offices. After this internal consultation procedure, a list of eligible projects is drawn up. Those cases in which the assessments differ from each other are presented to a panel of external academic experts from EU Member States and from the CEE partner countries. The outcome is a final list of JEP applications recommended for support. This list is sent to the Phare coordinator for information and the Ministry of Education in the CEE partner country concerned for comment and eventual approval. Upon approval the Commission begins with the financial control procedures. Upon their completion a final approval (or rejection) of proposed projects is done jointly by the European Commission and the Ministers of Education. The results of the selection are also presented to the TEMPUS Management Committee for comments on geographical/country and subject-related balance and for information about policy developments.

Thereafter, applicants are notified of the results, and contracts to successful applicants are dispatched. Upon return of the signed contracts to the ETF TEMPUS Department the funds for the first year of JEP activities are transferred to the contractor.

The selection of applications for Individual Mobility Grants (IMGs) also has a number of stages but is a less complex procedure. The NTOs receive and assess the applications from academic staff of their own country; the ETF TEMPUS Department receives and assesses the applications from academic staff of the EU Member States. The ETF TEMPUS Department then coordinates the submission of all IMG applications to the Commission for approval of those proposed for support. After the Commission has approved the selection of proposals the contracts are issued by the ETF TEMPUS Department. Contracts for academic staff from the CEE countries are sent to the NTOs for distribution.

As a rule, JEP applications are assessed in terms of four different aspects. The technical assessment is concerned with completeness and correctness of all forms and a check as to whether all partners have submitted letters of endorsement. The initial quality grading is a first check on the consistency and academic level of the proposed activities as well as on the distribution of tasks, the level of cooperation among partners and the management of the proposed project. The third aspect concerns the assessment by the NTOs and the academic experts in terms of correspondence with national needs and academic quality of the proposals. For each of these assessment procedures detailed guidelines and comparable assessment sheets have been developed to assure similarity and comparability of procedures in all CEE partner countries. The last assessment is more concerned with the correspondence of applications with the overall TEMPUS and Phare objectives and national higher education policies and involves the Phare coordinators as well as the Ministers of Higher Education from the CEE countries and the European Commission.

The most detailed and demanding assessment is usually done by the academic experts. The EC TEMPUS Office and later the ETF TEMPUS Department had proposed assessment criteria for this exercise which were adapted to the national situation to a certain extent by the NTOs. The criteria as proposed by the EC TEMPUS Office/ETF TEMPUS Department can be summarised as follows:

- objectives and content: aims and coherence of approach, preparation and organisation, aims and organisation of mobility
- management: division of tasks, commitment and involvement of partners, role in the East, financial arrangements, possibly complementary funding
- effects: benefit to CEE partner countries, integration and cooperation, regional activities
- country specific criteria: relevance in connection with Phare, compliance with national priorities.

During TEMPUS I all JEPs had to submit a report every six months about their activities and progress. After each year a more detailed report together with an application for renewal of contract was used as a basis for the eventual decision to continue support in the second and third year. In the last year of TEMPUS I the bi-annual reports were stopped when JEP funding changed from an annual to a multi-annual basis. The annual report was kept on and used as a basis for the decision to continue funding.

Selection procedures and selection criteria have basically remained the same during the first two years of TEMPUS II. Further developments can only be noted by the introduction of additional preferences, pre-selection criteria and objectives in the framework of existing procedures and criteria which have to be taken into account by applicants. Three issues can be pointed out in this respect:

- In TEMPUS II national priorities have been accorded a considerably higher status in the selection process of applications. In addition to national priorities, preferences have been introduced by most CEE countries for JEP applications. Applications for IMGs must also take special 'pre-selection criteria' and preferences into account. For the first time in 1996/97 preferences have also been introduced by some CEE partner countries for CME applications.

- In order to achieve a more integrated approach of TEMPUS activities taking place in the faculties and departments, endorsement letters have now to be accompanied by a statement of the central institutional level concerning the project's coherence with the development plan of the institution or the faculty as well as a description of this plan. This is intended to promote a higher awareness of strategic planning and institutional development in the framework of TEMPUS.

- With the gradual transfer of tasks and responsibilities from the TEMPUS Department in the ETF to the NTOs, the latter have become more and more responsible for parts of the assessment of applications. Thus, they have frequently taken over the assessment of JEPs as regards their compliance with national priorities and the assessment of applications for IMGs. Together with the TEMPUS Department in the ETF, they are also involved in the selection of successful JEPs for JEN grants. In addition, NTOs are involved in desk monitoring of JEPs and site visits organised by the Commission.

2.9   Amount of Grants

According to the TEMPUS I Guidelines for Applicants, the grant which can possibly be awarded for each TEMPUS activity is limited. As a rule, the actual grants awarded for the various activities are below the possible maximum.

Excluding mobility grants which have to be applied for under Action 2, Joint European Projects (Action 1) might be awarded a maximum grant of 200,000 ECU annually for up to three years. In 1993/94, the last year of TEMPUS I, the average grant per JEP was 117,000 ECU for newly accepted JEPs, 150,000 ECU for second year JEPs, and 159,500 ECU for third year JEPs. Another trend stated in the annual reports of the European Commission was that for each operational JEP year the proportion of grant allocated for administrative costs as well as for mobility increased. JEPs newly established in the first year of TEMPUS II (1994/95) could be awarded a maximum grant of 500,000 ECU for the full three year period of support. This was reduced to a maximum grant of 400,000 ECU for JEPs newly established in the second year of TEMPUS II. On average, the actual amount of funding allocated to JEPs newly established in the first two years of TEMPUS II was about 391,000 ECU.

Joint European Networks have been awarded a maximum grant of 15,000 ECU per year for a two year period of support.

The special measure of JEP+ projects for which applications could only be submitted in 1994/95 received a higher amount of funding because of its wider scope and national relevance. For the full three year period of support JEP+ projects could be awarded a maximum of 600,000 ECU.

A regulation for the breakdown of JEP budgets was introduced in the first year of TEMPUS II. Total staff costs could not exceed 50 per cent of the overall JEP grant awarded and were additionally limited to a maximum sum of 50,000 ECU per project and per year. Mobility grants constituted an independent item in addition to the JEP budget and were not included in staff costs. The amount of funding for administrative matters within JEPs was restricted to a maximum of 30,000 ECU per year of operation. The maximum amount of funding which could be used for administrative matters decreased from an average of 40 per cent of the total JEP grant in TEMPUS I to an average of about 25 per cent in TEMPUS II.

Mobility grants (Action 2) vary according to the duration of the period spent abroad, the direction of mobility (East to West or West to East) and the purpose of the stay abroad. In TEMPUS II they also vary according to the type of mobility.

Students from the EU going to one of the CEE partner countries for a period of study abroad received a maximum mobility grant of 5,000 ECU for one academic year during TEMPUS I. Students from the CEE countries going to study in one of the EU Member States received a maximum grant of 6,000 ECU for a period of one academic year. In addition, universities located in the EU Member States received a sum of 1,000 ECU for each student from the CEE countries they were hosting for a period of six months and more and of 500 ECU for each student from the CEE countries they were hosting for five months or less. The same amounts (5,000 and 6,000 ECU respectively) were awarded for practical placements of students for a period of twelve months.

Mobility grants for staff in TEMPUS I depended on destination, length of assignment, category of personnel, and – if applicable – the salary paid by the host institution. There were four categories of mobility grants for staff:

- teaching/training assignments: 15,000 ECU maximum for one academic year
- practical placements: 10,000 ECU maximum for a period of twelve months
- retraining/updating of knowledge (only for staff from the CEE countries): 15,000 ECU maximum for a period of twelve months
- (short) visit grants: at first staff from EU Member States were awarded a maximum of initially 1,500 (later of 2,000) ECU depending on the destination and length of stay abroad; staff from CEE countries were awarded a maximum of initially 2,500 (later of 3,000) ECU, depending on the destination and length of stay abroad.

Higher education institutions located in the EU Member States could be awarded a maximum of 2,500 ECU per person and per month to cover replacement costs for staff going abroad.

The average amount awarded for mobility grants was considerably lower and varied from country to country. Support awarded in the framework of Individual Mobility Grants (IMGs) in TEMPUS II varies according to the type of activity and duration of mobility:

- In 1994/95, the first year of TEMPUS II, short visits of staff from CEE countries to Western countries were supported with a maximum grant of 3,000 ECU. IMGs for short visits of staff from the Western countries spending some time abroad in CEE countries were supported with a maximum amount of 2,000 ECU.
- In the first TEMPUS II year a maximum amount of 15,000 ECU for one year was granted for teaching or training assignments at a partner institution abroad, for the purpose of mobility to update knowledge and skills as well as for practical placements.

In the second TEMPUS II year IMGs were only available to applicants from CEE partner countries wishing to visit partner institutions in the EU

Member States. Indications about the level of grant for the various purposes of individual mobility were not given in the Guidelines for Applicants of that year.

In 1996/97, IMGs were available again to staff from EU Member States. The level of support for IMGs in that academic year will be determined according to the length of stay abroad and the destination. Costs for travel and subsistence are distinguished and the latter grouped according to length of stay abroad and direction of mobility. No overall amounts of maximum support are indicated any longer.

Complementary Measures (Action 3) projects may receive grants of up to a maximum of 20,000 ECU annually per project. In 1992, the average grant awarded to Complementary Measures projects was 10,000 ECU. Preparatory visits in the framework of youth exchange activities could be awarded a maximum of 1,000 ECU for participants from CEE countries and a maximum of 750 ECU for participants from EU Member States. Youth exchange projects received 100 per cent of the costs for CEE participants and 50 per cent of the costs for EU participants up to a maximum of 10,000 ECU per project.

As in TEMPUS I, Complementary Measures projects (CMEs) in the first TEMPUS II year could receive a grant of up to 20,000 ECU per year. CME+ projects supported in the first TEMPUS II year received a maximum amount of 50,000 ECU for one year. In 1995/96, the second TEMPUS II year, CMEs were completely redefined and comprised three new strands of activities. The maximum duration of projects remained the same (i.e. one year). The maximum grant which can be awarded to the new types of CME projects is indicated as varying between 10,000 and 80,000 ECU (between 10,000 and 50,000 ECU in 1996/97) depending on the size and the scope of the project. For 1996/97, some CME projects are envisaged as having a duration of two years with the possibility of funding up to 100,000 ECU.

Chapter 3

Structural and Quantitative Development of the Joint European Projects

3.1 The Institutional Recipients of TEMPUS Support

This chapter provides a statistical overview of Joint European Projects (JEPs), that is, networks of organisations (institutions of higher education, enterprises and other organisations), which were awarded grants for the purpose of cooperative educational activities, structural development of higher education in Central and Eastern Europe and student and staff mobility. All JEPs are included which were supported by the TEMPUS Programme during the first phase, 1990/91 to 1993/94, and the first two years of the second phase, 1994/95 and 1995/96.

Furthermore, this chapter comprises information about the 'partners' – the persons or units of organisations involved in Joint European Projects. It should be noted that a department or an organisation might be involved in various networks. Each involvement in a network is counted as one 'partner'.

We identified the individual organisations participating in TEMPUS I, 1990/91 – 1993/94, and in TEMPUS II during the first two years, 1994/95 and 1995/96. This allows us also to establish the frequency of involvement in JEPs on the part of the individual organisations.

All figures are based on data provided by the TEMPUS Department in the ETF either in data bases[1] or in written documents.[2] The TEMPUS Department in the ETF is primarily interested in data regarding new ap-

---

1 Joint European Projects data base and Individual Mobility data base. The latter could not be used for statistical analysis because the content of the data base did not correspond to the figures published in the documents of the TEMPUS Department in the ETF.

2 Tables of student and staff mobility within JEPs.

plications and renewals of applications, that is, JEPs applying for a second or third year of TEMPUS support, and these data are stored in databases and described in official reports. The input of data from final reports sent by each coordinating unit of networks to the TEMPUS Department in the ETF started only recently and was still being processed during the evaluation period. Thus, the statistical analysis presented in this chapter is only based on data referring to the award decisions for TEMPUS support. It is possible that these data are actually not valid, that is that organisations were not active or not supported by TEMPUS, or that envisaged mobility did not take place. Therefore, the actual numbers of organisations, partners, mobile students and staff members might be lower than those reported in this chapter.

Due to the pluri-annual support for TEMPUS Joint European Projects, the selection of JEPs to be supported – including new applications and renewals of applications – does not only shape the TEMPUS reality in a single academic year but also determines to a certain extent the range of activities supported by TEMPUS in the subsequent years. Furthermore, the profiles of individual JEPs might change over time, for example the division of management functions between partners, the number of partners and organisations involved, etc. To provide appropriate figures about the development of TEMPUS, different types of views on available JEP data have to be taken into consideration:

(1) *General view on the TEMPUS Programme as a whole*: This analysis covers the whole period of TEMPUS I, 1990/91 to 1993/94, and the first two years of TEMPUS II, 1994/95 and 1995/96, and includes all organisations and partners that were awarded support for the first time in the framework of newly established JEPs or were awarded support repeatedly through a renewal of contract for a second or third year of JEP operation.

(2) *General view on the TEMPUS I period*: This analysis addresses the first phase of TEMPUS, 1990/91 to 1993/94, and includes all organisations and partners that were awarded support for the first time in the framework of newly established JEPs or were awarded support repeatedly through a renewal of contract for a second or third year of JEP operation.

(3) *General view on TEMPUS I JEPs*: This analysis refers also to the first phase of TEMPUS, but comprises only organisations and partners awarded support in the framework of JEPs starting in the first phase of TEMPUS but not necessarily completing their activities in the period between 1990/91 and 1993/94.

(4) *General view on the TEMPUS II period*: This analysis addresses the first two years of TEMPUS II, 1994/95 and 1995/96, and includes all organisations and partners awarded support for the first time in the framework of newly established JEPs or were awarded support repeatedly either through a renewal of contract for a second or third year of JEP operation starting during TEMPUS I or through a renewal of contract for a second year of operation for JEPs starting in the first year of TEMPUS II.

(5) *General view on TEMPUS II JEPs*: This analysis refers also to the first two years of TEMPUS II, 1994/95 and 1995/96, but comprises only all organisations and partners awarded support in the framework of JEPs starting in the second phase of TEMPUS.

(6) *View by TEMPUS year*: This analysis includes all organisations and partners awarded TEMPUS support for the respective academic year.

(7) *View by year of start of the JEP*: This analysis includes only organisations and partners awarded TEMPUS support in the initial year of the JEP, that is, the academic year in which the JEP was newly established.

(8) *View by year of operation of the JEP*: This analysis includes all organisations and partners awarded TEMPUS support for the respective year, that is, the first, second or third year of operation of the Joint European Project.

Special emphasis is put on the seventh type of analysis – the one concerned with the year of start of the JEP – because these figures show most clearly the development trends of the TEMPUS Programme. However, all types of views listed above were employed in this chapter in order to provide a comprehensive overview of the structural and quantitative development of TEMPUS Joint European Projects.

3.2 The Quantitative Expansion

In 1990/91, the year of inauguration of the TEMPUS Programme, 152 Joint European Projects were awarded support. Most of these JEPs (134) were continued in the second year of TEMPUS, while 318 JEPs were newly established (see Chart 3.1). Thus, the total number of JEPs was 452 in 1991/92. The third year of TEMPUS was characterised by a decrease in the number of new JEPs (240); however, the overall number of supported TEMPUS JEPs (641) reached a peak in 1992/93. In the fourth year, only 39 JEPs were newly established, mainly because the funding of the already running projects had to be secured. The total number of JEPs, including those receiving TEMPUS support for a second or third year of operation, amounted to 502 in 1993/94. Altogether 749 TEMPUS Joint European Projects were awarded support during the first phase of TEMPUS (1990/91–1993/94).

In 1994/95, the first year of the second phase of the TEMPUS Programme, 239 Joint European Projects were newly established. Additionally, 226 JEPs that had started during TEMPUS I received support either for a second or a third year of operation. In the following year, the second year of TEMPUS II, 219 JEPs were newly established, 238 TEMPUS II JEPs were awarded TEMPUS support for a second year of operation and 19 TEMPUS I JEPs for their third year (see Chart 3.1). Altogether, TEMPUS support was awarded during the first two years of TEMPUS II to 458 Joint European Projects newly established and to 226 JEPs that had started during TEMPUS I but had been awarded support repeatedly through a renewal of contract for a second or third year of operation. During the whole period of observation, 1990/91 to 1995/96, more than 1,200 JEPs were funded by TEMPUS.

Chart 3.1
Number of TEMPUS Joint European Projects, by Academic Year and Year of TEMPUS Support (absolute numbers)

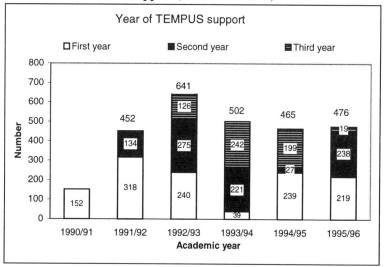

Source: Database of the European Training Foundation

About 435 higher education institutions participated in 1990/91, 813 in 1991/92, 1,047 in 1992/93, 910 in 1993/94, 986 in 1994/95 and 1,003 in 1994/95. Altogether, more than 1,400 institutions of higher education were involved in Joint European Projects between 1990/91 and 1995/96. Among them were more than 300 institutions of higher education from Central and Eastern Europe. By and large, the number of higher education institutions per individual country, in Central and Eastern Europe as well as in Western countries, reflects the size and diversity of the higher education systems. Countries with large numbers of institutions were represented by comparably large numbers of institutions in TEMPUS and vice versa.

The number of enterprises participating in TEMPUS varied between 117 in the year of inauguration and 359 in the third year of TEMPUS I. In TEMPUS II the respective number increased to 397 in the first year and to 476 in the second year. Altogether, about 900 enterprises participated officially in TEMPUS JEPs. However, the responses to the questionnaire suggest that the number of active enterprises was clearly smaller.

The number of other organisations involved grew from 127 in 1990/91 to 503 in 1992/93. In 1993/94, it decreased to 380 but increased again to 430 in 1994/95, the first year of TEMPUS II, and to 459 in 1995/96. Altogether, more than 1,000 other organisations participated in TEMPUS JEPs during the six years of observation.

3.3 The Profile of Networks and Participating Organisations

TEMPUS Joint European Projects as defined by the European Commission are networks of organisations (institutions of higher education, enterprises and other organisations) from Central and Eastern European partner countries, Member States of the EU and possibly other G24 countries. As minimal requirements for the award of TEMPUS support, the networks had to include:

- one institution of higher education from a Central or Eastern European country
- partner organisations from at least two different EU Member States, one of which must be a higher education institution.

Institutions of higher education, enterprises or other organisations from G24 countries may participate as partners in a JEP consortium. Beyond the minimal requirements concerning the number of countries and type of organisations necessary to create a Joint European Project, no formal restrictions were made regarding maximum size.

On average, Joint European Projects established during the first phase of the TEMPUS Programme comprised about 8 partners while the average number of partners were 10 per JEP during the second phase of the TEMPUS programme. A comparison of JEPs by the year in which they started (i.e. the year of first TEMPUS support) shows an increase in the average number of partners from 7.3 in 1991/92 to 13.9 in 1993/94 and afterwards, during the first two years of TEMPUS II, a decrease to 11.5 in 1994/95 and 9.2 in 1995/96. According to the initial award decisions, the average number of partners was:

- 7.7 in 1990/91 (2.2 from CEE countries, 5.4 from EU Member States and 0.1 from other G24 countries)
- 7.3 in 1991/92 (2.5, 4.6 and 0.2)
- 8.4 in 1992/93 (2.7, 5.5 and 0.2)
- 13.9 in 1993/94 (3.6, 9.9 and 0.5)
- 11.5 in 1994/95 (7.4, 3.9 and 0.2)
- 9.2 in 1995/96 (5.1, 4.0 and 0.1).

The composition of JEP partners by home country changed significantly from TEMPUS I to TEMPUS II. Whereas during TEMPUS I the majority of partners in the average individual JEP were from Western countries, this majority was lost in TEMPUS II as a consequence of two developments:

- the average number of Western partners in JEPs decreased to about 4 in the first two years of TEMPUS II
- the average number of partners from individual CEE countries in JEPs increased to more than five in the respective period.

The latter was at least partly due to national priorities of some of the CEE countries which required or preferred the participation of more than one higher education institution in individual JEPs.

In contrast to TEMPUS I, the participation of only one higher education institution per JEP from a single Central and Eastern European country was rather an exception in TEMPUS II (only 30 per cent of the JEPs starting 1994/95 or 1995/96 as compared to 60 per cent of TEMPUS I JEPs). Slightly more than 28 per cent of the JEPs starting in the second phase of TEMPUS comprised two, 19 per cent three and 12 per cent four or more higher education institutions from the same CEE country.

As Table 3.1 shows, the proportion of TEMPUS JEPs in which all participating organisations were higher education institutions was about 45 per cent. As regards the remaining JEPs, institutions of higher education cooperated in:

- 11 per cent of the JEPs only with enterprises

- 26 per cent of the JEPs only with other organisations
- 18 per cent with other organisations and enterprises.

A comparison of TEMPUS I and TEMPUS II JEPs shows only marginal changes regarding the institutional configuration.

The average number of countries represented in newly established TEMPUS Joint European Projects was:

- 5.2 in 1990/91 (1.7 from CEE countries, 3.2 from EU Member States and 0.2 from other G24 countries)
- 4.7 in 1991/92 (1.4, 3.1 and 0.2)
- 4.4 in 1992/93 (1.3, 2.9 and 0.2)
- 5.6 in 1993/94 (1.1, 4.1 and 0.4)
- 5.0 in 1994/95 (1.0, 3.9 and 0.1)
- 4.7 in 1995/96 (1.0, 3.6 and 0.1).

By and large, the number of countries per JEP did not change substantially over time. However, the number of JEPs including partners from more than one CEE countries decreased continuously to only one of the JEPs starting in 1995/96. The proportion of JEPs including organisations from non-EU G24 countries was with about 10 per cent of TEMPUS II JEPs – only half as high as the respective proportion of TEMPUS I JEPs. This shift in proportions was mainly due to Austria, Finland and Sweden joining the European Union in 1995.

Taking into account the minimal country configuration as defined by the rules for the establishment of TEMPUS Joint European Projects, about one-third of the JEPs were based on partners from one CEE country and two EU Member States at the time of start. A further 55 per cent of JEPs was characterised by the involvement of one CEE country and three or more partners from EU or other 'G24' countries. The most visible change in the country configuration of TEMPUS JEPs is the disappearance of JEPs involving organisations from two or more of the eligible CEE countries (multi-CEE JEPs). Only 1 per cent of JEPs starting in TEMPUS II can be considered as multi-CEE JEPs, whereas the respective proportion was 21 per cent of the JEPs starting during TEMPUS I (see Table 3.2). In contrast, the proportion of JEPs comprising 3 or more western countries increased from 32 per cent in 1990/91 to slightly more than 70 per cent in 1994/95 and 1995/96.

TEMPUS JEPs can be supported for periods of up to three years. While during the first phase of TEMPUS the JEPs had to apply for an extension of the contract in each year, the duration of the contract period under TEMPUS II is fixed in the initial award decision. However, the European Commission can discontinue the TEMPUS support if JEPs do not fulfil

Table 3.1
Institutional Configuration of TEMPUS Joint European Projects, by Year of Start (per cent of JEPs*)

	Year of start						Total
	1990/91	1991/92	1992/93	1993/94	1994/95	1995/96	
Only higher education institutions	44	44	51	62	41	42	45
Only higher education institutions and enterprises	7	14	10	10	10	10	11
Only higher education institutions and other organisations	24	30	22	18	26	25	26
Higher education institutions, enterprises and other organisations	24	12	17	10	23	23	18
Total	100	100	100	100	100	100	100
(n)	(152)	(318)	(240)	(39)	(239)	(219)	(1,207)

* Configuration of JEPs in the first year of TEMPUS support. Not including possible changes in the configuration during the second or third year of operation of the JEP.

Source: Database of the European Training Foundation

their contractual obligations. JEP grants are still paid annually upon the submission and positive acknowledgement of the JEPs annual activity report and revised budget and activity plans for the next year. About 91 per cent of TEMPUS I JEPs were awarded annual TEMPUS support for a period of three years and about 5 per cent received support for two years. Only 4 per cent of the JEPs discontinued their activities after one year, either because the JEP partners did not re-apply for a second year of support for various reasons or the contract was not prolonged by the European Commission. During the first two years of TEMPUS II, about 95 per cent of the JEPs starting in each year were awarded a three-year grant and slightly less than 5 per cent a two-year grant. Every year one JEP was established which eventually was supported for one year only.

The participation of higher education institutions, enterprises and other organisations in the individual TEMPUS JEPs was not necessarily constant over time. Partners could join the JEP activities at a later stage or discontinue their involvement before the end of the JEP. However, the data available show a high level of stability of participation within the TEMPUS II JEPs. Only a few JEP partners joined the project later, while less than 1 per cent dropped out before the end of the project.

The management of the JEP is divided into two functions: the coordination of the JEP activities ('coordinator') and the signing of the contract as well as the administration and distribution of funds ('contractor').

In the first year of TEMPUS, both management functions were combined and only partners from EU Member States were eligible for these tasks. In 1991/92, the second year of TEMPUS, the functions could be divided between two partners in the network. Partners from Central and Eastern European countries were eligible to become a coordinator but not to become a contractor. In 1992/93, this restriction was partly removed for organisations from Czechoslovakia and Hungary, in 1993/94 for Poland and Slovenia, and in 1994/95 for Romania and the Slovak Republic.

While during TEMPUS I the coordination of JEPs by partners from CEE countries was rather an exception (about one-quarter of the JEPs), it became the main mode during TEMPUS II (three-quarter of JEPs). The respective proportion increased continuously to about 40 per cent of TEMPUS II JEPs. By and large, the increasing number of CEE partners in charge of the management functions of JEPs is one of the most visible changes in the profile of JEPs over time.

In 44 per cent of the TEMPUS II projects, a single partner took over both the coordinating and contracting functions (as compared to more than 70 per cent of TEMPUS I JEPs). Thus, the division of management

Table 3.2
Country Configuration of TEMPUS Joint European Projects, by Year of Start (per cent of JEPs*)

	Year of start						Total
	1990/91	1991/92	1992/93	1993/94	1994/95	1995/96	
1 CEE and 2 EU Member States	32	36	43	23	26	29	33
1 CEE and 3 or more EU or other Western countries	32	44	42	69	73	71	55
Multi-CEE	36	20	15	8	1	0	12
Total	100	100	100	100	100	100	100
(n)	(152)	(318)	(240)	(39)	(239)	(219)	(1,207)

* Configuration of JEPs in the first year of TEMPUS support. Not including possible changes in the configuration during the second or third year of operation of the JEP.

Source: Database of the European Training Foundation

functions between partners becomes more prominent during TEMPUS II. One of the reasons for this development can be seen in the ongoing restrictions for partners from various CEE countries to take over the contracting function. JEP coordinators from respective CEE countries have to ask a Western partner in the network to take on the contracting function.

About half of the organisations participating in TEMPUS JEPs were institutions of higher education and a quarter each were enterprises and other organisations. By and large, the proportions of the various types of organisations involved in JEPs did not change substantially from TEMPUS I to TEMPUS II. While the proportion of higher education institutions slightly decreased, an increase in the proportion of enterprises can be observed.

The frequency of participation in JEPs differed by type of organisation. The vast majority of enterprises and other organisations (about 90 per cent each) participated solely in a single TEMPUS JEP each, whereas the institutions of higher education were active in about four TEMPUS JEPs on average. No differences between TEMPUS I and TEMPUS II can be observed in this respect.

3.4 Composition by Country

During the period observed, the number of Central and Eastern European countries eligible for the TEMPUS programme increased:

- In 1990/91, the first year of the TEMPUS programme only four countries were eligible for TEMPUS support: Czechoslovakia, Poland, Hungary and East Germany.
- In 1991/92 the pool of eligible CEE countries was widened by Bulgaria, Yugoslavia and Romania; institutions of higher education from the former East Germany were now treated as all other German institutions, that is, as institutions from the EU.
- In 1992/93 a further expansion in the number of eligible CEE countries took place by opening TEMPUS for organisations from Albania, Estonia, Latvia and Lithuania. Due to the political developments in Yugoslavia, eligibility for TEMPUS was discontinued except for the independent state of Slovenia. The separation of Czechoslovakia into two states, the Czech Republic and the Slovak Republic, further increased the number of CEE partner countries. Since 1992/93, altogether eleven Central and Eastern European partner countries have participated in TEMPUS.

Table 3.3
Participation of CEE Countries in New and Renewed TEMPUS Joint European Projects, by Academic Year
(absolute numbers)

| | Academic year | | | | | | |
	1990/91	1991/92	1992/93	1993/94	1994/95	1995/96	TOTAL
ALB	–	–	9	14	18	14	24
BG	–	53	86	66	61	60	149
CS[1]	39	124	163	–	–	–	170
CZ	–	–	–	81	43	34	115
EE	–	–	8	17	20	13	28
GDR[1]	12	–	–	–	–	–	12
H	63	161	179	125	69	74	281
LT	–	–	11	16	22	18	33
LV	–	–	11	15	23	13	31
PL	85	144	245	155	181	155	414
RO	–	69	104	87	54	60	169
SK	–	–	–	46	34	30	75
SLO	–	–	44	38	24	12	56
YU[1]	–	–	71	–	–	–	71

1) Eligible until the end of their formal existence

(–) Not eligible

Source: European Training Foundation: Survey of TEMPUS I (draft 2). Unpublished document, 1994.

- From 1993/94 to 1995/96 no further changes took place. Altogether, 11 CEE countries were eligible for TEMPUS support in the fourth year of TEMPUS.

Depending on the timing of eligibility for TEMPUS support but also on the available TEMPUS budget, large differences in the participation of the individual CEE countries in Joint European Projects can be observed. As Table 3.3 shows, the number of JEPs per individual Central and Eastern European country ranged from 24 in Albania[3] to 414 in Poland. The two other CEE countries eligible for support from the beginning of TEMPUS in 1990/91, the former Czechoslovakia and Hungary, were behind Poland the most often represented CEE countries in JEPs. On the other hand, only a small number of JEPs with partners from the Baltic States were awarded TEMPUS support.

As regards the EU Member States, partners from the United Kingdom participated in more TEMPUS Joint European Projects (63 per cent) than partners from any other Western country (see Table 3.4). In each year of TEMPUS, the United Kingdom was represented in a higher proportion of successful applications for new JEPs than any other Western country. The two other large EU Member States, Germany and France, participated in 48 per cent and 43 per cent respectively of the TEMPUS JEPs. A remarkably high proportion of JEPs included partners from The Netherlands (31 per cent). Other EU Member States that were represented in more than 20 per cent of the JEPs were Italy (31 per cent), Belgium (28 per cent) and Spain (24 per cent). The proportion of JEPs with partners from the new EU Member States – Austria, Finland and Sweden – was about 7 per cent each. Their involvement shows a considerable increase from 5 per cent in TEMPUS I to about 10 per cent in TEMPUS II. Partners from other G24 countries, which did not receive TEMPUS funds for their activities, participated in less than 3 per cent of the JEPs each.

The majority of CEE countries cooperated most frequently with partners from the United Kingdom in TEMPUS Joint European Projects. However, some exceptions can be observed as Table 3.5 shows:

- Albania cooperated most often with Italy (in 70 per cent of the JEPs in which Albania was represented) and Greece (48 per cent) in Joint European Projects
- Hungary with Germany (62 per cent)
- Romania with France (73 per cent).

---

3 A lower number of involvements, as in the case of Albania, could only be observed with regard to East Germany which is due to the fact that the eligibility of East Germany as a targeted country for TEMPUS was discontinued after the German unification.

Table 3.4
Participation of CEE and Western Countries in TEMPUS Joint European Projects, by Year of Start (per cent of JEPs*)

	Year of start							Overall country participation**
	1990/91	1991/92	1992/93	1993/94	1994/95	1995/96	Total	
ALB	–	–	3	13	2	2	2	2
BG	–	14	14	0	13	13	12	12
CS[1)]	25	24	15	–	–	–	12	14
CZ	–	–	–	0	6	9	3	10
GDR[1)]	8	–	–	–	–	–	1	1
EE	–	–	3	15	3	2	2	2
H	41	31	10	46	17	13	23	23
LT	–	–	5	13	2	5	3	3
LV	–	–	5	15	3	2	2	3
PL	56	20	42	3	38	30	34	34
RO	–	19	13	0	10	16	13	14
SK	–	–	–	5	6	6	3	6
SLO	–	–	8	0	2	3	3	4
YU[1)]	–	18	–	–	–	–	5	5

(continued)

(Table 3.4)

	Year of start						Total	Overall country participation**
	1990/91	1991/92	1992/93	1993/94	1994/95	1995/96		
AT	3	5	3	0	8	13	6	7
B	22	24	27	28	33	26	27	28
D	47	43	42	64	53	51	47	48
DK	15	9	13	18	16	15	13	14
E	24	16	22	44	30	21	23	24
FI	1	3	3	13	5	10	5	6
F	40	41	36	36	49	42	41	43
GR	15	14	13	18	23	15	16	17
I	26	27	27	44	36	30	30	31
IRL	11	10	11	15	21	13	13	14
L	0	0	0	0	0	0	0	0
NL	28	28	30	46	30	32	30	31
P	11	8	11	21	18	16	13	13
SE	1	1	4	13	10	13	6	7
UK	57	64	52	69	63	65	61	63

(continued)

(Table 3.4)

	Year of start						Total	Overall country participation**
	1990/91	1991/92	1992/93	1993/94	1994/95	1995/96		
AUS	1	1	0	0	0	0	0	0
CDN	0	1	1	0	0	0	1	1
CH	2	1	1	0	2	1	1	1
IS	0	0	0	0	0	1	0	0
J	0	1	0	0	0	0	0	0
N	1	1	2	5	3	2	2	2
TR	0	0	0	0	0	0	0	0
USA	3	4	2	10	2	1	3	3
Total	436	430	418	554	504	468	454	488
(n)	(152)	(318)	(240)	(39)	(239)	(219)	(1,207)	(1,207)

1) Eligible until the end of their formal existence

(–) Not eligible

* Including only countries represented by partners in the year of start of the JEP

** All partners, including those not participating the whole period of the JEP

Source: Data base of the European Training Foundation

Table 3.5
Cooperation between Individual EU Member States and CEE Countries in TEMPUS Joint European Projects
1990/91 – 1995/96 (per cent of JEPs*)

	ALB	BG	CS	CZ	GDR	EE	H	LT	LV	PL	RO	SK	SLO	YU	Total
								CEE countries							
AT	0	3	7	15	0	0	7	3	4	3	5	26	28	4	7
B	22	28	29	32	8	4	31	23	18	24	37	26	25	23	31
D	26	42	50	38	85	50	62	55	50	47	31	52	59	46	56
DK	0	9	16	29	0	33	12	55	46	15	8	0	13	5	16
E	9	20	27	32	38	17	29	13	25	21	26	23	16	14	27
FI	0	4	2	6	0	42	4	19	29	4	7	3	0	2	6
F	43	35	37	41	46	25	43	29	14	42	73	32	22	28	49
GR	48	35	11	6	15	0	19	3	14	13	20	0	3	14	19
I	70	29	13	29	0	0	35	10	29	26	35	29	50	4	16
IRL	4	19	29	15	8	13	16	10	14	16	9	23	9	44	35
L	0	1	0	0	0	0	0	0	4	0	0	3	0	0	0
NL	13	26	37	24	8	25	45	35	25	29	20	42	25	35	37
P	0	16	13	29	15	4	14	6	14	14	16	10	6	11	16
SE	0	4	1	18	0	38	5	35	32	5	3	10	6	4	7
UK	39	64	61	79	46	58	63	65	61	63	46	55	59	75	71
Total	274	334	335	394	269	308	384	361	379	321	337	332	322	307	393
(n)	(23)	(140)	(150)	(34)	(13)	(24)	(274)	(31)	(28)	(406)	(153)	(31)	(32)	(57)	(1,207)

* All partners, i.e. including those not participating the whole period
Source: Data base of the European Training Foundation

As regards the smaller EU members states, it is worthwhile mentioning that:
• Denmark cooperated relatively often with the Baltic States
• Belgium with Romania and the Czech Republic
• Greece with Bulgaria
• The Netherlands with Hungary, the Czech Republic and Slovenia.

In several CEE countries, the inclusion of partners from more than one organisation became a national priority during TEMPUS II. Thus, it is not surprising to note that some of these countries often were represented by at least two partners in the respective TEMPUS II JEPs. These 'multi-institutional' JEPs were most frequent in the Slovak Republic (97 per cent of the JEPs in which this country participated), Bulgaria (93 per cent) and Romania (92 per cent). On the other hand, the respective proportion was lowest in the case of Albania (40 per cent of the JEPs with Albanian participation) and Slovenia (42 per cent). Multi-institutional participation of Western countries in TEMPUS II JEPs was most common for France (47 per cent of JEPs with French partners) and Germany (33 per cent).

Altogether, about 11,000 representatives from the various countries participated in the 1,207 Joint European Projects starting during the first phase of TEMPUS and the first two years of the second phase of TEMPUS. Thus, an average TEMPUS Joint European Project was formed by nine partners from higher education institutions, enterprises and other organisations. A comparison between TEMPUS I and TEMPUS II shows a slight increase in the proportion of partners from CEE countries among all partners from 33 per cent to 38 per cent. As Table 3.6 shows, partners from CEE countries most often came from Poland, Romania and Hungary and least often from the Baltic States, Albania and Slovenia. Among the Western countries, partners from the United Kingdom, France and Germany most frequently participated in TEMPUS JEPs.

As described in Chapter 3.3, individual higher education institutions participated on average in about four TEMPUS II Joint European Projects while the vast majority of enterprises and other organisations participated solely in a single JEP each. The frequency of participation of the various types of organisations did not differ substantially between Central and Eastern European and Western countries.

However, some differences in the type of organisations participating in TEMPUS II JEPs can be observed as regards the individual countries (see Table 3.7).

Table 3.6
Number of TEMPUS Joint European Projects, Partners and Organi-
sations 1990/91 – 1995/96, per Country (absolute numbers and per cent*)

	Joint European Projects		Partners		Organisations	
	Number	Per cent	Number	Per cent	Number	Per cent
ALB	24	2.0	31	0.3	9	0.3
BG	149	12.3	417	3.8	121	3.6
CZ	115	9.5	294	2.7	89	2.6
CS[1]	170	14.1	143	1.3	119	3.5
GDR[1]	12	1.0	19	0.2	10	0.3
EE	28	2.3	46	0.4	17	0.5
H	281	23.3	792	7.3	184	5.4
LT	33	2.7	69	0.6	25	0.7
LV	31	2.6	65	0.6	27	0.8
PL	414	34.3	1,047	9.6	339	10.0
RO	169	14.0	604	5.5	248	7.3
SK	75	6.2	162	1.5	51	1.5
SLO	56	4.6	90	0.8	36	1.1
YU[1]	71	5.9	62	0.6	41	1.2
AT	80	6.6	126	1.2	39	1.1
B	338	28.0	513	4.7	128	3.8
D	587	48.6	1,087	10.0	305	9.0
DK	168	13.9	245	2.2	80	2.4
E	284	23.5	394	3.6	97	2.9
FI	70	5.8	89	0.8	31	0.9
F	513	42.5	1,148	10.5	507	14.9
GR	204	16.9	285	2.6	69	2.0
I	236	19.6	640	5.9	162	4.8
IRL	299	24.8	186	1.7	33	1.0
L	4	0.3	4	0.0	4	0.1
NL	371	30.7	562	5.2	139	4.1
P	160	13.3	209	1.9	46	1.4
SE	85	7.0	113	1.9	38	1.1
UK	760	63.0	1,323	12.1	329	9.7
AUS	4	0.3	4	0.0	2	0.1
CDN	9	0.7	9	0.1	5	0.1
CH	18	1.5	40	0.4	11	0.3
IS	2	0.2	2	0.0	1	0.0
J	3	0.2	4	0.0	2	0.1
N	25	2.1	33	0.3	9	0.3
TR	3	0.2	3	0.0	3	0.1
USA	37	3.1	43	0.4	37	1.1
Total	1,207	100.0	10,903	100.0	1,918	100.0

(1) Eligible until the end of their formal existence
* All partners and organisations, including those not participating the whole period
Source: Database of the European Training Foundation

Table 3.7
Type of Organisations Participating in TEMPUS Joint European Projects 1990/91 – 1995/96, by Country (per cent*)

	Type of organisation				
	HE institution	Enterprise	Other organisation	Total	(n)
ALB	89	0	11	100	(9)
BG	26	38	36	100	(121)
CZ	30	28	42	100	(89)
CS[1]	41	18	41	100	(119)
GDR[1]	90	0	10	100	(10)
EE	52	24	24	100	(17)
H	43	20	38	100	(184)
LT	60	0	40	100	(25)
LV	48	4	48	100	(27)
PL	27	38	36	100	(339)
RO	16	52	32	100	(248)
SK	35	26	39	100	(51)
SLO	33	36	31	100	(36)
YU[1]	51	22	27	100	(41)
AT	44	28	28	100	(39)
B	45	27	28	100	(128)
D	50	26	24	100	(305)
DK	49	26	25	100	(80)
E	51	18	32	100	(97)
FI	77	19	3	100	(31)
F	46	22	32	100	(507)
GR	48	23	29	100	(69)
I	35	20	44	100	(162)
IRL	55	30	15	100	(33)
L	50	0	50	100	(4)
NL	53	18	29	100	(139)
P	72	11	17	100	(46)
SE	61	21	18	100	(38)
UK	53	27	20	100	(329)
AUS	50	50	0	100	(2)
CDN	100	0	0	100	(5)
CH	82	0	18	100	(11)
IS	100	0	0	100	(1)
J	88	0	13	100	(2)
N	78	0	22	100	(9)
TR	67	0	33	100	(3)
USA	90	5	5	100	(37)
Total	52	25	23	100	(3,393)

(1) Eligible until the end of their formal existence
* Including organisations not participating the whole period
Source: Database of the European Training Foundation

In Central and Eastern Europe:

- the proportion of enterprises among all participating organisations from individual countries was highest in Romania (52 per cent), Poland and Bulgaria (38 per cent each)
- institutions of higher education participated most frequently in Albania (89 per cent) and Lithuania (60 per cent)
- other organisations were most frequent in Latvia (48 per cent).

In EU Member States:

- the proportion of enterprises was highest in Ireland (30 per cent) and Austria (28 per cent)
- higher education institutions were most frequent in Finland (77 per cent) and Portugal (72 per cent)

other organisations were most common in Italy (44 per cent).By and large the proportion of enterprises and other institutions among the partners can be considered as remarkably high, in accordance with the aim of the TEMPUS Programme to establish links between higher education and the economic and public sectors.

During the first phase of TEMPUS, the management functions (i.e. those of the coordinator and the contractor) were most often taken over by partners from the EU Member States. This was partly due to the regulations set up by the European Commission from the beginning of TEMPUS in 1990/91 that excluded partners from CEE countries from taking over these tasks and partly, as one might expect, due to difficulties in conforming with the demands of these tasks faced by CEE partners in the first years of political and economic reforms.

As already mentioned above, the accessibility of partners from individual CEE countries to the management functions were continuously widened over the years. Thus, it is not surprising to note that in accordance with the growing experience in administrative and financial tasks the management functions within JEPs were considerably more often taken over by partners from the CEE countries during TEMPUS II.

Altogether, 44 per cent of the TEMPUS Joint European Projects were coordinated by partners from Central and Eastern European countries. While the respective proportion was only about one-quarter of the TEMPUS I JEPs, it increased to about three-quarters of the TEMPUS II JEPs. This figure clearly underlines the willingness and ability of CEE partners to take stronger responsibility for the whole process of implementation of TEMPUS-supported educational and structural matters. Organisations from Poland, Hungary and Romania acted more often as coordinators of JEPs than organisations from the other CEE countries.

Table 3.8
Country of Coordinator of TEMPUS Joint European Projects, by Year of Start (per cent of JEPs*)

	Year of start						Total
	90/91	91/92	92/93	93/94	94/95	95/96	
ALB	–	–	0	0	0	0	0
BG	–	1	3	0	6	10	4
CS[1]	x	3	6	–	–	–	2
CZ	–	–	–	0	6	7	2
GDR[1]	x	–	–	–	–	–	–
EE	–	–	0	8	1	1	1
H	x	7	4	41	13	12	9
LT	–	–	0	3	0	3	1
LV	–	–	0	0	2	1	1
PL	x	1	10	0	24	22	11
RO	–	8	4	0	8	15	7
SK	–	–	–	0	5	6	2
SLO	–	–	5	0	2	3	2
YU[1]	–	8	–	–	–	–	2
AT	0	0	0	0	0	1	0
B	6	5	6	3	4	2	4
D	17	9	7	13	3	3	7
DK	3	3	5	0	1	0	2
E	4	1	3	0	0	0	1
FI	0	0	0	0	0	0	0
F	16	11	12	5	7	2	9
GR	4	4	3	8	3	0	3
I	7	5	5	3	3	1	4
IRL	1	1	1	0	1	0	1
L	0	0	0	0	0	0	0
NL	12	8	9	0	1	3	6
P	1	1	1	3	0	0	1
SE	0	0	1	0	1	0	0
UK	29	23	15	15	8	6	16

(continued)

(Table 3.8)			Year of start				Total
	90/91	91/92	92/93	93/94	94/95	95/96	
AUS	0	1	1	0	0	0	1
CDN	0	0	0	0	0	0	0
CH	0	0	0	0	0	0	0
J	0	0	0	0	0	0	0
N	0	0	0	0	0	0	0
TR	0	0	0	0	0	0	0
USA	0	0	0	0	0	0	0
Total	100	100	100	100	100	100	100
(n)	(152)	(318)	(240)	(39)	(239)	(219)	(1,207)

(1) Eligible until the end of their formal existence

(-) Not eligible

(x) Not eligible for coordination (as coordinator)

* Country of coordinator in the year of start of the JEP. Not including changes in the management functions between partners in the second or third year of operation of the JEP.

Source: Database of the European Training Foundation

Among the Western countries, partners from the United Kingdom clearly stand out in terms of taking over the role of JEP coordinator (16 per cent of all JEPs). In addition French (9 per cent), German (7 per cent), and Dutch (6 per cent) partners often acted as coordinators.

During the first phase of TEMPUS, partners from CEE countries played a marginal role as contractors in TEMPUS Joint European Projects (4 per cent of the JEPs). This reflects the fact that only four CEE countries were eligible to take over the financial responsibility in TEMPUS I. In 1992/93, the first year in which partners from Czechoslovakia and Hungary became eligible for the contracting function, 5 per cent of the newly-established JEPs were contracted by partners from these countries. In about one-third of the relatively small number of Joint European Projects established in the last year of TEMPUS I, partners from Hungary were in charge of the financial administration.

During the first two years of TEMPUS II, partners from Bulgaria, the Czech Republic, Hungary, Poland, Romania, the Slovak Republic and Slovenia were eligible to take over the contracting function. Altogether, in 39 per cent of the TEMPUS II Joint European Projects the contractor was a member of an organisation from Central or Eastern Europe. With about

Table 3.9
Country of Contractor of TEMPUS Joint European Projects, by Year of Start (per cent of JEPs*)

	Year of start						Total
	90/91	91/92	92/93	93/94	94/95	95/96	
ALB	–	–	x	x	x	x	x
BG	–	x	x	x	x	x	x
CS[1]	x	x	2	–	–	–	0
CZ	–	–	–	0	5	7	2
GDR[1]	x	–	–	–	–	–	x
EE	–	–	x	x	x	x	x
H	x	x	3	36	8	8	5
LT	–	–	x	x	x	x	x
LV	–	–	x	x	x	x	x
PL	x	x	x	x	13	16	6
RO	x	x	x	x	x	7	1
SK	–	–	–	0	5	5	2
SLO	–	–	x	0	1	2	1
YU[1]	–	x	–	–	–	–	x
AT	x	x	x	x	0	1	0
B	7	7	8	3	8	4	7
D	16	16	12	10	8	8	12
DK	3	4	7	5	3	0	3
E	4	1	3	3	2	1	2
FI	x	x	x	x	0	0	0
F	18	17	18	5	17	10	16
GR	3	4	3	8	3	0	3
I	6	6	8	5	5	2	6
IRL	2	1	1	3	2	1	1
L	0	0	0	0	0	0	0
NL	13	11	11	0	4	7	9
P	1	2	1	5	0	1	1
SE	x	x	x	x	0	0	0
UK	28	31	23	18	16	16	23
Total	100	100	100	100	100	100	100
(n)	(152)	(311)	(239)	(39)	(239)	(219)	(1,199)

(1) eligible until the end of their formal existence; (-) = not eligible; (x) = not eligible for contracting (as contractor)

* Country of contractor in the year of start of the JEP. Not including changes in the management functions between partners in the second or third year of operation of the JEP.

Source: Database of the European Training Foundation

13 per cent of all Joint European Projects in 1994/95 and 17 per cent in 1995/96, Poland was the most frequent CEE contractor country, followed by Hungary with 8 per cent of the JEPs each in both years. Partners from CEE countries eligible for contracting of the JEPs made use of this possibility in more than half of the respective TEMPUS II JEPs, among them partners from the Slovak Republic most often took the contracting function, in 80 per cent of the TEMPUS II JEPs, with partners from the Slovak Republic.

Among Western countries, partners from the United Kingdom most often acted as JEP contractors (23 per cent of the TEMPUS I and TEMPUS II JEPs). A further 16 per cent of the JEPs were contracted by partners from France, 12 per cent by partners from Germany and 9 per cent by partners from The Netherlands (see Table 3.9). Partners from the remaining EU Member States only played a minor role in taking over responsibility for the financial administration of TEMPUS Joint European Projects.

During TEMPUS I most of the CEE countries were underrepresented in the management functions in comparison to their overall number of partners in Joint European Projects. This situation has completely changed during TEMPUS II. With the exception of Albania, all other CEE countries are now overrepresented in the management functions (coordinator or contractor). Accordingly, the proportion of coordinators and/or contractors of the majority of Western countries is below their respective proportion of partners in all TEMPUS II JEPs. The only exceptions can be observed as regards the United Kingdom (which constitutes 'only' 11 per cent of the partners in TEMPUS II Joint European Projects but 16 per cent of the contractors) and France (10 per cent of partners and 14 per cent of contractors).

3.5 Subject Areas and Objectives

The subject areas represented in TEMPUS Joint European Projects were partly pre-determined by the objectives of the PHARE Programme. The national priorities of the CEE partner countries played an important role in this respect. Two subject areas clearly stood out during the first phase of TEMPUS: engineering/applied sciences (20 per cent) and management and business studies (18 per cent). Undoubtedly these two areas were viewed as most important for the economic development of the Central and Eastern European countries. Although the proportion of newly established Joint European Projects in these two subjects decreased slightly during TEMPUS II (17 and 16 per cent), the proportion of TEMPUS II JEPs in engineering/applied sciences as well as in management and business studies was higher than in any other subject area. A remarkable proportion of 10 per cent of all TEMPUS JEPs was concerned with social sciences and 8 per cent with environmental protection. Other subjects represented by more than 5 per cent of the JEPs were computer and medical sciences (7 per cent each) and agriculture and natural sciences (6 per cent each). At the end of the scale, we note humanities, art and design and law each comprising 1 or 2 per cent of the JEPs.

Table 3.10
Subject Area of TEMPUS Joint European Projects, by Year of Start
(per cent of JEPs)

Subject area*	Year of start						Total
	90/91	91/92	92/93	93/94	94/95	95/96	
Agr	4	6	6	15	6	6	6
Arc	1	2	3	3	3	2	2
Art	1	2	0	0	1	0	1
Com	8	8	8	10	9	4	7
Eng	18	23	19	13	13	21	19
Env	7	5	8	3	12	8	8
Hum	1	2	1	3	1	1	1
Lan	7	7	4	3	3	5	5
Law	3	2	2	0	3	2	2
Man	24	17	16	13	18	15	17
Med	6	7	9	10	6	5	7
Nat	7	6	6	10	4	8	6
Soc	7	9	10	8	11	12	10
Tea	3	3	5	8	3	5	4
Other	5	2	3	3	7	6	4
Total	100	100	100	100	100	100	100
(n)	(152)	(318)	(240)	(39)	(239)	(219)	(1,207)

* Explanation see Table 3.11

Source: Database of the European Training Foundation

As Table 3.10 shows, some changes in the proportion of Joint European Projects established in the various subject areas can be observed over time. The proportion of newly established JEPs in engineering decreased continuously from 23 per cent in 1991/92 to 13 per cent each in 1993/94 and 1994/95. After that the respective proportion of JEPs increased again to 21 per cent in 1995/96, the second year of TEMPUS II. The number of JEPs in management and business studies which had decreased continuously during TEMPUS I, from 24 per cent in 1990/91 to 13 per cent in 1993/94, increased in the first year of TEMPUS II to 18 per cent of the new JEPs and than decreased again to 15 per cent of new JEPs in the second year of TEMPUS II. By and large, a certain variation in the proportions of newly established JEPs in the individual subject areas can be observed over the time. However, the general subject area spread did not change substantially.

Almost all of the Central and Eastern European countries participated in a wide range of different subject areas in TEMPUS JEPs. However, different priorities can be identified, as Table 3.11 shows. TEMPUS Joint European Projects with

- Albanian partners were most often in management sciences and agriculture (21 per cent)
- Bulgarian partners in engineering (20 per cent)
- partners from the Czech Republic in management (17 per cent) and engineering (15 per cent)
- Estonian partners in social sciences (18 per cent)
- Hungarian partners in management (14 per cent) and social sciences (13 per cent)
- Lithuanian partners in social sciences (18 per cent)
- Latvian partners in engineering (23 per cent)
- Polish partners in management (22 per cent) and engineering (19 per cent)
- Romanian partners in engineering (27 per cent)
- Slovakian partners in engineering (19 per cent each)
- Slovenian partners in engineering (23 per cent) and management studies (19 per cent).

The highest diversity of JEPs in terms of different subject areas could be observed in the case of Hungary.

Large Western countries with frequent JEP participation, notably the United Kingdom, were highly represented in most of the subject areas covered by TEMPUS II Joint European Projects. With the exception of humanities, agriculture, law, environmental protection, computer science, art and design, natural sciences and so called other subjects, British organisations participated in more Joint European Projects (between 55 and 75 per cent) than any other Western country (see Table 3.12). In some of

Table 3.11
Subject Areas of TEMPUS Joint European Projects 1990/91 – 1995/96, by Central and Eastern European Countries (per cent of JEPs*)

	ALB	BG	DS	CZ	EE	GDR	H	LT	LV	PL	RO	SK	SLO	YU	Total
							\multicolumn{8}{c}{CEE countries}							
Agr	21	10	7	5	7	8	7	9	10	4	5	6	2	3	6
Arc	4	3	2	1	4	0	2	3	0	2	2	3	4	3	2
Art	0	0	4	2	4	0	1	0	3	1	1	2	2	0	1
Com	8	11	5	4	4	8	7	12	3	9	4	9	6	5	7
Eng	4	20	19	15	11	31	12	12	23	19	27	19	23	25	19
Env	4	10	10	11	4	0	8	6	3	9	5	9	4	8	8
Hum	4	1	1	1	7	8	2	0	0	0	2	0	2	0	1
Lan	0	3	13	9	7	23	8	3	0	5	2	9	4	5	5
Law	4	1	3	4	0	0	3	0	0	1	0	3	2	0	2
Man	21	12	10	17	4	0	14	6	10	22	15	14	19	20	17
Med	13	8	8	5	7	0	7	9	3	5	9	5	8	8	7

(continued)

(Table 3.11)

							CEE countries								Total
	ALB	BG	DS	CZ	EE	GDR	H	LT	LV	PL	RO	SK	SLO	YU	
Nat	13	5	9	7	11	8	7	3	10	7	9	6	6	3	6
Soc	0	10	4	9	18	0	13	18	16	9	11	4	10	12	10
Tea	4	2	6	4	7	8	5	3	13	2	1	6	8	3	4
Other	0	5	1	4	7	8	5	15	6	5	5	4	2	2	4
Total	100	100	100	100	100	100	100	100	100	100	100	100	100	100	100
(n)	(24)	(146)	(103)	(164)	(28)	(13)	(280)	(33)	(31)	(413)	(169)	(117)	(52)	(59)	(1,199)

Agr = Agricultural sciences/agrobusiness
Arc = Architecture, urban/regional planning
Art = Art and design
Com = Computer sciences
Eng = Engineering studies/applied sciences
Env = Environmental protection
Hum = Humanities/philological sciences
Lan = Languages studies

Law = Law
Man = Management and business
Med = Medical sciences
Nat = Natural sciences and mathematics
Soc = Social sciences
Tea = Teacher training
Oth = Other subjects

* All JEP partners, i.e. including those not participating the whole period

Table 3.12
Subject Areas of TEMPUS Joint European Projects 1990/91 – 1995/96, by Central and Eastern European Countries (per cent of JEPs*)

								CEE countries								Total
	Agr	Arc	Art	Com	Eng	Env	Hum	Lan	Law	Man	Med	Nat	Soc	Tea	Other	
AT	3	3	10	3	5	11	20	7	17	3	10	13	6	10	10	7
B	40	14	20	21	22	21	33	23	43	28	39	29	38	19	36	28
D	44	41	50	52	53	59	53	56	65	30	35	68	48	46	64	48
DK	18	14	20	12	11	23	13	11	4	10	20	19	13	15	18	14
E	21	31	0	26	23	20	27	15	39	23	34	23	24	17	30	24
FI	5	3	0	0	8	3	0	3	13	3	11	9	5	6	16	6
F	41	34	50	43	44	29	47	30	61	44	51	51	43	19	60	42
GR	19	17	0	17	18	19	7	11	30	15	15	16	15	10	30	17
I	33	28	10	28	38	24	47	18	48	26	41	41	28	15	22	31

(continued)

(Table 3.12)

	CEE countries														Tea	Other	Total
	Agr	Arc	Art	Com	Eng	Env	Hum	Lan	Law	Man	Med	Nat	Soc	Tea	Other	Total
IRL	29	17	20	10	9	17	0	10	4	15	16	12	13	15	16	14
L	0	0	10	0	0	0	0	0	0	0	0	0	1	2	0	0
NL	41	14	40	20	15	34	32	20	48	29	43	45	45	38	42	31
P	15	3	0	12	17	17	0	7	9	16	14	16	10	6	16	13
SE	4	3	0	6	5	9	0	2	9	5	8	21	11	6	10	7
UK	60	55	70	36	66	54	27	69	61	69	59	55	60	75	68	63
Total	373	279	300	313	334	338	397	280	452	317	395	419	358	298	438	344
(n)	(73)	(29)	(10)	(89)	(227)	(94)	(15)	(61)	(23)	(298)	(80)	(75)	(119)	(48)	(50)	(1,201)

Agr = Agricultural sciences/agrobusiness
Arc = Architecture, urban/regional planning
Art = Art and design
Com = Computer sciences
Eng = Engineering studies/applied sciences
Env = Environmental protection
Hum = Humanities/philological sciences
Lan = Languages studies

Law = Law
Man = Management and business
Med = Medical sciences
Nat = Natural sciences and mathematics
Soc = Social sciences
Tea = Teacher training
Oth = Other subjects

* All JEP partners, i.e. including those not participating the whole period

the other subject areas, Germany was the major player. France was highly represented in law (61 per cent) and medical sciences (51 per cent).

Other EU Member States tended to be strongly represented in the following subject areas:

- Austria participated in a relatively large proportion of Joint European Projects in the humanities and law
- Belgium in law, agriculture and social sciences
- Denmark in environmental sciences, arts and design and medical sciences
- Spain in law and architecture
- Greece in law
- Ireland in agriculture and arts and design
- Italy in law and humanities
- The Netherlands in social sciences and natural sciences
- Sweden in natural and social sciences.

TEMPUS Joint European Projects in environmental protection, computer sciences, engineering and business studies most often involve enterprises. It is also not surprising to note that enterprises did not play any role in teacher training and art and design.

Joint European Projects are awarded TEMPUS support to promote the development of the higher education systems of the eligible countries and to encourage cooperation between them and academic or industrial partners in the European Community. Financial support is awarded for a wide range of activities classified as:

- cooperative educational measures (e.g. curriculum development, continuous education and retraining of staff members, open and distance learning, etc.)
- structural development of higher education institutions (upgrading of facilities, creation of new and restructuring of existing institutions, etc.)
- exchange of students and staff members between partner institutions.

Due to changes in the classification system of JEP activities used in the administration of applications since the beginning of TEMPUS, a comparison between TEMPUS I JEPs and TEMPUS II JEPs with regard to the educational and structural activities is not possible. Thus, the following description clearly distinguishes between objectives and activities of JEPs newly established prior to and after the beginning of TEMPUS II.

The available data on the award of TEMPUS support for Joint European Projects newly established in the first phase of TEMPUS suggest that most of the JEPs were concerned with various areas of activities:

- 15 per cent of the JEPs were awarded TEMPUS support for all three areas of activities named above
- 22 per cent for cooperative educational measures and for structural development
- 22 per cent for cooperative educational measures and for mobility of students and staff
- 7 per cent for structural development and for mobility of students and staff.

Support for activities in a single area was received by

- 21 per cent of the JEPs for cooperative educational measures
- 9 per cent of the JEPs for mobility of students and staff
- 4 per cent of the JEPs for structural development.

Table 3.13
Profile of Activities of TEMPUS Joint European Projects, by Year of Start (per cent of JEPs)

	Year of start				Total
	90/91	91/92	92/93	93/94	
Educational measures, structural development and mobility	18	17	10	10	15
Educational measures and structural development	11	22	29	28	22
Educational measures and mobility	22	28	15	13	22
Structural development and mobility	11	6	7	5	7
Only educational measures	20	22	23	8	21
Only structural development	6	2	4	8	4
Only mobility	12	4	11	28	9
Total	100	100	100	100	100
(n)	(152)	(316)	(231)	(39)	(738)

Source: Database of the European Training Foundation

As Table 3.13 shows, the proportion of TEMPUS Joint European Projects active in all three areas decreased from 18 per cent of the JEPs starting in 1990/91 to about 10 per cent each of JEPs starting in 1992/93 and 1993/94. On the other hand, the proportion of newly established JEPs awarded TEMPUS support for cooperative educational measures and structural development but not for mobility increased from 11 per cent in 1990/91 to 29 per cent in 1992/93 and to a similar proportion in 1993/94.

An especially high proportion of the small number of JEPs starting in the last year of TEMPUS I were solely concerned with the mobility of students and staff.

Although some changes in the profile of activities of JEPs can be observed over time, the overall balance between the different types of activities did not change substantially. About 80 per cent of the JEPs starting between 1990/91 and 1993/94 were awarded TEMPUS support for cooperative educational measures and about half for the mobility of students and staff and for structural development of CEE higher education institutions. The information available in the database of the TEMPUS Department in the ETF allows us a more detailed description of some of the JEP activities.

As regards cooperative educational measures:
- 57 per cent of all TEMPUS I Joint European Projects were awarded support for curriculum development
- 19 per cent for the development of continuing education and retraining schemes
- 16 per cent for intensive training courses
- 3 per cent for open and distance learning
- 7 per cent for general or other cooperative education/training activities.

As regards structural development:
- 35 per cent were awarded support for the upgrading of facilities within departments or institutions in CEE countries
- 7 per cent for the creation of new institutions
- 6 per cent for re-structuring of existing institutions
- 4 per cent for the development of university – industry cooperation
- 2 per cent for structural development in general or other structural development.

Activities differed according to subject areas. TEMPUS I Joint European Projects in computer sciences (68 per cent), engineering (55 per cent) and natural sciences (48 per cent) were concerned most frequently with upgrading of facilities, whereas this activity only played a marginal role in teacher training (13 per cent), art and design (14 per cent), management and business (16 per cent) and social sciences (17 per cent). Support for mobility of students and staff was awarded to all JEPs in arts and design and to 79 per cent of JEPs in language studies but only to 38 per cent of JEPs in law. Curriculum development was most common in architecture (83 per cent) and engineering (68 per cent), whereas it was least frequent in art and design (43 per cent) and teacher training (45 per cent).

Looking at individual countries, we note that about three-quarters of the partners in Bulgaria and Lithuania were concerned with curriculum development whereas the respective proportion was about one half of the JEPs in most other CEE countries. Upgrading of facilities was most frequent in Albania (64 per cent) and Romania (49 per cent) and least frequent in Hungary, the Czech Republic and Poland. TEMPUS Joint European Mobility of students and staff members was most frequently represented in the Slovak Republic (75 per cent) and in Hungary (66 per cent).

The majority of networks awarded the first TEMPUS support during the second phase of the programme was classified as 'Structural JEPs' (86 per cent), that is, they were awarded support for cooperative measures in the field of teaching and education or for structural development of departments, faculties or institution(s) of higher education. A further 11 per cent of TEMPUS II JEPs were classified as 'Mobility JEPs', that is, networks of higher education institutions, enterprises and other organisations awarded TEMPUS support for the organisation of student mobility. A special type of Structural JEPs, the so called 'JEP+', was introduced in 1994/95, the first year of TEMPUS II, to foster activities beyond the level of departments or faculties – on the institutional or supra-institutional level. The objectives of these projects had to be clearly defined by the national authorities of the CEE partner countries and was published in a special supplements to the guide for applicants. The total number of JEP+ projects awarded support was 11 in 1994/95 (5 per cent). Because of difficulties in the application and selection procedure, no new JEP+ projects could be proposed in the second year of TEMPUS II.

Following the new classification of TEMPUS JEPs introduced with the beginning of the second phase of TEMPUS by the European Commission:

- 39 per cent of the TEMPUS II JEPs were concerned with the introduction of new course programmes
- 17 per cent with the restructuring of already existing course programmes
- 11 per cent with the creation of a network for the organisation of student mobility
- 10 per cent with the restructuring of departments, faculties or institutions
- 8 per cent with the development of universities' capacities in continuing education and retraining schemes for university staff
- 7 per cent with the development of universities' capacities to cooperate with industry
- 5 per cent with the creation of new departments, faculties or institutions

- 4 per cent with the review and improvement of university management.

Some changes in the objectives of JEPs can be observed between the first and the second year of TEMPUS II. While the proportion of JEPs concerned with the creation and restructuring of departments, faculties and institutions or with the improvement of the university management decreased slightly, an increase in the proportion of JEPs concerned with the introduction or restructuring of course programmes or with the organisation of student mobility can be observed. However, the changes are in most cases small and might be rather co-incidental.

As Table 3.14 shows, some differences in the objectives of TEMPUS II JEPs can be observed according to the participating CEE countries:

- Albania (50 per cent of the JEPs with partners from Albania) and Estonia (22 per cent) were most often concerned with the restructuring of departments, faculties or institutions
- Poland (48 per cent) and Bulgaria (47 per cent) were frequently concerned with the introduction of new course programmes
- The Slovak Republic and Slovenia developed often the universities capacities to cooperate with the industry (48 and 33 per cent) and continuing education/retraining schemes (30 and 42 per cent)
- Latvia (22 per cent) and the Czech Republic (21 per cent) most often were concerned with the creation of departments, faculties or institutions
- Latvia (22 per cent), Lithuania, Romania (21 per cent each) and the Czech Republic (18 per cent) most often were awarded TEMPUS support for the organisation of student mobility
- The Czech Republic was frequently involved in JEPs aiming to review and improve the university management.

The focus of objectives of TEMPUS II JEPs did not only differ according to CEE countries involved but also according to the subject areas in which JEP activities were undertaken. The introduction of new course programmes was the JEP objective in more than half of TEMPUS II JEPs in architecture (55 per cent), agriculture (54 per cent), social sciences (52 per cent) and environmental protection (51 per cent). Retraining of staff and development of continuing education capacities were most often the JEP objective in teacher training (27 per cent), languages (22 per cent) and humanities (20 per cent), whereas the organisation of student mobility was most frequent in natural sciences (22 per cent) and management and business studies (16 per cent).

Table 3.14
Objectives of TEMPUS II Joint European Projects 1994/95 and 1995/96, by Central and Eastern European Countries (per cent of JEPs*)

Objectives of JEPs	CEE countries											Total
	ALB	BG	CZ	EE	H	LT	LV	PL	RO	SK	SLO	
Creation of department, faculty or institution	10	12	21	11	1	14	22	1	7	4	8	5
Restructuring of department, faculty or institution	50	3	3	22	14	7	11	5	9	4	8	10
Review and improvement of university management	10	2	21	11	4	7	11	6	2	4	8	4
Development of capacities for cooperation with industry	20	5	18	33	3	7	11	11	9	48	33	7
Development of continuing education/retraining schemes	10	8	18	22	7	7	22	6	7	30	42	8
Introduction of new course programmes	0	47	18	0	37	14	22	48	39	11	0	39
Restructuring of existing course programmes	0	22	0	0	19	21	0	13	5	0	0	17
Organisation of student mobility	0	2	0	0	14	21	0	10	21	0	0	11
Total	100	100	100	100	100	100	100	100	100	100	100	100
(n)	(10)	(60)	(33)	(9)	(70)	(14)	(9)	(155)	(56)	(27)	(12)	(449)

* All JEP partners, i.e. including those not participating the whole period

3.6   Student and Staff Mobility

From the outset of the TEMPUS Programme mobility of staff and students was seen as an important measure to promote higher education reforms in the Central and Eastern European countries through cooperation with partners from Western countries. Altogether 27,252 students were awarded a mobility grant in the framework of TEMPUS I and TEMPUS II JEPs:[4]

- 23,295 mobility grants for students from CEE countries to stay for a period of study in a Member State of the EU
- 3,924 mobility grants for students from the EU going abroad to a CEE country
- 133 mobility grants for students moving from one CEE country to another.

TEMPUS was expected from the outset to serve primarily students from CEE countries. However, lack of interest and language barriers kept the West–East student mobility on a small scale.

The number of mobility grants awarded to students in the framework of TEMPUS Joint European Projects increased from 1,218 in 1990/91 to 6,408 in 1992/93 and then decreased continuously to 6,166 in 1993/94, 6,072 in 1994/95 and 4,356 in 1995/96. Poland and Hungary clearly stood out in the number of students sent to the EU but also in the number of students received from Member States of the EU (see Table 3.15).

Although the TEMPUS regulations originally allowed the provision of mobility grants for students and staff on an individual basis, priority was given to applicants intending to be mobile in the framework of a Joint European Project. In 1992, the support of student mobility on an individual basis was officially discontinued. Overall, less than 5 per cent of student mobilities supported by TEMPUS during the period of observation were granted on an individual basis. On the other hand, mobility grants for staff members *were* awarded on a small scale on an individual basis – actually, about 10 per cent of the overall TEMPUS grants for staff mobility.

TEMPUS mobility grants for academic and administrative staff members in the framework of Joint European Projects were provided for teaching

---

4   The available figures are based on applications and renewals of applications. The real figures about student mobility as provided in the annual and final reports of the JEP are not currently or are only partly included in the databases of Torino.

and training assignments, practical placements in enterprises, short visits, retraining and updating periods, participation in intensive courses, etc. Altogether, about 51,597 mobility grants for staff were awarded during six years of TEMPUS:

- 29,923 mobility grants for staff members going from a CEE country to the EU
- 21,017 mobility grants for staff members from EU Member States to spend a period abroad in a CEE country
- 657 grants for staff mobility within the CEE countries.

The number of staff mobility grants awarded in the framework of JEPs increased more or less continuously over time and peaked with about 13,800 in 1994/95, the first year of TEMPUS II. A decrease in the number of staff mobility grants can be observed in the second year of TEMPUS II to about 12,100.

In fact, 41 per cent of the TEMPUS II mobility grants were awarded to persons from Western countries spending some time in Central and Eastern European countries (as compared to 38 per cent of mobility grants for Western partners during TEMPUS I). As regards the individual CEE countries, Poland, Hungary, Romania and Bulgaria clearly stood out in the exchange of staff members (see Table 3.16).

A comparison to ERASMUS underscores the strong emphasis TEMPUS places on staff mobility. Staff exchange is expected to contribute to the restructuring of departments the training of staff and to the interaction between CEE countries and the EU on a departmental level. Student mobility seems to be a supplementary activity, possibly contributing to long-term changes with regard to the internationalisation of the higher education and economic systems of the CEE partner countries.

Table 3.15
Number of Student Mobility Grants Awarded Within Joint European Projects, by Academic Year
(absolute numbers)

	ALB	BG	CZ	CS	EE	GDR	H	LT	LV	PL	RO	SK	SLO	YU	Total
	Number of students sent to EU Member States by individual CEE countries														
1990/91	–	–	–	154	–	9	403	–	–	467	–	–	–	–	1,033
1991/92	–	70	–	500	–	–	844	–	–	879	316	–	–	138	2,747
1992/93	50	295	–	979	36	–	1,417	65	52	1,763	817	–	138	–	5,612
1993/94	65	321	608	–	63	–	1,178	89	138	1,496	842	289	164	–	5,253
1994/95	79	277	404	–	106	–	819	197	202	1910	528	391	149	–	5,061
1995/96	42	259	199	–	31	–	538	162	72	1387	638	212	50	–	3,589
Total	236	1,222	1,211	1,633	236	9	5,199	513	464	7,902	3,141	892	501	138	23,295

(continued)

(Table 3.15) Number of students received from EU Member States by individual CEE countries

	ALB	BG	CZ	CS	EE	GDR	H	LT	LV	PL	RO	SK	SLO	YU	Total
1990/91	–	–	–	28	–	25	74	–	–	58	–	–	–	–	185
1991/92	–	–	–	70	–	–	160	–	–	53	57	–	–	12	352
1992/93	–	29	–	165	1	–	230	11	–	250	84	–	16	–	786
1993/94	6	57	126	–	8	–	191	19	40	261	91	36	38	–	873
1994/95	4	47	145	–	9	–	188	17	41	380	89	8	0	–	1011
1995/96	0	41	94	–	1	–	166	5	2	223	120	49	16	–	717
Total	10	174	365	263	19	25	1,009	52	83	1,225	441	93	70	12	3,924

Source: European Training Foundation: Survey of TEMPUS I (draft 2). Unpublished document, 1994.

Table 3.16
Number of Staff Mobility Grants Awarded Within Joint European Projects, by Academic Year (absolute numbers)

Number of staff sent to EU Member States by individual CEE countries

	ALB	BG	CZ	CS	EE	GDR	H	LT	LV	PL	RO	SK	SLO	YU	Total
1990/91	–	–	–	141	–	33	224	–	–	326	–	–	–	–	724
1991/92	–	259	–	636	–	–	678	–	–	786	498	–	–	291	3,148
1992/93	47	607	–	1,181	57	–	1,103	83	95	1719	901	–	221	–	6,014
1993/94	124	620	671	–	62	–	971	133	116	1,536	1,041	351	251	–	5,876
1994/95	208	857	553	–	146	–	1,009	279	260	2,851	834	320	232	–	7,551
1995/96	212	877	510	–	114	–	980	221	163	2,120	888	401	123	–	6,610
Total	591	3,220	1,734	1,958	379	33	4,965	716	607	9,338	4,162	1,072	827	291	29,923

(continued)

(Table 3.16)   Number of staff received from EU Member States by individual CEE countries

	ALB	BG	CZ	CS	EE	GDR	H	LT	LV	PL	RO	SK	SLO	YU	Total
1990/91	–	–	–	119	–	17	192	–	–	256	–	–	–	–	584
1991/92	–	150	–	405	–	–	455	–	–	550	287	–	–	203	2,050
1992/93	48	341	–	649	33	–	790	36	45	1,173	575	–	104	–	3,794
1993/94	73	344	417	–	56	–	496	90	89	931	575	210	155	–	3,436
1994/95	161	682	522	–	183	–	691	167	299	2,122	661	236	203	–	5,925
1995/96	166	638	381	–	105	–	859	214	152	1,667	824	277	146	–	5,428
Total	448	2,155	1,320	1,173	377	17	3,483	507	585	6,699	2,922	723	608	203	21,017

Source: European Training Foundation: Survey of TEMPUS I (draft 2). Unpublished document, 1994.

3.7   Financial Support for Joint European Projects

The financial approach of the TEMPUS Programme could be considered as full-funding of activities. In this respect the TEMPUS Programme differs from most other EU Programmes, which cover only parts of the costs of supported projects. In the first phase of TEMPUS, Joint European Projects were awarded on average 397,000 ECU for a three year period,[5] and 391,000 ECU were awarded for the respective period during TEMPUS II. While the average support provided for individual JEPs increased continuously from 104,000 ECU in the first year of operation to 172,000 ECU in the third year during TEMPUS I, a continuous decrease can be observed in TEMPUS II (see Table 3.17):

- in the first year TEMPUS II JEPs were awarded about 137,000 ECU
- in the second year 132,000 ECU
- in the third year 123,000 ECU.

Table 3.17
Average Amount of TEMPUS Support Allocated to Joint European Projects in Each Year of Operation, by Year of Start (mean of support in 1,000 ECU)

Year of operation	First year	(n)	Second year	(n)	Third year	(n)
TEMPUS I						
1990/91	108	152	160	134	179	126
1991/92	88	315	147	275	165	242
1992/93	122	237	156	220	182	206
1993/94	111	39	130	28	129	20
Total	104	743	152	629	172	368
TEMPUS II						
1994/95	139	239	134	238	127	228
1995/96	135	219	130	218	118	209
Total	137	458	132	456	123	437

Source: Database of the European Training Foundation

---

5   Because no figures about real costs are available, the following analysis is based on the funds allocated to the Joint European Projects.

The available data allow us to distinguish between TEMPUS funds allocated for administrative matters (e.g. staff costs, overheads, etc.), for equipment and for mobility.

- The amount of *TEMPUS funds allocated for administrative matters* of the Joint European Projects decreased from about 50,000 ECU per year of JEP operation starting in 1990/91 to about 30,000 ECU in each year of operation of TEMPUS II JEPs starting in 1995/96. In the same period, the respective proportion of funds in the overall annual budget of the JEPs decreased from about 40 per cent to about 25 per cent.

- By and large, the amount of *TEMPUS funds allocated for the provision of equipment* did not change over time (on average about 30,000 ECU per year of operation). However, one difference between TEMPUS I and TEMPUS II seems to be noteworthy. While during TEMPUS I the support allocated for equipment was usually highest in the second and third year of operation, the respective allocations for TEMPUS II JEPs were highest in the first year of operation.

- The amount of *TEMPUS funds allocated for staff and student mobility* was clearly higher in TEMPUS II than in TEMPUS I. The average amount was 73,000 ECU per year of operation for TEMPUS II JEPs as compared to 58,000 ECU for TEMPUS I JEPs. This figure corresponds to an increase in the proportion of mobility funds in the annual budget of the JEPs from about 40 per cent on average in TEMPUS I JEPs to more than 50 per cent in TEMPUS II JEPs.

3.8 Complementary Measures

In addition to TEMPUS Joint European Projects (Action 1) and Individual Mobility Grants (Action 2), support is provided for Complementary Measures (Action 3). As Complementary Measures were introduced to facilitate the major TEMPUS activities organised in Joint European Projects, it is not surprising to note, that the objectives of CMEs were adapted over time. During the first phase of TEMPUS, support was awarded for Complementary Measures mainly to foster and strengthen links between participants in higher education:[6]

- grants to associations: associations or consortia of universities were supported to facilitate the participation of organisations within the

---

6 See TEMPUS Vademecum, Academic year 1990/91. EC TEMPUS Office Brussels, 1990, p. 16.

partner CEE countries in the activities of European associations, notably associations of universities

- support for publications and other information material: this kind of support was provided to organisations and individuals for publications and other information of particular importance in view of the overall TEMPUS objectives
- support for surveys and studies: TEMPUS support was awarded to organisations for surveys and studies designed to analyse the development of the higher education systems in CEE partner countries and their interaction with the European Union and other Western countries.

In the first year of TEMPUS II, 1994/95, a fourth type of Complementary Measures was supported:

- CME+ projects designed to give the national authorities of the eligible countries the means to reach practical objectives in accordance with their policy for the development of higher education in their country. In view of this overall planning strategy, the national authorities predefine the objectives, expected outcomes and local patterns of CME+ projects.

In 1995/96, the objectives of Complementary Measures were changed. The special type of CME+ projects were no longer supported. Instead, three main strands were provided for:

- institutional restructuring and development at university/faculty level
- support for the dissemination of TEMPUS results including, where appropriate, dissemination of comparable results achieved in programmes other than TEMPUS
- support for the formulation of national higher education policies.

Although the special measure of CME+ were only supported during the first year of TEMPUS II, the objectives connected with this measure (i.e. development and restructuring of the higher education system beyond the level of departments and faculties) are now integrated in the first and third strands of CMEs. However, national authorities from individual CEE countries are no longer in the position to predefine objectives and outcomes of CMEs.

The information available about Complementary Measures during TEMPUS I is rather limited. Although databases were created and partly used for administrative purposes,[7] these databases were not maintained continually and did not correspond to official figures in the annual TEM-

---

7   CME data base of the European Training Foundation.

PUS reports of the European Commission. Although regarding most of the following analysis no data are available for the CMEs supported during the first phase of TEMPUS, some basic information could be collected from descriptions of individual projects and official reports.

During the six years of TEMPUS covered by this study, an overall number of 248 CMEs was supported, among them 138 CMEs in the first phase of TEMPUS and 110 in the first two years of the second phase.

Prior to the change of objectives of CMEs in 1995/96
- 37 per cent of the CMEs were awarded support for publication and information activities
- 36 per cent of the projects were concerned with surveys and studies
- 23 per cent were for associations and consortia of higher education institutions
- 6 per cent were CME+ projects.

Although 14 proposals for CME+ projects were offered by the national authorities of the individual CEE countries in 1994/95, only 7 projects were finally supported. The limited number and the quality of applications for these projects was mentioned by EU officials as the main reason for the refusal of the European Commission to award TEMPUS funds to the remaining CME+ projects.

In 1995/96, the second year of TEMPUS II:
- 77 per cent of the CMEs were concerned with institutional restructuring and development
- 14 per cent with the dissemination of TEMPUS results
- 9 per cent with the formulation of national higher education policies.

Most of the Complementary Measures projects in the second year of TEMPUS II were classified as feasibility studies (65 per cent). This was the case for all CMEs concerned with formulation of national policies and about three-quarters of CMEs concerned with institutional restructuring and development.

Support provided through CME and especially CME+ projects not only aimed to assist the development of faculties and single institutions, but also to contribute to the development of the higher education systems in the partner CEE countries. As Table 3.18 shows, in only about one-third of the CMEs was the focus of the activities directed towards a single institution. The majority of CMEs either focused on several institutions in the targeted country (42 per cent) or the higher education system itself (17 per cent. The proportion of CMEs focusing only on one single institution substantially increased from 28 per cent in 1994/95 to 38 per cent in

1995/96, whereas the proportion of CMEs concerned with matters on a transnational level decreased from 16 per cent to merely 1 per cent.

The most common country configuration of CMEs was one CEE country and two or three Western countries. However, in 1994/95 about one-quarter of the CMEs were multi-CEE CMEs, that is, including two or more partners from different CEE countries. In contrast, only one multi-CEE CME was awarded support in the second year of TEMPUS II.

Table 3.18
Institutional Focus of Complementary Measure Projects, by Academic Year (per cent)

	Academic year*		
	1994/95**	1995/96	Total
Single institution of higher education	28	38	36
Group of institutions of higher education	40	42	42
National higher education system	16	18	17
Transnational CEE countries	16	1	5
Total	100	100	100
(n)	(25)	(78)	(103)

*   Information missing for CMEs supported during the first phase of TEMPUS, i.e. 1990/91 – 1993/94
** Information missing for 7 CMEs
Source: Analysis of documents of the European Training Foundation

Almost 60 per cent of the TEMPUS II CMEs were contracted by partners from Member States of the European Union. However, the country with the highest number of TEMPUS II CME contractors was a CEE country, Poland (20 per cent of the CMEs), followed by The Netherlands (14 per cent) and the United Kingdom (13 per cent). The proportion of CEE partners taking over the contracting role increased from 35 per cent in 1994/95 to 45 per cent in 1995/96.

The majority of TEMPUS II CMEs were coordinated by partners from CEE countries. The respective proportion increased from about 50 per cent in 1994/95 to 75 per cent in 1995/96. As Table 3.19 shows, the largest number of coordinators was from Poland (21 per cent), Romania and Bulgaria (13 per cent each).

Table 3.19
Country of the CME Contractor and Coordinator, by Academic Year
(per cent of CMEs)

	Contractor			Coordinator		
	1994/95	1995/96	Total	1994/95	1995/96	Total
BG	0	0	0	6	15	13
CZ	13	6	8	9	5	6
EE	x	x	x	0	3	2
H	3	3	3	3	4	4
LT	x	x	x	3	0	1
LV	x	x	x	3	3	3
PL	16	22	20	13	24	21
RO	0	10	7	3	17	13
SK	0	3	2	3	4	4
SLO	3	1	2	3	0	1
AT	0	1	1	0	0	0
B	9	6	7	19	1	6
D	3	4	4	0	1	1
DK	0	1	1	0	0	0
FI	0	1	1	0	0	0
F	9	6	7	6	4	5
GR	0	3	2	0	0	0
I	9	5	6	0	0	0
IRL	0	1	1	0	0	0
NL	25	9	14	22	3	8
P	0	3	2	0	1	1
UK	9	15	13	3	7	6
CH				0	1	1
Total	100	100	100	100	100	100
(n)	(32)	(78)	(110)	(32)	(78)	(110)

(x) not eligible for contracting (as contractor)

Source: Database of the European Training Foundation

While during TEMPUS I the average funding per CME remained quite stable over time (about 10,000 ECU each year, see Table 3.20), the budget allocated to CMEs under Action 3 and the average financial support available per CME increased considerably under TEMPUS II:

- In 1994/95 a CME received an average grant of 17,300 ECU and the overall budget for CMEs was 554,000 ECU.
- In 1995/95 the average grant was 41,100 ECU per CME and the overall budget 3,206,000 ECU.

The increased overall budget for Complementary Measures underlines an increasing importance of this measure in the framework of the TEMPUS Programme.

Table 3.20
Number of Projects Awarded TEMPUS Support for Complementary Measures and Allocation of TEMPUS Funds, by Academic Year (in absolute numbers and ECU)

	Number of CME projects	Annual budget	Average support per CME project
1990/91	40	377,650	9,441
1991/92	37	435,500	11,770
1992/93	42	409,800	9,757
1993/94	19	188,595	9,926
1994/95	32	554,246	17,320
1995/96	78	3,206,200	41,105

Source: Database of the European Training Foundation

3.9 Youth Exchange

Additionally, and not much linked to the other activities supported by the TEMPUS Programme, grants were awarded for youth exchange activities. By the end of TEMPUS I, this kind of support was discontinued.

The amount of TEMPUS funds allocated to youth exchange activities was slightly higher in each year of TEMPUS I than the funds allocated to complementary measures (see Table 3.21). An increasing number of projects was awarded support for organising reciprocal exchange of young people between the European Union and the CEE partner countries lasting at least 10 days. The respective number of projects was 65 in 1990/91, 66 in 1991/92, 106 in 1992/93 and 114 in 1993/94. On average, about 300 young people participated in one project. Information about the home country of participants and the directions of mobility is not available.

Table 3.21
Number of Projects, Participants and Amount of TEMPUS Funds Allocated for Youth Exchange, by Academic Year (absolute numbers and allocation in million ECU)

| | Academic year | | | | Total |
	1990/91	1991/92	1992/93	1993/94	
Number of projects	65	66	106	114	351
Number of participants	2,118	1,074	3,532	3,663	10,387
Amount of TEMPUS funds (MECU)	0.60	0.51	0.86	1.11	3.08

Source: European Training Foundation: Survey of TEMPUS I (draft 2). Unpublished document, 1994

3.10   Joint European Networks

In 1993/94, a pilot phase was introduced to support Joint European Networks (JENs), a new measure which officially started in 1994/95. The aim of the JENs is to maintain the achievements of Joint European Projects through supporting a limited number of projects which have successfully completed their maximum three-year period. The grant awarded for a maximum of additional two years serves to achieve self-sustainability of project activities and to disseminate the results of the JEPs beyond the faculty or department in the CEE country.

About 30 JENs (24 per cent of the JEPs starting in 1990/91 for a support period of three years) were awarded TEMPUS support during the pilot phase, in 1993/94, and a further 83 JENs (34 per cent) were established in 1994/95, the first year of TEMPUS II. Altogether, these networks comprised about 950 partners from CEE partner countries and Western countries.

Each JEN received support for a period of two years. JENs starting in 1993/94 received on average about 12,000 ECU in their first year and 14,000 ECU in their second year of operation, while a fixed amount of

15,000 ECU for each year was granted to JENs starting in 1994/95. Altogether, 3,259,000 ECU were allocated to the about 110 JENs starting in 1993/94 and 1994/95.

Looking at the profile of JEPs and JENs in terms of numbers of participants, subject areas or activities, no differences can be observed between JEPs that were accepted to become JENs and the remaining JEPs of the respective years of start. However, it is worthy noting that JEPs with British coordinators or contractors more often were continued as JENs than JEPs with coordinators or contractors from other countries.

Chapter 4

Policy Formation and Administration of the TEMPUS Programme in the Central and Eastern European Partner Countries

4.1 The System of Policy Formation and Administration

The TEMPUS Programme has a rather complex system of decision-making and administration characterised by a number of framework regulations (e.g. Council decision, Vademecums or Guidelines for Applicants, competences of key actors in decision-making processes) on the one hand and by a certain openness and incomplete definition of concrete aims and objectives on the other. The features of openness and incomplete definition of aims are not arbitrary because there are three basic arenas in which relevant discussions and decisions take place. These are the European level, the national level of the CEE partner countries and the field of higher education. The interaction in these arenas has a certain potential for conflict. In this chapter we will concentrate on the level of national policy formation and patterns of administration of the TEMPUS Programme in the CEE countries and on the competences and roles of the actors in the various processes of policy formation and administration.

The general framework of TEMPUS Programme regulations is complemented by three important levels of decision-making:

- On the supra-national level the original decision of the EU Council was made concerning the introduction of the TEMPUS Programme. After consultation with all countries taking part in TEMPUS, every three to four years a decision is made about the continuation of the programme as such, possible changes in its basic structure, and its main objectives and areas of support.

- On the national level of the CEE partner countries annual decisions are made about national TEMPUS policies and award of TEMPUS support.
- In the field of higher education the institutions and academic staff are responsible for all decisions concerning applications for TEMPUS support and involvement in the actual TEMPUS activities and networks.

Apart from these levels of decision-making there is a system of permanent administrative assistance for TEMPUS activities as well as policy formation taken over by the EC TEMPUS Office/ETF TEMPUS Department and the National TEMPUS Offices (NTOs) in the CEE countries.

Concerning policies and administration of TEMPUS we find a number of actors with official competences in the decision-making processes related to the programme: the European Commission, the Higher Education Ministries and the Phare responsibles in the CEE countries, representatives from the higher education institutions, academic experts, etc. The actors and their competences are indicated in a flow-chart contained in the annual reports about the TEMPUS Programme published by the European Commission (see pp. 15 – 18; 32 – 36). These competences may differ from the actual role the actors are playing in the policy and administration processes. For the functioning of the TEMPUS Programme the success of interaction and interdependence of these roles has turned out to be more important than a distinct separation of their tasks and functions.

Apart from the basic decisions taken in 1990 and 1993 by the EU Council about the introduction and continuation of the TEMPUS Programme itself as well as the general framework for TEMPUS activities eligible for support, there are four main processes of policy formation and decision-making on the national level of the CEE countries:

- the determination of the national budget for TEMPUS
- the establishment of national priorities
- decisions concerning the selection of applications for TEMPUS support
- permanent administrative activities for TEMPUS carried out by the NTOs.

The first three decisions are taken annually in a regular sequence in which decision-making competences on the various levels and of the various actors involved are fixed whereas advisory competences are not. Apart from these policy and award decisions taken once a year we also have permanent administrative activities in the framework of TEMPUS which

are carried out by the ETF TEMPUS Department[1] and the National TEM-
PUS Offices (NTOs) in the CEE countries. From this structure of decision-making about policies and permanent administrative tasks the competences can be derived of the various actors involved. As their actual role
differs from their official competences, we will concentrate our analysis
on the roles the various actors actually play in the processes of policy
formation and administration.

One important focus of our analysis is concerned with the relationships
between the key actors on the national level (i.e. Education Ministers,
Phare responsibles, higher education institutions). Other important foci of
our analysis are the routine administration and management of the TEM-
PUS Programme carried out by the NTOs and the relationship between
the NTO and the key actors on the national level on the one hand and the
ETF TEMPUS Department on the other.

From what has been said so far about the interaction of key actors in
policy decisions for and administration of the TEMPUS Programme on
the national level in the CEE countries, we can derive a number of questions which will be relevant for the following analyses:

- What are the national policies and what kind of policy development for
  and administration of the programme takes place on the national level?
- Are the overall TEMPUS objectives reflected in national policies?
- Does the steering system (i.e. policy formation and programme administration) on the national level function?
- What is the impact of the national system of policy development and
  administration on the actual TEMPUS-related educational activities in
  the networks of higher education departments and institutions?
- What kind of limits does the national system of steering have and what
  are its blind spots concerning impacts and effects?

Our analyses in this chapter are based on visits to all of the eleven CEE
partner countries currently participating in TEMPUS. During each of
these visits we carried out a series of interviews with the following key
actors:

- a representative from the Ministry of Education responsible for TEM-
  PUS

---

1 As the tasks and responsibilities of the former EC TEMPUS Office have been
   taken over by the TEMPUS Department of the European Training Foundation
   (ETF) since January 1995, we will refer only to the latter in the following
   chapters.

- directors and staff members of the NTOs
- the national PHARE responsibles
- a representative from the EU Delegation (except in the Baltic States)
- academic experts involved in the assessment of applications.

In addition, we visited a number of higher education institutions involved in TEMPUS activities in each CEE country. At these institutions we carried out interviews with the rector or vice-rector, officers of the international relations office, deans of faculties and departments, academic staff members acting as coordinators, contractors or partners in TEMPUS projects, and staff and students participating in TEMPUS-supported mobility. For complete coverage of administrative units in the countries involved in the TEMPUS Programme we also conducted telephone interviews with the national TEMPUS Contact Points in all EU Member States.

4.2   Steering Bodies and Relevant Actors

4.2.1 Higher Education Ministries

In most of the CEE partner countries the Ministries of Education are responsible for designing an overall higher education reform and renewal strategy for which TEMPUS can be most effectively used as an instrument. The Ministries are mostly represented by a Vice-Minister responsible for TEMPUS. There are a few exceptions (Albania, Lithuania, Slovenia) in which the responsibilities for TEMPUS were or still are assigned - sometimes partially, sometimes completely – to the Ministry of Science and Technology. In one of these cases TEMPUS was originally thought of as being a support programme for research in the other cases responsibilities for higher education were either divided among several Ministries or higher education was – at least in the first years after 1989 – not in the hands of any proper Ministry at all.

Apart from designing the overall reform strategy, the Ministry of Education is basically involved in four other processes of policy formation and decision-making in the framework of the TEMPUS Programme:

- budget negotiations for TEMPUS with the Phare responsibles
- determination of the national priorities for TEMPUS in consultation with the European Commission
- final decisions about the acceptance of JEP applications in consultation with national authorities and the European Commission
- monitoring and controlling the work of the NTO.

The actual role of the Education Ministries in these processes of policy formation and decision-making varies from country to country but is generally less pro-active than we expected. One of the reasons for this is that many of the tasks involved in filling out these responsibilities are delegated to intermediary bodies (see pp. 98 – 104). As a rule the Ministries are chairing these bodies so that a decisive influence is still secured. As our analyses have shown, the actual influence of the Ministries on the steering mechanisms of the TEMPUS Programme on the national level is less dependent on the formal responsibilities than on a pro-active role adopted by the Ministries. There are considerable differences in the degree of commitment to TEMPUS by the various Ministries in the partner countries. Due to a lack of national higher education development plans in the first phase of TEMPUS (i.e. TEMPUS I) – in quite a few of the partner countries there were also no higher education laws – there was no real basis for a focused and pro-active role of the Ministries with respect to an overall steering mechanism which would have provided a national framework for the TEMPUS activities in the higher education institutions. An exception to this situation has been found in Albania. Here, however, TEMPUS responsibilities on the ministerial level are divided between the Ministry of Education and the Committee for Science and Technology, the latter having ministerial status. Ministerial involvement in and procedural commitment to TEMPUS seems also to be dependent to a certain degree on the proportion of TEMPUS support in the overall budget for higher education in any one country.

The situation characterised above created a rather open and unstructured frame for the reflection of TEMPUS objectives in the national higher education policies. A number of other actors and newly created bodies became involved in policy decisions and the establishment of steering mechanisms. To these actors and bodies the Ministries of Education in the CEE countries have often delegated their role in shaping TEMPUS policies and strategies on the national level. At the same time an increasing interest of Phare responsibles in TEMPUS could be noted. In a number of countries Phare responsibles have become involved in the processes to establish TEMPUS priorities. Increasingly, TEMPUS budget negotiations are connected to certain conditions to take Phare objectives more strongly into account. And even the opportunity to intervene into processes of project applications and selections is sometimes used more extensively now than in the first years of TEMPUS in order to achieve a stronger reflection of Phare objectives in TEMPUS activities. This situation of less pro-active Ministries of Education and increasingly pro-active Phare Coordination Units creates an interesting configuration for conflict because Phare intervention into TEMPUS is not always appreciated by the other actors. There are two main reasons for this:

- On the one hand we find a conflict of interest between two ministries in which the Ministry of Education usually is in the weaker position and therefore tends to guard its spheres of influence. In addition, the national budget for higher education is still rather low in most of the CEE countries so that the TEMPUS budget adds to the overall funding which is needed to implement higher education reforms.

- On the other hand we noted that Phare involvement is not necessarily a sign of genuine interest in TEMPUS as such but sometimes rather the attempt to bring TEMPUS into line with the tasks of the department or Ministry in which Phare is located. A frequent argument in this context is: as Phare finances the TEMPUS budget, TEMPUS might as well be more supportive in order to achieve the Phare objectives.

We can conclude from this configuration that it may be difficult to reach a joint policy agreement between Phare and TEMPUS. This seems to hold true not only for the national level of the Central and Eastern European countries but also for the supra-national level. However, in the CEE partner countries the arguments coming from the side of the Phare responsibles overlap in certain issues (e.g. improvement of university/industry relations) with policies for the higher education sector, so that usually compromises have been found by way of negotiations and finding a consensus.

4.2.2 TEMPUS Advisory Boards

In all of the partner countries some kind of advisory or sometimes supervisory board for TEMPUS has been established. The mandate of these boards as well as the composition of their members vary to a certain degree from country to country, although their function is quite similar in that they constitute an arena in which all relevant actors can discuss national TEMPUS policies. These boards are usually involved in the policy decisions, in some cases also in the management of the TEMPUS Programme on the national level. They either play an advisory and consultative role or have been accorded decision-making powers. We have found that the different boards are successful in different ways. In general, however, their most important task is to discuss and propose the national TEMPUS priorities. In some countries they are consulted on further issues related to policy decisions and administrative processes of the TEMPUS Programme. As a rule, these boards serve as a body to achieve consensus and to balance the interests of all authorities and interest groups involved in TEMPUS. Frequently, the NTOs are their executive body or secretariat.

Usually, the advisory boards are involved in the following processes of policy formation and/or decision-making:

- discussion of national TEMPUS policies and an overall strategy for the TEMPUS Programme
- discussion of and recommendations for the draft proposal of national priorities submitted by the NTO after consultation with the Ministry of Education
- monitoring the work of the NTO
- in some cases selection of academic experts (Hungary, Slovakia)
- in some cases assessment of applications (Hungary, Albania)
- in some cases discussion of national selection strategies for TEMPUS project applications (Bulgaria).

Apart from the Education Ministry and the director of the NTO, the following officials and groups are usually represented in these advisory or supervisory boards (in some countries called councils or committees):

- the national Phare coordinator
- representatives of higher education (e.g. from the Council of Rectors, sometimes also additional academic members of higher education institutions)
- in some countries representatives of other Ministries apart from the Ministry of Education
- sometimes representatives of industry
- in some cases representatives of the EU and/or other organisations involved in international cooperation (e.g. EU Delegation in Romania, Cultural Foundation in Hungary).

The following paragraphs give an account of the interrelations between advisory or supervisory boards and NTOs at the time this survey was conducted.

Under TEMPUS I and further until mid-1995, the *Albanian* TEMPUS Supervisory Board had 13 members, 11 of whom represented science and research (vice-rectors of higher education institutions; representatives of research institutions and of the Committee for Science and Technology, being equivalent to a Ministry; and individual professors). These members were appointed by the Prime Minister. Natural member of the Board is the Director of the NTO. The chairperson is the director of the higher education department in the Ministry of Education. Since mid-1995, the person responsible for Phare in the Council of Ministers and representatives of further Ministries are also represented in the Board. The Board makes the budget proposal for TEMPUS, discusses and decides about the national TEMPUS priorities, is involved in the national selection of project applications and also appoints the academic experts for the assessment of applications.

A certain amount of independence similar to that in Poland and Romania has only recently been achieved by the *Bulgarian* TEMPUS Office. In November 1994, the Bulgarian TEMPUS Office was established as a semi-autonomous unit together with the National TEMPUS Consultative Council to represent national authorities and society in TEMPUS decisions. Members of this Consultative Council are: the Ministry of Education and other Ministries responsible for specialised higher education institutions, the Phare Coordinator, representatives from the National Rectors' Conference, representatives from industry and the Director of the NTO. The Consultative Council participates in the establishment of national TEMPUS priorities and in the determination of selection strategies for TEMPUS project applications, and it supports and supervises the work of the NTO.

The equivalent to a TEMPUS advisory board in the *Czech Republic* is the Commission for International Relations of the Academic Council. The Academic Council has approximately 100 members, one representative from each faculty of all higher education institutions in the country. For special issues smaller working groups or commissions are formed from among the members of the Academic Council. One of these is the Commission for International Relations. The chairperson is nominated by the Academic Council and has the right to nominate the other nine members of the Commission. Chairperson and Commission members change every three years. The mandate of the Commission in terms of TEMPUS is to discuss national TEMPUS priorities and to be responsible for the assessment of applications, that is, to act as academic experts for JEP, IMG and CME applications. Commission members may ask additional experts of their choice for cooperation and support in the assessment exercise. In order to have a wider range of opinions and proposals for the national TEMPUS priorities the NTO asks a number of ministries in a written letter to make their preferences known. However, these ministries are not involved in any discussions and decisions concerning the final draft version.

The *Estonian* TEMPUS Advisory Board has 15 members: a representative of the Ministry of Education who acts as the chairperson of the Board, the Director of the NTO, two representatives each from all big higher education institutions and one representative each from all small higher education institutions, and some individual professors who are known to be actively involved in higher education policy formation. On the basis of proposals made by the NTO the TEMPUS Advisory Board discusses the TEMPUS budget proposal and the national priorities. It is also involved in the nomination of academic experts for the assessment of applications.

The *Hungarian* Supervisory Board is called the TEMPUS Steering Committee and was the only steering body responsible for TEMPUS during TEMPUS I. Its 35 members represent all institutions and interest groups which are involved in TEMPUS. Apart from representatives of the Hungarian Rectors' Conference and representatives from those higher education institutions that are not members of the Rectors' Conference, the Steering Committee consists of representatives from the Ministry of Culture and Education and from the Ministry of Industry and Trade responsible for Phare. Additionally, there are also representatives from the Ministry of Labour, the Ministries of Agriculture, Industry and Trade, International Economic Relations, and Social Welfare. The NTO, representatives from industry and commerce as well as representatives of student organisations are also members of the Committee. Finally, there are members representing Unions and the National Committee of the European Cultural Foundation. Chairperson of the Committee which decides in all matters concerning TEMPUS on the national level is a former director of the NTO.

The TEMPUS Advisory Board in *Latvia* was established by the Ministry of Education on the initiative of the NTO. The Director of the NTO is a member of the Board. The following members of the Board are appointed by the Ministry of Education: the Head of the Department of Higher Education and Science and another member of the Department, the Director of the Strategic Planning Unit of the Ministry of Education, and the Director of the Foreign Relations Department of the Ministry of Education. Further ministries and individuals are invited by the Ministry of Education to participate in the board meetings: Ministry of Welfare, Ministry of Culture, Ministry of Agriculture, the Pro-rectors of Riga Technical University, of the Latvian University, of the Latvian Academy of Medicine, of the Latvian University of Agriculture, and of the Latvian Academy of Music. The Head of the Phare Coordination Unit is also invited. The mandate of the TEMPUS Advisory Board is to assist the Ministry of Education in decisions concerning policy development for the TEMPUS Programme, to develop proposals for national TEMPUS priorities and the TEMPUS budget, to discuss TEMPUS problems and legal aspects of the TEMPUS Programme.

When *Lithuania* first became a TEMPUS partner country, in 1992, there was no ministry responsible for higher education. Higher education as an area of responsibility and policy formation was assigned to the Ministry of Education only at the beginning of 1995. In 1992, there was the Agency for Higher Education, Research and Development which – in close cooperation with the Science Council – made proposals and decisions concerning national TEMPUS priorities. The Science Council was asked to carry out the assessment of TEMPUS applications by academic experts and organised this procedure independently. During the period of TEMPUS I the Agency for Higher Education, Research and Development was replaced by the Board of Experts on Higher Education and Research. This Board consists of three representatives from each of the following bodies: the Rectors' Conference, the Academy of Sciences, the Science Council, and the Board of Directors of State Research Institutions. All four bodies acted as experts and advisers on higher education and research for the government. The chairperson of the Board of Experts was a personal adviser of the Prime Minister in all matters concerning higher education. Officially the Board of Experts is asked for opinions and comments on national TEMPUS priorities, the assessment of applications and other TEMPUS-related issues but delegates these tasks to the Rectors' Conference which has become one of the most important and powerful bodies concerning TEMPUS matters in Lithuania.

The *Polish* TEMPUS Advisory Board heads the Foundation for the Development of Higher Education which was set up in December 1993 and constitutes the Polish TEMPUS Office. The Foundation was established in order to make the NTO more independent from the Ministry of Education. The Advisory Board consists of nine members who are appointed by the Minister of Education: the Director of the Polish TEMPUS Office, the Vice-Minister of Education, the Phare coordinator, representatives of the Polish Council for Higher Education and representatives of the higher education institutions. Apart from monitoring the work of the NTO the Advisory Board of the Foundation has taken over the task of formulating recommendations, that is, drafting the first proposal for the national TEMPUS priorities each year. During this process close consultation with the Phare coordinator and the academic community is ensured, while at the same time national higher education policy is taken into account. Board meetings take place approximately four times a year.

The *Romanian* TEMPUS Office was established as an independent unit headed by a supervisory board which is called the National TEMPUS Committee (NTC). Originally, members of the NTC were five representatives from the Ministry of Education, five representatives from the Council of Rectors, one representative from the Department of European Integration which is a department of the Council of Ministers and also responsible for Phare, and the Director of the Romanian TEMPUS Office. Meanwhile, in addition, the Ministry of Labour and Social Protection and the National Bank of Romania are represented in the NTC. The Head of the European Delegation in Bucharest as well as the Ministry of Foreign Affairs are invited to all meetings of the NTC. They have no decision-making power but are involved in hearings and recommendations. The chairperson of the NTC is the Secretary of State for Reform, Coordination, Management and Resources located in the Ministry of Education. The NTC is predominantly involved in drafting a proposal for the national TEMPUS priorities each year and meets about three times during this stage.

The *Slovak* Advisory Board consists of six delegates from the Association for the Development of International Cooperation of the Slovak Universities and two representatives from the Board of Slovak Universities, the Director of the Department for Foreign Assistance in the Ministry of Foreign Affairs who is responsible for Phare, and the director of the NTO. Chairperson is the Secretary of State responsible for higher education in the Ministry of Education. The six delegates from the Association for the Development of International Cooperation are appointed by the Association. Legally, the NTO is the secretariat of this Association for which the Advisory Board acts as board of directors. Decisions of the Board are prepared by discussions and decisions of the Association. Seen from an organisational perspective the steering of the TEMPUS Programme lies with the Association. The Advisory Board serving as board of directors influences the decision-making processes and ensures the acceptance of decisions. Seen from a legal perspective, Association, Advisory Board and NTO together form an independent unit with a recognised legal status. All TEMPUS-related matters are decided by the Board.

Slovenia's TEMPUS Advisory Board has been established by the Ministry of Education. It is necessary to emphasise this fact because the NTO is attached to the Ministry of Science and Technology's Department of Foreign Cooperation. The NTO Director is at the same time the head of this Department. This link is not favoured by the Ministry of Education. The Slovenian TEMPUS Advisory Board has seven members: the Vice-Minister of Education who is the chairman of the Board, the rectors of the two Slovenian universities, representatives from the Ministries of Science and Technology, of Foreign Affairs and of Culture, and the Director of the NTO. Membership in the Board is not strictly exclusive and the two universities often delegate more than one representative to participate in the meetings. The mandate of the Board is to have a general overview of TEMPUS matters, to make proposals for the steering of the TEMPUS Programme, for national TEMPUS priorities and even for concrete TEMPUS projects, to discuss any problems related to TEMPUS as well as future strategies concerning the TEMPUS Programme. The Board does not meet very often and lost a certain amount of influence once TEMPUS had been firmly established in Slovenia. Decisions of the Board are not binding.

In some of the countries under review here, the legal status of these advisory or supervisory boards is unclear or problematic. In Hungary and Albania they do not have a legally autonomous status, although in both of these countries the boards have considerable steering and decision-making powers. Irritations and conflicts might also arise when Ministries of Education delegate their decision-making power to these boards but have to re-establish this power in their dealings with the European Commission.

It is, in principle, an optimal model to give the responsibilities for the steering of the TEMPUS Programme to such a board representing all interest groups. In practice, the functioning of this model depends on a number of further factors. One of these factors is the size of the board: the larger the number of members the bigger the danger that not all representatives participate in the meetings or that decisions are made in exclusive and smaller groups, the legitimacy of which is questionable. In contrast to this, the fewer the members of such a board are, the more likely that its decisions and/or proposals are criticised by those social groups and authorities being involved in TEMPUS but excluded from representation in the board. A small size of the board may also have an impact with regard to limitations and blind spots in the national steering – for example policy formation, decision-making, administrative mechanisms and routines – of the TEMPUS Programme.

4.2.3 National TEMPUS Offices

The tasks and responsibilities of the National TEMPUS Offices refer to the two basic dimensions of the national TEMPUS steering system: (a) that of policy formation and preparation of related decisions and (b) that of giving all necessary administrative support for carrying out the programme activities in the higher education institutions. This double role is not always easy to maintain and needs a considerable amount of leadership, professionalisation and political tact. NTOs can be characterised as key actors for the TEMPUS Programme because they do not only constitute the link between the Ministries of Education, the advisory or supervisory boards and the higher education institutions but, compared to other actors involved in TEMPUS on the national level, they also have the most intensive and frequent contact to the supra-national level (European Commission and ETF TEMPUS Department). As a rule, the NTOs are also informed about TEMPUS-related matters in the other CEE countries because of regular meetings of NTO Directors organised by the ETF TEMPUS Department.

The distinctive ways in which the NTOs are dealing with their tasks and responsibilities in each of the CEE countries are shaped to some extent by the self-understanding of the NTO Director. We can basically distinguish between three types of NTO leadership accounting for certain differences in strategies and efficiency of the various NTOs: the manager/administrator, the politician/civil servant and the professorial academic. The manager/administrator tends to put an emphasis on the smoothness and efficiency of administrative procedures and management of the office and its staff. The politician/civil servant tends to appreciate good formal and informal relations with all authorities and groups involved in TEMPUS affairs. The academic tends to take care of intellectual quality of the various issues for which proposals and drafts are produced as well as selection criteria for applications. This type of NTO Director usually also keeps closer ties to the higher education institutions.

The responsibilities of the NTOs in all partner countries have gradually become more complex and diverse. Depending on the degree of professionalisation achieved, the ETF TEMPUS Department has transferred more and more responsibilities to the NTOs, especially in terms of the various assessment procedures of applications and of project monitoring. As a rule, there are seven main activities in the context of TEMPUS Programme administration which are carried out by the NTOs:

- the preparation of proposals for priorities, special actions and strategic documents concerning the national policy formation of the TEMPUS Programme for the national authorities and bodies involved in the respective decision-making processes.

- the provision of information, consultancy and advice to national and foreign institutions interested in applying for a TEMPUS grant. This includes country-wide information about priorities, individual advice for applicants, support in finding and linking potential partners, distributing general and special information material on TEMPUS activities, and participating in various national and European TEMPUS meetings.

- the establishment and maintenance of data bases for JEPs, IMGs and CMEs
- the supervision and organisation of and participation in the assessment and selection of applications. This includes the guidance of academic experts, adaptation of assessment criteria, participation in the bilateral discussions with the ETF TEMPUS Department, preparation of selection reports and provision of results to the applicants
- the monitoring of on-going projects. This includes an assessment of all reports submitted by the projects as well as carrying out and participating in site-visits
- the organisation of special actions such as national TEMPUS conferences or events
- the management of contracts, including the operational contract of the NTO and appropriate staff training and development, the contracts for IMG grantholders and special action contracts from funds which have not been spent.

The legal status of most of the NTOs is one of semi-autonomy. However, there are some exceptions. During TEMPUS I the Bulgarian NTO was a department of the Ministry of Education and became an independent unit only in November 1994. In Albania, the NTO is a department subordinated to the Committee of Sciences and Technology, the latter having ministerial status. In Slovenia the NTO, though autonomous, is attached to the Ministry of Science and Technology. The Director of the NTO is at the same time the Head of the Ministry's Department of Foreign Cooperation and thus a high ministerial official and senior civil servant. The legal status of the Hungarian NTO was under dispute at the time our study was conducted.

The operational budget for the NTOs is provided by the ETF TEMPUS Department in Torino on the basis of contracts and a detailed description of tasks. It is supposed to comprise around one per cent of the national TEMPUS budget. However, actual proportions differ considerably as a comparison among the various NTOs shows. In many cases national funding is provided for premises and other basic resources (i.e. heating and electricity). The operational budget also covers NTO staff salaries. The level of staff salaries is usually determined according to the salary level of comparable government officials, public servants or academic staff of universities in the respective country and on the basis of an agreement between the national Ministry responsible for TEMPUS and the European Commission.

Although the number of full-time and part-time staff in each of the NTOs varies, most of the NTOs complain about being understaffed and consequently overworked. This is due to the fact that not only TEMPUS activities expanded in each of the countries but also the ETF TEMPUS Department has gradually delegated more and more tasks and responsibilities to the NTOs in tune with their growing degree of professionalisation and efficiency.

In general, the NTOs have a predominantly administrative role for TEMPUS, but all of them are deeply involved in preparing all relevant decisions. This gives them a relatively high degree of informal influence on the shape of the TEMPUS Programme far beyond their legal status and their official functions. For instance, most of the NTOs prepare all decisions concerning the budget required for TEMPUS and the national priorities by formulating draft proposals or briefings for the Ministries of Education and/or the advisory boards. Depending on their strategic skills and the extent of formal and informal cooperation and contacts to the authorities in charge of formal decisions, they can shape the TEMPUS Programme to a considerable degree. In sum, the efficiency and effectivity of the TEMPUS Programme is largely dependent on the work of the NTOs.

As the NTOs are involved in one way or another in practically all important decisions concerning the policy and administration of TEMPUS on the national level and often act as a communicative link between the key actors in TEMPUS on all three levels (supra-national, national and institutional), their tasks and responsibilities require a lot of mediation and balancing skills. Their general achievements in this respect are remarkable. Except for Bulgaria, which is the only country having had a succession of NTO directors and staff because of political changes, all other NTOs have enjoyed some continuity in terms of leadership and staff. This has certainly led to the fact that their role has become stronger and more powerful over time. As a result, they have also become more self-assured in their role vis-à-vis the European Commission and the ETF TEMPUS Department. The gradual transfer of responsibilities from the ETF TEMPUS Department to the NTOs has contributed to this process. At the same time the NTOs are also well informed about the TEMPUS activities in the universities and spend substantial time and effort in gathering information and opinions of all actors involved. This gives them a relatively high degree of legitimacy. Overall we can say that the NTOs together with the advisory boards are largely responsible for the degree to which the steering system for TEMPUS is functioning on the national level. Thus, their informal role is much more influential than their official responsibilities.

With the gradual transfer of tasks from the ETF TEMPUS Department to the NTOs and the increasing professionalisation of the NTOs themselves, the relationship between the NTOs and the ETF TEMPUS Department has somewhat changed. There is a growing criticism of the NTOs in terms of the ways the ETF TEMPUS Department is handling certain matters. This criticism is less directed towards the desk officers responsible for the respective CEE country than towards the overall management and administration of TEMPUS by the ETF TEMPUS Department as such. The main points of this criticism are as follows:

- The NTOs frequently feel that the ETF TEMPUS Department does not properly take into account their increased expertise and professionalisation but is often too prescriptive in its instructions. Instead of being treated as equals and colleagues, they feel as is they are being treated as service units for those higher up in the hierarchy.

- Some NTOs complained about being often made responsible in their respective country for mistakes and shortcomings of the ETF TEMPUS Department or the European Commission.

- There is a growing dissatisfaction in many of the NTOs about the contractual situation of their staff members. Having to work in an international context and to perform according to European standards, NTO staff members consider their salaries as too low and not commensurate to salaries that would be offered in the private sector to persons with the same qualification.

- With regard to the gradual transfer of tasks from the ETF TEMPUS Department to the NTOs, the latter feel often left alone with the ensuing problems in their own country. These problems are especially related to issues of coming into conflict with legal regulations concerning taxes on grants, value-added taxes or customs regulations for equipment, the legal status of the NTO being not sufficiently defined in order to carry out those tasks. The NTOs might have to take over duties which they are not legally entitled to do or for which they have to strike a balance between legal correctness (on the national level) and outside expectations (on the supra-national level).

- According to the NTOs, the ETF TEMPUS Department has up to now prevented any form of exchange of information and experiences as well as cooperation among the NTOs not supervised by the ETF TEMPUS Department. Meetings of the NTO Directors are always organised in a way that they cannot meet among themselves to discuss a common standpoint or to influence the agenda. Wishes for discussion have been ignored.

- Many NTOs complained about a lack of support in establishing and updating TEMPUS data bases. Statistics published by the ETF TEMPUS Department are often incorrect and software does not work properly.

- For the NTOs the transition from the EC TEMPUS Office in Brussels to the ETF TEMPUS Department in Torino has disrupted procedures and routines and, for technical reasons, made communication more difficult.

Overall the NTOs would like the ETF TEMPUS Department to be more supportive and understanding in terms of problems arising for the NTOs and more collegial in its way of communication and cooperation. They would also like the ETF TEMPUS Department to be more conscientious in terms of deadlines and transfer of contracts and grants and more exact in terms of exchange of data and statistics. Finally, many NTOs would like a salary for their staff members which is commensurate to the expected work and performance.

4.2.4 The TEMPUS Contact Points in EU Member States

In each Member State of the European Union TEMPUS 'Contact Points' have been established to provide information on TEMPUS and assistance to institutions, organisations and individuals in the respective country interested in participating in the programme. Compared to the National TEMPUS Offices which were established in the Central and Eastern European countries on a similar administrative level, the TEMPUS Contact Points have fewer competences and responsibilities. In contrast to the NTOs, the TEMPUS Contact Points are neither involved in any kind of assessment of applications for TEMPUS projects nor do they officially play a role in national decision-making processes related to TEMPUS. Although representatives of the Contact Points are frequently members of the EU TEMPUS Management Committee, they more often act as experts and advisers than as decision-makers. The main activities of the TEMPUS Contact Points in EU Member States are information and advice.

Those national ministries politically responsible for TEMPUS – in most countries the Ministry of Education – have also taken over the establishment and the main funding of the Contact Points. Two major modes of institutionalisation can be distinguished. In some countries the Contact Point was established within the respective Ministry itself (e.g. in

Luxembourg, Spain, Portugal); in other countries the Contact Point was contracted out to an already existing unit, agency or association (e.g. the German Academic Exchange Service in Germany, the Rectors' Conference in Denmark, Nuffic in the Netherlands, or, up to 1995, the British Council in the United Kingdom). The latter type of Contact Point is often in charge of the administration of other European Programmes as well, such as SOCRATES and LEONARDO.

Whereas in most countries the TEMPUS-related tasks were assigned to one Contact Point, it was decided in four EU Member States to establish two Contact Points, either for different target groups – in France and Germany for higher education institutions on the one hand and enterprises on the other and in Belgium for the Dutch-speaking community on the one hand and for the French-speaking community on the other - or to provide two contact partners between which all those seeking information or advice can choose freely, as is the case in Greece.

All Contact Points are embedded into a larger administrative context. Therefore, it is quite difficult to estimate their 'real' size in terms of staff available for the TEMPUS-related work. In most cases the staff of the Contact Points has to accomplish the TEMPUS work in addition to other tasks. In some of the EU Member States one person is primarily in charge of the TEMPUS work; in others the work is distributed among several persons (up to twelve). Calculated in full-time equivalents, the professional staffing of the Contact Points varies between one-third of a post up to about one and a half. In general, some secretarial assistance is provided additionally. Overall, staff members of the Contact Points are satisfied with the existing structure and resources of their Contact Point. However, it was mentioned in a few cases that more staff would enable them to do more in terms of TEMPUS-related activities.

As described above, the Contact Points have two main tasks – the provision of information and advice. In terms of time spent on these tasks, information activities are the dominant occupation. Three areas of information can be distinguished:

* the TEMPUS Programme for those interested in participation
* TEMPUS decisions for those already involved in the programme
* national TEMPUS participation and developments to the public and national authorities.

The emphasis put on the various information tasks has changed over time. In the beginning the Contact Points had to do quite a lot of public relations work in order to make the TEMPUS Programme known as widely as possible and to ensure proper participation of EU partners in it. In the meantime, the proportion of work addressing TEMPUS 'newcomers' decreased, whereas the information on TEMPUS decisions (e.g. approval of applications, amount of grant awarded, etc.) has increased considerably. This affects particularly the 'larger' EU Member States with many TEMPUS participations.

Nonetheless, general information remains the most voluminous activity of the Contact Points in all EU Member States. Each year one or two national TEMPUS information days are organised in each country, usually in cooperation with the ETF TEMPUS Department. Beyond this, the various Contact Points developed their own ways of handling information issues as it seemed appropriate to the situation in the country and the structure of the Contact Point itself. For example, international relations offices at higher education institutions are often used as multipliers; in some countries the Contact Point publishes articles about TEMPUS in relevant newspapers and journals, in other countries the Contact Points concentrate their effort on the distribution of information material produced by the ETF TEMPUS Department. Staff members of many of the Contact Points participate in information events organised by higher education institutions, organisations, enterprises, etc. Personal contacts of the Contact Point staff are used very frequently to gather information and sometimes also to link project partners.

Although some of the EU Member States, namely France, Germany and Denmark, have made some effort to involve enterprises in TEMPUS activities, the main target group for general information is higher education institutions in the country. The Contact Points in some of the EU Member States exclusively address higher education institutions and leave it to them to interest enterprises in participation.

The information about TEMPUS decisions and new developments (e.g. changes in priorities) is communicated to TEMPUS participants and applicants either through regular TEMPUS Newsletters or equivalent bulletins or directly by telephone, fax or e-mail in case of decisions about approval of applications.

In general, information on national TEMPUS facts or developments – such as participation rates – is prepared by the Contact Points in the context of regular (annual) reports and presented only to the national ministries in charge of TEMPUS. The main data source are statistics provided by the ETF TEMPUS Department. Due to the limited number of staff in the Contact Points, such additional statistical information and analyses, e.g. as provided by the German Contact Point, are the exception. There were some complaints about regularity and quality of information supplied by the ETF TEMPUS Department. Information considered to be important for the work of the Contact Points is frequently not sent automatically to them but only upon request. Statistics often seem to be incorrect. Overall, communication between the ETF TEMPUS Department and the national Contact Points in EU Member States has been more difficult since the technical assistance for the programme relocated in Torino due to technical reasons.

The second task of the Contact Points – that is, giving advice – is primarily related to applications for TEMPUS projects. In most cases, staff of higher education institutions seek such advice, for example how to shape the envisaged project, where to put the emphasis, and sometimes how to formulate the application. The proportion of application-related advice within the overall activities of a Contact Point differs considerably. Whereas some Contact Points reported frequent requests for advice, others stated that application-related advice only plays a minor role.

Due to the administrative structure of the TEMPUS Programme the Contact Points act as a kind of mediator between the ETF TEMPUS Department and the TEMPUS participants from the respective EU Member State. Correspondingly, the Contact Points cooperate primarily with these two groups of actors. In addition, there are usually close contacts to the respective national ministries. Some of the Contact Points also cooperate with selected NTOs, e.g. assisting them in finding appropriate Western partners, visiting the respective CEE country for information or exchange of expertise, providing assistance for residence permits, etc.

In the course of our telephone interviews we asked staff members of the national TEMPUS Contact Points what they would consider to be serious problems for the TEMPUS activities. Two issues were mentioned frequently: long decision-making processes and delays in the transfer of funds and grants. Some contracts come so late that originally planned activities cannot take place at all or cannot be carried out properly.

We also wanted to know whether staff from TEMPUS Contact Points would intervene in cases of conflicts between JEP partners from their country and from CEE countries and whether they were involved in any kind of project monitoring or site-visits. The answer to these questions was negative. If partners cannot resolve a conflict among themselves it is usually the desk officer from the ETF TEMPUS Department responsible for the CEE country involved who would try to take over as mediator.

In contrast to the NTOs in the Central and Eastern European countries which have at least some opportunities to cooperate with each other during meetings of the NTO Directors, there is almost no cooperation among the national TEMPUS Contact Points in the EU Member States. This fact is strongly regretted by respective staff members. There is also very little exchange of information, except for some personal contacts and rare official meetings of Contact Point staff organised by the ETF TEMPUS Department.

4.2.5 National Phare Coordinators

The tasks of the national Phare coordination are not assigned to the same ministry or governmental unit in all of the partner countries.

- The Albanian Phare coordination is located in the Department for Economic Development and Foreign Aid in the Council of Ministers.
- In Bulgaria, Phare coordination is the responsibility of a recently established Commission for European Integration in the Council of Ministers.
- In the Czech Republic there is a Phare Unit in the Centre for Foreign Assistance which is part of the Ministry of Economy.
- The Estonian Phare Unit is part of the Department for International Cooperation which in turn is located in the Ministry of Finance.
- In Hungary, the Phare coordination is assigned to the Ministry of Industry and Trade.
- In Latvia, the Phare coordination is the responsibility of the Foreign Assistance Programme Co-ordination Department in the Ministry of Finance.
- In Lithuania, the Phare coordination is undertaken in the Technical Assistance Division of the European Integration Department located in the Ministry of Foreign Affairs.
- In Poland, the Phare coordination is located in the Office of the Undersecretary of State for European Integration and Foreign Assistance, which in turn is part of the Council of Ministers.
- In Romania, the Phare coordination is located in the Department for European Integration of the Romanian Government.
- In the Slovak Republic, Phare coordination is the responsibility of the Ministry of Foreign Affairs.
- In Slovenia, the national Phare Coordinator is Head of the Phare Unit in the Ministry of Science and Technology and also acts as Counsellor to the Government.

The actual involvement of the national Phare Coordinators in TEMPUS varies from country to country. Most Phare Coordinators are members of the TEMPUS advisory or supervisory boards. There are two domains in the TEMPUS-related decision-making processes in which the Phare Coordinators are involved on grounds of their office: (a) the determination of the proportion of the national Phare budget for TEMPUS, in consultation with the national government and the European Commission, and (b) taking part in the decisions about the national TEMPUS priorities in order to ensure their compatibility with the Phare priorities. They also have the opportunity to comment on the list of JEP applications recommended for approval and funding before it is finalised by the Minister of Education and the European Commission.

On the basis of the respective national Phare indicative programmes and the corresponding government decisions, most of the CEE countries have decided upon a fixed proportion of the annual Phare budget being allocated to TEMPUS. Although there is some margin for variation this is not so high that it will greatly unsettle expectations about the level of the TEMPUS budget. In fact, during TEMPUS I the annual TEMPUS budget increased in most of the CEE countries.

4.2.6 Academic Experts

The selection of national academic experts for the assessment of JEP applications and the organisation of the respective procedures differ considerably in the CEE partner countries.

- In Albania, the members of the TEMPUS Supervisory Board carry out the assessment themselves and nominate additional experts if no member of the Board has sufficient expertise to assess a specific application.

- In Bulgaria, the rectors of the universities recommend academic experts from their institutions to the NTO. The NTO matches experts with applications to be assessed. Names of experts are kept secret.

- In the Czech Republic, the ten members of the Academic Council's Commission for International Relations carry out the assessment of JEPs, IMGs and CMEs. They might draw a few more experts recommended by the NTO into the assessment exercise or just give a special application to a colleague. All applications are assessed by only one expert and recommendations are established after a discussion of assessment results in the Commission.

- In Estonia, the academic experts are nominated by the TEMPUS Advisory Board and invited by the NTO to serve in the assessment exercise. The NTO also makes proposals to the Board concerning the nomination of experts. Until 1994, the NTO organised the assessment of each application by three experts who did not know of each other.

- In Hungary, the TEMPUS Supervisory Board proposes candidates to be confirmed by the Ministry of Education. Names of experts are kept secret.

- In Latvia, it is the NTO which proposes candidates in consultation with the chairperson of the TEMPUS Advisory Board. The proposal is confirmed by the Advisory Board.

- During TEMPUS I the assessment of TEMPUS applications in Lithuania was carried out by the Board of Experts on Higher Education and Research, which acted as an equivalent to the TEMPUS advisory boards.

- In Poland, the NTO asks known experts from various fields to serve in the assessment. Some experts propose possible further candidates themselves. For each subject area there is a relatively stable core group of academic experts serving in the assessment every year.

- In Romania, experts are nominated by the NTO in consultation with the Vice-Minister for Education. The proposed candidates are confirmed by the Minister of Education. Their names are kept secret.

- In the Slovak Republic, the representatives of the higher education institutions in the Association for the Development of International Cooperation of the Slovak Universities propose candidates to be confirmed by the supervisory board. Names of experts are kept secret.

- In Slovenia, the NTO establishes a list of academic experts in all subject areas to be covered and sends them the applications to be assessed. The names of the experts are kept secret. As a rule, each application is assessed by a single expert. Only in cases of uncertainties or irregularities is an additional expert asked to assess.

Originally, guidelines for the selection of academic experts as well as a format for the assessment sheets to be filled out by them were recommended by the EC TEMPUS Office. This was necessary to establish comparable data base input and to guarantee a certain degree of comparability of criteria and procedures. The NTOs have the option to adapt the assessment sheets according to their country's specific situation and needs and most of them have done so.

In most of the CEE partner countries the work of the academic experts is appreciated. Often they are also asked to serve in national TEMPUS evaluation exercises (e.g. site-visits, evaluation studies of all JEPs in a certain subject area). In some of the countries where the names of the experts are kept secret, we have come across a certain amount of suspicion with regard to the possibility of influence being used in the assessment exercise. As a rule, experts are not allowed to asses applications from their own institution in order to prevent favouritism. All experts receive a honorarium for their service.

The role of the academic experts in the processes of policy formation and related decision-making as well as TEMPUS administration is limited and more indirect than direct. Nevertheless, they do play a certain role in a number of issues:

- In those countries in which the expertise of the academic experts is also used in various kinds of national TEMPUS evaluation exercises, the results of these studies might serve as a basis for decisions concerning changes in priorities or selection criteria.

- In Poland, academic experts have played an active role in changes concerning the format of the assessment and specifications of selection criteria. In other countries experts have told us that they have some leeway in emphasising certain criteria while neglecting others.

- Usually, academic experts have emphasised the fact that their involvement in the assessment exercise provides them with a good overview of what is going on in their field at other higher education institutions in the country. In some cases national co-operative activities have been started on the basis of this knowledge which might also extend to joint TEMPUS project applications.

4.2.7 EU Delegation

With the exception of the Baltic States for which the representation of the EU is taken over by the EU Delegation in Sweden, the EU is represented in all CEE countries by a Delegation located in the respective capitals. The EU Delegation has Embassy status. Among other things, the EU Delegations are responsible for supervising and advising Phare activities in the respective countries. We therefore assumed that they also might play a certain role for TEMPUS. Except in Romania, the Slovak Republic and Slovenia, members of the EU Delegation are not regularly involved in the TEMPUS affairs of the CEE countries. However, the EU Delegations often have a supporting and advisory, sometimes even interventionist role concerning the solution of practical problems such as obtaining tax exemptions for Individual Mobility Grants, helping students to obtain visas or getting exemptions from customs for equipment bought with TEMPUS funds. Depending on the problem at hand they might become involved in negotiations either with the national government of the respective country or the Embassies of the EU Member States. They often do so upon request from the NTO.

In Romania, the involvement of the EU Delegation in TEMPUS matters is quite different from that in other CEE countries. The Head of the EU Delegation is quite deeply involved in consultations and advice on strategic issues, especially the establishment of national priorities. The Delegation is also helpful in certain practical matters, such as contacting embassies or consulates of EU Member States in case of difficulties Romanian academic staff or students face in obtaining visas for TEMPUS-supported mobility. In fact, the involvement goes as far as being the driving force in the conception and formulation of an application for a special JEP (formerly JEP+) in the area of Economics (under TEMPUS II). The EU Delegation is invited to all meetings of the NTC and their recommendations concerning priorities and TEMPUS strategies are taken into account. Special efforts have been made to achieve a closer relationship between Phare and TEMPUS and to develop an integrated strategy. Thus, the EU Delegation has put a special emphasis on promoting the idea of developing a higher education reform strategy that closely takes into account the needs of the economy.

Attempts to influence national TEMPUS priorities and initiate concrete project proposals have also been made by the EU Delegation in Slovenia. This was done, it seems, out of concern about an overemphasis of TEMPUS priorities and projects in Slovenia on science and technology and a neglect of other fields in need of renewal and restructuring (e.g. social sciences).

In the Slovak Republic, the EU Delegation has put an emphasis on information about other EU programmes in order to establish better links between them and TEMPUS. It is also involved in hearings concerning the establishment of national TEMPUS priorities. On occasion, the Delegation has acted as an intermediator in conflicts between the NTO and other EU bodies.

The examples show that there is a role to play for the EU Delegations, especially in the area of links between Phare and TEMPUS. Apart from the issues raised in our examples, Phare has a number of cross-border activities dealing with common problems of neighbouring countries, and also tries to link projects and activities on a national scale with regard to certain problems (e.g. transport or waste disposal). Such activities, although eligible for TEMPUS support, have so far been somewhat neglected. However, efforts to establish better links between Phare and TEMPUS might not always be wholly appreciated by the Ministries of Education on the one hand and the higher education institutions – the respective faculties and departments becoming involved in TEMPUS-supported activities – on the other. For example, a stronger reflection of Phare objectives in TEMPUS priorities might lead to the potential exclusion of those disciplines and subject areas not having a direct or at least indirect impact on economic restructuring and renewal.

4.2.8 Higher Education Institutions

The involvement of higher education institutions in TEMPUS can be located basically on three levels:

- involvement of representatives of the higher education institutions (e.g. rectors or vice-rectors and possibly other academic staff members) in the advisory boards (see pp. 96 – 98)
- involvement of units of the university administration (international relations officers, finance officers) responsible for information about the TEMPUS Programme, in advising applicants and, in some cases, managing TEMPUS funds for the faculties or departments involved in TEMPUS projects
- involvement of faculties and/or departments in TEMPUS-supported activities in the cooperative framework of TEMPUS projects.

In most of the CEE partner countries the NTOs have encouraged a stronger involvement of the university administration in TEMPUS activities at the institutional level and to make TEMPUS part of an integrated institutional development strategy. Concerning these issues the level of action undertaken by the institutional management varies to a considerable extent independent from existing support structures for TEMPUS at the institutions (e.g. TEMPUS contact persons in all faculties and/or departments).

In all of the CEE countries institutional leadership and management has been rather weak. This is not surprising because the institutional autonomy which was gained after 1989 gave the faculties a key role in the university administration. Attempts made by rectors or the central administrative level of the universities to play a stronger role have been resisted by the academic community as a trend towards centralisation. This has had considerable consequences for institutional planning and institutional development strategies. During TEMPUS I and still at the beginning of TEMPUS II it was an exception in most of the CEE countries for the central university administration to receive a copy of the TEMPUS applications or of JEP reports. Exceptions were Slovakia and Albania as well as individual institutions in the various partner countries. The Rector or Vice-Rector responsible for international affairs usually knows the number and the subject of the TEMPUS projects, because he or she signs the letter of endorsement, but is mostly unfamiliar with the details of the work and the results. Only in exceptional cases have measures been taken by the rector, vice-rector or the central university administration to introduce strategies for participation and involvement of the faculties and departments pertaining to the institution as a whole, to pre-select offers from institutions abroad to become involved as a partner, to initiate targeted project proposals from own staff or to encourage staff members to become contractors or coordinators. As a consequence most TEMPUS activities during TEMPUS I were neither integrated into an overall institutional reform and development strategy nor were results disseminated and equipment shared. TEMPUS projects in any one institution could be characterised as a number of little islands unconnected with each other.

Nevertheless, institutions are to a varying degree involved in the consultative process for the determination of national TEMPUS priorities and, in some countries, in the selection of academic experts for the assessment of JEP applications. In most countries the NTOs have managed to have at least one TEMPUS contact person at each institution to whom all important TEMPUS information is sent. Most NTOs also arrange meetings of all contact persons at least once a year to explain about the new priorities and the procedures of application and selection.

For example, in the Polish higher education institutions there is often not enough clarity about the national TEMPUS priorities and their changes each year. This is especially the case when departments or faculties are invited from partners abroad to participate in a project and do not become involved in writing the application. This sometimes leads to activities being organised out of context with no proper knowledge of objectives, contract and general TEMPUS framework.

In Bulgaria, the higher education institutions are strongly involved in the consultative process about national TEMPUS priorities. Usually, the rectors receive an information letter with the draft proposals for next year's priorities and are asked to encourage discussions about them in their institution and send comments and suggestions back to the NTO. The Minister of Education also presents the draft proposal to the Council of Rectors for discussion and comments.

In Albania, the TEMPUS Programme is administered with a top-down approach. National priorities specify subject areas as well as institutions from which applications are expected. Deans and vice-rectors coordinate TEMPUS activities at their respective institutions. JEPs are linked at an early stage to the needs of other departments.

As a rule, JEP activities of the departments receive some support from the central administration. However, in four of the countries under review, the finance departments have refused to administer JEP funds because they did not feel competent enough to do so. It is more often the case that faculties or departments prefer to administer TEMPUS funds themselves because they feel that otherwise they might lose control over the money or have to pay for central services. The latter was frequently found in those universities in which the finance department administered TEMPUS funds.

In general, the lack of institutional development plans which could function as a framework for TEMPUS activities was not only due to the fact that faculties insisted on being autonomous. The following issues contributed to the problem as well:

- Institutional planning seems to be very difficult in the large universities which are often spread over the city. It is easier in the smaller universities but these usually have only very few JEPs.

- Links between similar TEMPUS activities at various universities in one country are not frequent. The competition among higher education institutions for TEMPUS support tends to contribute to a differentiation into haves and have-nots. However, it must be noted here that this trend is being counterbalanced in some of the partner countries since the start of TEMPUS II by introducing preferences in the national priorities providing increased opportunities for weaker institutions to participate in TEMPUS projects.

- International relations offices responsible for TEMPUS and/or TEMPUS contact persons in the higher education institutions have often developed a high level of expertise and understanding concerning TEMPUS. However, these positions are sometimes filled by young women who are not recognised as experts by the institutional management.

4.3   Processes and Activities

4.3.1   The TEMPUS Programme

The administration of the TEMPUS Programme in the CEE partner countries is influenced by three areas of policy formation and decision-making:
- the determination of the TEMPUS budget
- the establishment of national priorities

- decisions concerning the selection of applications for TEMPUS support.

As we have pointed out in the previous sections of this chapter, several groups of actors are involved in these processes of policy formation and decision-making while the NTOs are responsible for the technical assistance and continuous administrative activities (e.g. information, advice, support, monitoring, preparation of selection procedures) connected to the operation of the programme on the national level. In addition, the NTOs play an important and usually informal role in the preparation of all decisions concerning the policy formation on the national level. Under TEMPUS I this role was especially important since there were often no higher education laws or formulated overall higher education reform and renewal strategies. At the beginning of TEMPUS I there was not even a Ministry responsible for higher education in one case, and till today some countries have experienced frequent changes of government or Ministers responsible for higher education. Initiatives for projects were often started by Western partners and applications from the departments and faculties of the higher education institutions had to comply with the TEMPUS objectives and the national priorities of the respective CEE partner country. The framework of regulations established by the Council decision and the increasingly detailed guidelines for applicants on the one hand and the development of national TEMPUS priorities on the other provided the most important framework for links between the activities proposed for TEMPUS support by the applicants and the TEMPUS objectives. However, it has been a characteristic feature of TEMPUS I that the TEMPUS-supported activities (educational cooperation, structural development, student and staff mobility) in the higher education institutions were not always clearly linked with the overall main TEMPUS objectives (reform of higher education, renewal of the economy). There are several reasons which may support this assessment:

- During TEMPUS I the programme was frequently seen less as part of a general process of transformation than as a sometimes substantial additional part of the budget available to higher education. The difficulty in establishing overall higher education development strategies explains at least in part the limited engagement of most Ministries of Education in TEMPUS. This has changed to a certain degree in TEMPUS II.

- The ad-hoc approaches which were developed under TEMPUS I on the institutional level do not only reflect the fact that TEMPUS I was established in 1990 as a kind of emergency measure, the basic operations of which remained more or less the same. They also reflect the lack of institutional development plans due to the weak position of the rector and a considerable degree of autonomy for faculties and of academic freedom for professors.

- The degree to which TEMPUS objectives may be achieved on the level of a higher education system as a whole is further influenced by the balance of participating higher education institutions (i.e. geographical coverage, inclusion of smaller or weaker institutions, etc.) and by activities concerning the dissemination of results of TEMPUS activities. In TEMPUS I, project support tended to concentrate in the large universities and/or in those institutions located in the capital and other main centres of higher education. It also concentrated on those institutions already cooperating with Western institutions. Dissemination of results and cooperation among institutions in the same country were not the rule. In general, the selection of applications based on quality criteria tended to exclude the weaker and often most needy institutions.

- Achievements of TEMPUS activities could not always be kept up on the same level because of lack of funding after TEMPUS support had stopped (e.g. for maintenance and continuous updating of computers and software, periodicals, laboratory consumables) or because newly developed curricula were not recognised on the national level.

The weak link between project activities and overall TEMPUS objectives has contributed to the fact that under TEMPUS I two kinds of activities often lacked coherence or remained coincidental:

- Policy formation for and administration of the TEMPUS Programme focused more the programme itself (i.e. carrying out the activities for which support was granted according to the rules and regulations) and were less clearly connected to an overall higher education reform and renewal strategy on the national level. A typical feature was the island character of the TEMPUS projects in the institutions.

- The contribution of TEMPUS activities to economic renewal and restructuring was seen as an indirect and long-term impact of TEMPUS. With some exceptions project or content related connections between TEMPUS and Phare did not exist (e.g. cooperation between TEMPUS and Phare projects or reciprocal information and exchange of experiences and results).

These developments have, however, been recognised in several CEE countries as hampering the impact of TEMPUS on the systems level. Efforts have been made to increase cooperation and consultation between TEMPUS and Phare and also to design a national strategy for higher education reform and renewal towards the end of TEMPUS I and under TEMPUS II. These changes include a better definition of national aims to be achieved with the help of TEMPUS (e.g. through a differentiation of national TEMPUS priorities) and have also led in some countries to a more important role of the Phare responsibles in developing and/or establishing TEMPUS strategies and priorities.

4.3.2 Phare Participation

In all countries under review the budget negotiations between Phare and TEMPUS became routinised during TEMPUS I. Thus, a relatively high stability of planning for TEMPUS was ensured although the TEMPUS selection schedule still operates on an estimated budget in the beginning of the procedures due to incoherent decision-making schedules between Phare and TEMPUS.

In some countries, namely Poland, Hungary and Romania, the role of the national Phare Coordinator in the procedures of establishing national TEMPUS priorities has become more important over time. Depending on the political context in which Phare coordination is located (e.g. Ministry of Economic Development, Department for European Integration, etc.) on the national level, there is a trend to insist more strongly on issues of economic renewal or European integration to be reflected in the national TEMPUS priorities as well as incorporated into the preferences for the selection of JEP applications. In some countries, however, a more active role of the Phare responsibles in the national TEMPUS Committees or Advisory Boards has led to conflicts among the political actors involved in TEMPUS on the national level (see pp. 96 – 89).

Our interviews in the CEE countries have shown that the actual role of the Phare Coordinator in a number of TEMPUS-related decisions does not always meet with agreement on the side of the higher education policy makers. In most countries the conflict remained latent and has never broken out. In some cases, however, it has become manifest. The conflict concerns the issue that some Phare responsibles would like to integrate TEMPUS activities for which support is granted more strongly into the policy of their department or unit in the respective Ministry or the Council of Ministers. This may include the wish, for example, to have a certain number or percentage of JEPs accepted in a certain field or discipline. Accordingly, they expect that applications from these fields are given preference in the selection and award of TEMPUS support. This wish may or may not coincide with national TEMPUS priority proposals of other groups and key actors or with selection criteria established for project proposals. A stronger insistence of the national Phare Coordinator to have Phare objectives better reflected in national TEMPUS priorities has led in some of the CEE countries to a certain shift of TEMPUS projects from science and technology to business and economics as well as to some of the social sciences (e.g. law).

In this context we have come across one case only in which the Phare responsibles addressed the European Commission in order to achieve recognition of their preferences for TEMPUS activities. This case was concerned with the attempt to pre-determine a certain number of JEPs to be accepted in a specified subject area regardless of the outcome of the quality assessment. The problem could be solved eventually by way of finding a compromise among the key actors involved on the national level.

A pro-active role of the Phare responsibles in TEMPUS-related policy formation and decision-making could not be found in all CEE partner countries. Where this is not the case the high degree of disbursement of the TEMPUS budget in contrast to that of the other Phare sub-programmes is often viewed as the main factor for not having to worry about TEMPUS. Seen from this perspective, TEMPUS has become the best functioning programme in the framework of Phare and therefore seems to cause less concern.

The relationship between TEMPUS and Phare may also become difficult in negotiations about the TEMPUS budget itself. The fact that the NTO is neither involved in the initiation of concrete projects nor in the application and selection of proposals as the Programme Management Units of other Phare sub-programmes, may lead to the view of the Phare Coordinator that the TEMPUS budget proposal is not sufficiently legitimised and that the Phare coordination does not have sufficient control over the financial means allocated to TEMPUS. This view tends to lead to lower budget allocations from Phare for TEMPUS. In a few countries, additional circumstances have played a role in conflicts concerning the determination of the TEMPUS budget. The proportion of the national Phare budget allocated for TEMPUS was in one case not determined individually but as part of the overall allocation for the Phare Human Resources Development Programme which also includes funds for general and vocational education. It was then left to the Ministry of Education to determine the respective proportions. In another case, the budget allocation for TEMPUS was substantially reduced because of the decision to allocate approximately one-third of the whole national Phare budget to the Cross Border Programme and distribute the rest of the Phare budget among the other Phare sub-programmes according to pre-determined proportions. Thus, TEMPUS received a considerably lower budget than was expected and than it had received in the previous years.

4.3.3 National Priorities

In the framework of policy formation, the national TEMPUS priorities establish a link between the general objectives of the TEMPUS Programme on the one hand and national higher education policies in the CEE countries on the other. Until 1992, national TEMPUS priorities were almost identical for the countries involved. In 1993, national priorities started to diverge. This divergence was not due to a change in TEMPUS regulations but rather was a sign of different speeds of general development, a differentiation in processes of policy formation and differences in the development of the respective higher education sectors. However, due to the shift towards multi-annual funding for TEMPUS projects, the call for JEP applications was cancelled in most of the CEE countries in 1993/94. Thus, only a very limited overall number of new JEPs was accepted and the new national priorities could hardly be implemented. In 1994, national priorities diverged even more and also became more detailed and refined in some of the CEE countries. Currently we can distinguish between three types of priorities:

- subject or subject area related priorities
- structural or thematic priorities applying to all subjects
- a mixture of the first two.

In general, there is no shared policy among the CEE countries which seems to be one of the reasons – among others – for the low acceptance of regional JEPs. Concerning the subject area related priorities, there was an emphasis on science and technology in the beginning of TEMPUS. This can be explained by the fact that Western contacts were more frequently established in these fields and finding partners was easier. The gradual inclusion of humanities, teacher training and social sciences reflected the view in the partner countries that these subjects needed renewal because they were more ideologically distorted. There were also new fields in this area (e.g. business and management studies) which did not exist before. Susequently the sciences and technical subjects felt excluded although they are still strongly represented in the overall number of accepted JEPs (see also pp. 51 – 65).

The annual establishment of national priorities can be described as a sequence of four steps:

- The Education Ministry asks the NTO to submit a draft proposal for priorities or a strategy paper on which proposals for priorities can be based. This proposal might or might not be changed by the Minister and is then adopted as an official document for the national consultation process.

- The next step is the national consultation process about the proposal, usually taking place in the TEMPUS advisory boards, sometimes also involving opinions and recommendations from all higher education institutions. In some of the CEE countries it is not the NTO but the TEMPUS Advisory Board which submits a draft proposal for national priorities to the Minister.

- The Education Minister establishes the list of national priorities based on this consultation process and sends it as an official document to the European Commission.

- The national priorities are submitted for advice to the EU TEMPUS Committee and the European Commission. The Commission may comment on them and even ask for revision. After this consultation between the European Commission and the CEE partner countries, the final version of national TEMPUS priorities is published. In two cases national priorities submitted by a CEE country were changed by the Commission and published without final consultation and approval of the changes by the CEE country concerned. This has led to considerable problems and concerns.

The establishment of national priorities is not only the area of policy formation in which the largest number of actors is involved; it is also the area which has experienced the highest degree of development and change over time. The process of establishing national priorities has not been accorded an equal importance in all countries under review here. In those countries where national priorities are established by only a small group of actors or are kept very general, policy formation has evolved either in different areas of the national TEMPUS steering system or takes place on the governmental level.

There are five major issues of potential tensions or problems concerning the establishment of national priorities:

- Revisions proposed or even undertaken by the European Commission might not properly reflect the actual situation in the respective CEE country.

- Interests of Phare responsibles and the Ministry of Education might diverge.

- Faculties and departments of higher education institutions might feel excluded from TEMPUS participation when their subject area is not reflected in the priorities.

- The growing divergence of national TEMPUS priorities among the CEE partner countries has led to a decrease in regional cooperation and thus to a growing disinterest in regional JEPs. The only exception in this respect are the Baltic States, where some efforts at regional cooperation are still undertaken (e.g. in the Euro Faculty Project).
- Finally, the annual establishment of priorities may create an information problem. Not only must potential applicants continuously be kept up-to-date, but in some countries priorities are published at such a late stage that project proposals cannot be matched properly with priorities.

There have been three stages in the importance of national TEMPUS priorities for TEMPUS project applications and their selection. In the beginning of TEMPUS I national priorities were not much more than an indicative list. Since 1993, national TEMPUS priorities have become more influential and binding in the selection of applications for TEMPUS support. Under TEMPUS II the match between priorities and applications is conditional for the award of funding. In those countries where national priorities are a relatively refined and detailed mixture of subject area related priorities and thematic or structural priorities, some higher education institutions or some disciplines or subject areas tend to feel excluded.

Concerning the process of establishing national TEMPUS priorities and its impacts, various issues were addressed during our visits:

- Although key actors are involved in the establishment of national priorities, some faculties and departments complained about lack of information and felt excluded from opportunities for application.
- There are still substantial differences among the partner countries concerning the extent to which higher education institutions are involved in the process of establishing national priorities. In Romania, for example, the Rectors' Conference is represented in the Supervisory Board discussing the priorities, but at least up to 1995 the Rectors' Conference did not meet regularly and not all members were informed automatically. In contrast to this, all rectors in Bulgaria receive a draft proposal of the priorities with the request for comments. In Slovenia and Estonia the rectors and possibly other representatives of all higher education institutions are actively involved in the establishment of national priorities through membership in the TEMPUS Advisory Board.
- It is not at all clear to what degree detailed priorities may come into conflict with the emphasis on quality criteria in the selection procedures. A proposal might fully comply with the national priorities but not have the required quality and vice-versa. Our experiences have

shown that solutions to this problem are still rather ad-hoc in most of the countries. An exception in this respect is Albania.

- During TEMPUS I national priorities often constituted the only written document which reflected in one way or another national higher education policies. Some Education Ministries expressed a relatively low interest in national TEMPUS priorities. The process of establishing national priorities each year seems to have led, in some countries at least, to the awareness of the need to create a more focused overall policy for higher education and link it more strongly to the needs of the economy.

4.3.4 Selection Procedures

JEP applications in TEMPUS go through several assessment procedures, partly on the national level and partly on the EU level. Three groups of actors are usually involved: the NTO, academic experts and the ETF TEMPUS Department. The award decisions are made jointly by the Education Minister and the European Commission after consultation with the Phare Coordinator.

The assessments cover various aspects of the applications:
- the technical assessment (completeness of forms, etc.) done by the ETF TEMPUS Department
- the priority assessment done by the NTO with parallel checks of the ETF TEMPUS Department in some cases
- the academic quality assessment including an assessment of the JEP management and an assessment of the budget proposed is done by the academic experts.

The number of layers and stages of the JEP selection procedure as well as the number of actors involved make it a rather complex exercise. However, this procedure is the only one in which the all objectives interrelate.

Each of the actors or groups of actors involved in the selection procedure has a certain amount of leeway to express personal preferences and opinions in terms of the quality and characteristics of TEMPUS activities. For example, each application is usually assessed independently by two academic experts. If they disagree a third expert is asked for an assessment or the case is discussed in bilateral consultations, possibly supported by the opinion of EU academic experts. Criteria for the various assessments were originally proposed by the EC TEMPUS Office including a format for the assessment sheets, thus supporting comparability and management of the data-bases. Nevertheless, the NTOs have been free to adapt or complement criteria and assessment sheets according to their needs of information and the national situation.

The processes of assessment and selection have been gradually refined in the course of TEMPUS I. In most of the partner countries we found no cause for concern and all actors involved seemed to be quite satisfied with the way the overall process has turned out. All CEE countries have managed to establish varied mechanisms aimed at preventing undue particularistic influence.

The assessment and selection procedures of applications during TEMPUS I tended to create a potential for problems in two areas. First, some applications received high grades in the quality assessment but did not particularly comply to the national priorities or vice-versa, that is, some applications fully complied to national priorities but received somewhat lower grades in the quality assessment. These applications became an object for discussion in the framework of the bilateral consultations. The selection procedure has usually been kept flexible enough to find solutions for difficulties and imbalances.

Second, the emphasis on quality tended to exclude those institutions or faculties from TEMPUS support which needed it most for their reform and renewal. Thus, during TEMPUS I, certain institutions and subject areas tended to be excluded In some of the CEE partner countries attempts were made to remedy this by including the neglected subject areas concerned explicitly into the national priorities and by formulating a preference for acceptance of those applications in which well established institutions cooperated with one or more smaller and weaker institution from the same country within one project.

The NTOs have often tried to offer special advice and help to these smaller and weaker institutions in order to enable them to formulate a good application. A certain balance is sought also in the choice of academic experts so that they do not only come from the well established and usually prestigious and big institutions. The efforts seem to have worked best in those CEE countries in which the experts were given the opportunity to discuss their assessments among each other and come to an agreement as a group.

From the standpoint of the well established and prestigious institutions, however, there is another bias implicitly contained in the assessment procedures. It is possibly re-inforced by the fact that academic experts frequently come from these institutions as well but are not allowed to assess applications coming from their own departments or institutions. Concerning the institutional level, the argument is that if a certain institution is well recognised in any one subject and the dominant assessment criterion is quality, then it is impossible that an application coming from this institution is rejected. Concerning the level of the individual academic expert and assessor the argument is that if an application coming from their own department is rejected, then it is due to the envy or non-understanding of experts less qualified than they are themselves.

4.3.5 Funding of Activities

The funding of TEMPUS activities within the projects is determined on four levels of decisions. In addition, we found that for certain activities the time factor plays an important role.

The first level is the determination of the TEMPUS budget. The certainty of a relatively routinised procedure which has been established was necessary for the planning of TEMPUS activities because of the differing time schedules of decision-making in Phare and in TEMPUS. Budget allocations in Phare are finalised each year at such a late date that TEMPUS selection procedures are almost finished. This means the number of TEMPUS projects for which funds may be awarded might either change rather late or – in case of a lower budget than expected – all projects might receive a lower support. The former solution seems to have a higher impact on national policies than the latter insofar as in such a case the number of applications which can be accepted is insufficient to cover each priority with at least one project. In contrast to this, the latter solution which is usually finalised by the European Commission might produce an untenable situation for the projects themselves in terms of carrying out all activities planned in the framework of the project and laid down in the contract while at the same time having to work on a budget considerably lower than applied for.

The second level of funding decisions concerns the amount of support awarded to individual TEMPUS projects (i.e. JEPs, CMEs, IMGs), which is decided by the European Commission after consultation with the Ministries of Education. Taking the example of JEP support, few projects are awarded either the maximum amount of support as laid down in the EU guidelines or the full amount of support they have applied for. Nevertheless, all activities stated in the application are usually contained in the JEP contract. And the fulfillment of the contract is closely monitored. Two solutions are possible: the distribution of funds among partners is reduced for each partner or for each activity. The solution must be found among the JEP partners themselves. A project may face a crisis when the support granted is so low that the contract cannot be fulfilled properly anymore.

The third level is the funding of the activities themselves. The proportion of funds for each of the activities within one JEP must be indicated in the application and is laid down in the contract. Funds for mobility cannot simply be used to buy computers and vice-versa. All changes of contract must be applied for and projects are closely monitored with regard to their finances. Financial irregularities not complying to the official rules were sometimes a cause in TEMPUS I to stop a JEP. The level of funding for the individual activities has been judged differently by CEE partners involved in JEPs. Funds for structural support were greatly appreciated and often considered generous although never enough. The amount of funds for curriculum development did not seem to be a problem but there were frequent complaints about lack of financial support for publication and dissemination of results (including costs for printing new textbooks). Mobility grants for staff were usually considered as being sufficient but becoming tight when hotel accommodation was needed abroad. Finally, grants for student mobility were considered much more frequently to be on the low side or even insufficient.

The fourth level is the distribution of funds among partners in a JEP. Apart from a great deal of praise and gratefulness for large amounts of unpaid or only minimally paid work of Western contractors, coordinators and partners in support of the JEP activities were also made aware of some criticism related to the impression that in one way or another TEMPUS funds go back to the Western partners. In some cases problems were also caused by demands of Western partners for high levels of overheads and administrative costs (in some cases up to 20 per cent). In serious cases the NTO and the ETF TEMPUS Department may act as intermediators in certain conflicts or the ETF TEMPUS Department might even suggest stopping a JEP, but, as a rule, these conflicts are seen as part of the cooperation process which the partners have to solve among themselves.

While we have come across only one case of conflict on the first level, the second, third and fourth levels are more often a source of problems affecting cooperation among partners. In one of the CEE countries the Rectors' Conference has been dissatisfied with the level of the budget which was allocated for TEMPUS from Phare. The rectors addressed themselves to the Prime Minister and received his support for their demands. However, this had negative consequences for the relationships between Phare responsibles and other TEMPUS actors because two years in a row Phare was forced to change its annual indicative programme.

There were more frequent cases during TEMPUS I in which CEE partners had difficulties in receiving a copy of the contract and information about the JEP budget and the amounts of funding allocated to the various activities. Some CEE partners did not even request information on these issues. A greater awareness of their importance has changed the situation to a certain degree. We also note that with growing experience in international cooperation dissatisfaction of CEE partners increased about the low coverage of their own administrative costs in the framework of JEP activities.

The success and impact of JEP activities is dependent on two different time factors: (a) delays in the transfer of project funds and (mobility) grants and (b) the end of JEP support after three years. For the recipients in the CEE countries it is often not quite clear who or what causes delays in the transfer of grants. Delays seemed to be quite frequent and often resulted in severe problems for carrying out a planned activity, especially with regard to mobility. In some cases the recognition arrangements had to be cancelled when students arrived in the middle rather than at the beginning of a term; in other cases delays in the transfer of mobility grants (three months and more) for staff caused serious problems for the arrangement of personal, professional and administrative matters.

The ending of JEP support after three years has been made less harsh by the introduction of JENs (Joint European Networks) at the end of TEMPUS I providing support for a limited period of time to wrap up activities and disseminate results. During the first years of TEMPUS I the lack of such an opportunity has frequently caused some disappointment. Generally, the dissemination of results seems to have been neglected to a certain extent in most of the CEE countries.

In summarising, it can be said that the funding of TEMPUS activities in the CEE countries does not constitute an issue for serious concern on the level of national and supra-national decision-making. The reverse can be said about individual recipients and faculties or departments involved in JEPs. Discrepancies between contractual conditions to be fulfilled in the framework of a JEP and amount of support actually awarded were not sufficiently taken into consideration. Delays of grants occur to such an extent that it seems to be less and less acceptable.

4.3.6 Monitoring and Controlling

There are a number of monitoring and controlling activities built into the administrative processes of the TEMPUS Programme for which the ETF TEMPUS Department on the one hand and the NTOs for their respective countries on the other are responsible. We can basically distinguish between monitoring and controlling activities on three levels:

- The European Commission monitors TEMPUS activities by organising site-visits to a number of JEPs in the CEE partner countries. The results of these visits are documented in the framework of reports. It is also responsible for publishing the annual report about the TEMPUS Programme as a whole on the basis of documentation provided by the ETF TEMPUS Department.

- The EC TEMPUS Office/ETF TEMPUS Department monitors administrative procedures of the NTOs as well as TEMPUS-supported activities at the higher education institutions in each CEE country through permanent contact with the NTOs and frequent visits to the JEPs. Desk monitoring is done on the basis of NTO and project reports. In addition, the ETF TEMPUS Department is responsible for building up and continuously updating a TEMPUS data base which is fed by input from the NTOs of the partner countries and by the outcomes of the annual selection procedures for the various TEMPUS activities. Finally, it may scrutinise TEMPUS JEPs in which there is cause for concern to financial audits.

- The NTO is responsible for continuous monitoring of all TEMPUS activities in the country. This includes desk monitoring by taking note of all incoming project reports, keeping contact with all TEMPUS-supported projects as well as advising and supporting projects in cases of difficulties (e.g. delays in transfer of funds, customs and tax regulations, visa problems, problems among partners or with the institution). Several of the NTOs have started to organise their own site-visit programmes, mainly visiting JEPs, and initiating evaluation exercises in their country. For these site-visits and evaluations they are frequently supported by the academic experts serving in the assessment of JEP applications.

Towards the end of TEMPUS I the EC TEMPUS Office had started to gradually transfer more and more responsibilities to the NTOs, a process which is currently still going on. NTOs have taken over more reponsibilities in the assessment procedures preceding the decisions about selection of applications and award of funding. Some of the NTOs have also taken over the payment of IMGs to the grantholders. The work of the NTOs themselves is monitored quite closely by the ETF TEMPUS Department and – usually – by the Ministry of Education or the TEMPUS advisory boards in the respective countries. For example, they have to send a financial statement to the ETF TEMPUS Department every four to eight weeks in addition to their biannual and annual activity reports.

In general, we have found no serious dissatisfaction concerning the monitoring and controlling activities in the CEE countries under review. In those cases in which JEPs have been stopped on the basis of results of monitoring, controlling or financial auditing, some kind of settlement was reached that was acceptable to all parties involved. A hearing of all JEP partners before the decision was made to stop the support of a JEP turned out to be instrumental.

The administrative logic of the TEMPUS Programme can be characterised as a mix of more or less formal short-term and incremental feedbacks and long-term feed-backs. Both of these feedbacks produce a multitude of small and short-term revisions of programme elements with limited scope. Up to the time this study was conducted, no strategic long-term reflection and revision of the TEMPUS Programme had been undertaken. Small revisions have served the continuous adaptation and development of activities but have tended to make the information issue much more complex and harder to deal with for all people involved, especially the NTOs and potential applicants.

4.4 Achievements, Impacts and Policy Development

The TEMPUS Programme is characterised by a certain openness and incomplete definition of higher education target areas so that the CEE partner countries have the opportunity to adapt the scheme and its resources to their respective national needs. These have to be formulated in the framework of national TEMPUS policy decisions.

The processes of TEMPUS policy formation on the national level are divided into different steps and stages of decision-making and involve a number of different actors. Processes and actors have been analysed in detail in the previous sections of this chapter. The findings show that a rather complex structure of TEMPUS policy formation, decision-making and administration has been established in the CEE partner countries. The structure is quite similar in all CEE partner countries. To summarise our findings with regard to this structure we will focus on three main questions:

- What are the processes of policy formation (including decision-making) and administrative routines which have been established?
- How functional are these processes and routines and which policy is actually realised?
- What are the effects of these processes and routines with regard to the TEMPUS project activities carried out in the higher education institutions?

4.4.1 Policy Formation for TEMPUS

Policy formation and decision-making for TEMPUS take place on basically two different levels involving a number of actors from each of these levels:

(1) On the national level decisions are made about the financial resources (TEMPUS budget) and about national TEMPUS priorities identifying structural, educational and subject-related areas of reform and renewal. In addition, academic experts are nominated and selected to serve in the quality of assessment of applications.

(2) On the level of the higher education institutions project proposals are initiated or initiatives from Western partners are taken up on the basis of interests of individual academic staff members, concepts of reform and renewal of individual departments or faculties and possibly institutional development plans. All applications need an official letter of endorsement signed by the rector or vice-rector, thus expressing more or less directly the approval and consent of the central institutional level to the proposed project.

Against the background of the most important areas of national policy formation and the interests of the actors involved in the respective processes and procedures, TEMPUS can be characterised as a programme which needs a continuous formal as well as informal dialogue of all actors involved. The procedures established in all CEE partner countries to arrive at the necessary policies and decisions do not clearly separate actors and levels of decision-making power (e.g. supra-national, national, institutional level) but rather have intensified the efforts at coordination and cooperation.

In response to centrally planned economies and societies, resistance against and rejection of any central planning persisted so that a typical feature of the implementation of TEMPUS in the CEE partner countries was a lack of explicitly formulated overall higher education policies on the national level and frequently also a lack of development plans on the level of the higher education institutions. Thus, the processes of policy formation continuously had to strike a balance between:

- the EU in the sponsor role wanting to achieve certain overall objectives with the programme and the CEE countries in the role of a beneficiary with more or less defined individual demands and needs
- the educational and the economic objectives of national authorities (Education Ministries and Phare responsibles)
- the national authorities and the higher education institutions

- among the various higher education institutions, the various disciplines and subjects themselves.

Although each domain of policy formation and decision-making has one clearly identifiable key actor, cooperation is required as well with the other actors. Thus, continuous coordination turned out to be necessary. For example, the TEMPUS budget is decided by the national Phare Coordination Unit on the basis of an estimated budget proposal submitted by the Ministry of Education. Here, economic policies have to be coordinated with educational policies. National priorities are decided by the Ministry of Education on the basis of proposals from the higher education sector. Here, overall educational policies have to be coordinated with interests and policies of institutions and faculties or departments. Therefore, the overcomplexity of the stages of policy formation and decision-making involving actors from all levels created a certain amount of centripetal pressure towards:

- a single major decision-making arena, the TEMPUS advisory or supervisory boards
- a managerial unit serving as a moderator and trouble shooter for most of the administrative procedures involved in TEMPUS, the National TEMPUS Offices.

The size and the composition of the members of the boards vary considerably from country to country. However, the majority of them count a representative of the Ministry of Education, a representative of the national Phare coordination unit, the director of the National TEMPUS Office and representatives from the higher education institutions among their members. During the meetings of these boards policy formation is discussed and negotiated; in case of supervisory boards the relevant decisions are made by way of seeking consensus and finding compromises among all actors. In Slovakia, the status of the board is reinforced by vesting it with an independent legal status.

Efficiency and actual functioning of the boards vary to a certain extent according to their status (advice or decision-making, legal status), their organisational structure (number of meetings per year, involvement in all or only some of the relevant policy questions), their size (number of members), and the composition of their members (representation of all relevant actors or only some of them). One of the most important factors for the activities of the boards is, however, the role played by the National TEMPUS Offices.

In all CEE countries we found that the National TEMPUS Offices have an exceptional importance for the successful steering of the TEMPUS

Programme. Formally, their assignment is the provision of administrative support to TEMPUS policy-makers and TEMPUS activities at higher education institutions in their respective countries. To carry out these tasks they have to be in close cooperation with the ETF TEMPUS Department on the one hand and with the faculties and departments of higher education institutions in which TEMPUS activities actually take place on the other hand. Because of their position between the supra-national and the institutional level, the NTOs do not only possess the most comprehensive information but they are also in a position to make recommendations for and prepare all relevant policy decisions on the national level.

The involvement of the NTOs not only in the administrative procedures but also – though frequently in an informal way – in policy formation has led to a significant degree of competence and as a result to considerable influence on the national steering of the TEMPUS Programme. Thus, the NTOs have a strong position in the coordination of the various policy formation and decision-making processes as well as in the coordination of the interests of various actors involved in them. In many of the national TEMPUS advisory and supervisory boards common recommendations or joint decisions are made on the basis of proposals from the NTOs. This cumulation of competences is well accepted and even appreciated in the CEE countries but also might represent a certain risk for the balance of power and influence on the national level. However, during our interviews we could not note frequent problems in this respect. However, a case under dispute was Hungary.

Overall, the processes and procedures for TEMPUS policy formation and administration on the national level gained a relatively high degree of stability and even routinisation over time. Exceptions could be found if there was a conflict of interests and an individual actor had tried to push his position by addressing authorities not generally involved in the TEMPUS-related procedures but having more political power or by choosing forms of lobbying outside the established arena for dialogue and cooperation. Overall, we came across three cases in which the structure of dialogue, cooperation and finding a consensus through negotiations was deliberately suspended in the six years of TEMPUS operations under review.

4.4.2 *The Functioning of the Operational System*

The operational system of TEMPUS policy formation and administration in the CEE partner countries has been well established during the period of TEMPUS I. This can be characterised as one of the major achievements in the framework of TEMPUS considering the complex structure of steering which had to be taken into account, the ongoing instabilities of the transformation processes, and the novelty of European support programmes. Towards the end of the TEMPUS I period we found a relatively smoothly functioning form of policy formation including all relevant actors and a routinised steering and administration of the TEMPUS Programme in almost all CEE countries.

The growing importance of the NTOs and the boards for mediating and balancing the interests and objectives of the various actors involved in TEMPUS policy formation and decision-making tended to counterbalance the influence of national key actors in the various processes of policy formation and decision-making and led to a certain shift in responsibilities. In some cases tasks and decisions were deliberately delegated (e.g. to the boards); in other cases we found a tacit handing over of tasks (e.g. to NTOs) in the face of routinisation of decision-making processes and increased competence in the administration of TEMPUS.

Each of the four key actors (Ministries of Education, Phare responsibles, higher education institutions, and the EU) has basically three possibilities to influence parts of the steering system of the TEMPUS Programme by either exercising a programmatic control (i.e. decisions concerning programme revisions and policy formation), or a bureaucratic control (i.e. decisions concerning the administrative structure), or opting for a bottom-up approach (i.e. deliberate grass-roots approach or 'laissez-faire'). Any of these options entails further decisions bearing upon the effects of TEMPUS. For example:

- definitions of the role and shape of the national higher education system
- prioritisation or balance of structural sectors and subjects to be supported by TEMPUS
- definition of institutional beneficiaries
- targeted improvement of quality or coverage of all institutions and subjects
- optimisation by matching of resources or channelling TEMPUS support to the weakest institutions and those subjects most needing renewal and reforms.

The Ministries of Education could:

- define the programme more strongly by integrating it into the framework of a formulated policy for the higher education sector on the national level

- influence the programme by a stronger bureaucratic control of the NTOs
- intentionally follow a bottom-up approach by leaving the policy decisions for TEMPUS to the higher education institutions.

The actual involvement of the respective ministries in these processes of policy formation and decision-making varies considerably among the CEE countries. On the whole, a more pro-active involvement of the ministries in TEMPUS could have been expected because TEMPUS is also supposed to achieve impacts on the level of the higher education systems in the CEE partner countries. A coherent and integrated higher education development strategy existed in none of the CEE partner countries during TEMPUS I. In most of the CEE countries we found a rather close cooperation of the Ministries of Education with the NTOs. However, the growing professionalisation of the latter led to the tacit agreement that the NTOs could be depended upon when decisions had to be prepared, proposals had to be drafted, briefings were needed, or preliminary negotiations had to be conducted. The majority of the NTOs has to report regularly to the Ministry, but this is less understood as a form of bureaucratic control than as a form of keeping the Ministry informed about what is going on in TEMPUS on the national level.

In contrast to the argument that a critical mass of TEMPUS projects in any one country will more or less automatically lead to positive impacts on the systems level or that it will lead to the achievement of TEMPUS objectives, it could also be argued that TEMPUS impacts and effects might improve beyond the level of faculties and departments if TEMPUS were integrated into an overall higher education development strategy and complemented by institutional development strategies. Such an argument proposes to integrate TEMPUS activities into a coherent and supportive rather than prescriptive framework which might create better complementarity and synergy effects among TEMPUS projects and thus improve the general impacts of the programme for the institutional and national level. However, it cannot simply be assumed that educational activities have a direct impact on institutional management and administrative frameworks.

The *Phare responsibles* have a somewhat ambiguous role in the steering of the TEMPUS Programme on the national level. On the one hand, TEMPUS is one of Phare's subprogrammes and the TEMPUS budget comes from the Phare resources. On the other hand, the logic of the TEMPUS Programme was structured on the model of incentive programmes like ERASMUS and thus has a somewhat different legal structure. The NTOs cannot be compared to the Programme Management Units which have been established for the other Phare sub-programmes, and control and decision-making structures in TEMPUS are much more decentralised. In general, the Phare responsibles have much less influence on and control of TEMPUS policies and activities than they have in the other Phare sub-programmes.

Nevertheless, the participation of Phare responsibles in the main domains of policy formation and decision-making is arranged in all CEE countries by their membership in the TEMPUS advisory boards. We have found examples of Phare responsibles choosing any of the three options listed above (programmatic, bureaucratic and bottom-up). Because of a difference in the sectors which are addressed by TEMPUS (higher education) and Phare (economy), we had assumed a possible conflict in terms of the interests and objectives of the key actors from these two sectors. The general assumption that a well educated society contributes to economic growth and prosperity might not establish sufficiently direct and immediate links between the two programmes and the anticipation of long-term effects might not satisfy the urgency and envisaged speed of the transformation processes. It could have been a standpoint suggesting itself to Phare responsibles to force TEMPUS into a direction in which only those projects and disciplines will be supported (e.g. business studies, applied sciences and technology, university-industry relations, technology transfer, etc.) which have a direct and visible impact on the economy, thus excluding all those having an only indirect impact or none at all. We did not find such an approach to TEMPUS in any of the CEE partner countries.

The involvement of *higher education institutions* in TEMPUS policy formation on the national level is usually given through their representation in the TEMPUS advisory or supervisory boards. In the larger CEE countries the national rectors' conference delegates two or three of its members to the board. In the smaller CEE countries having only few higher education institutions, it is frequently the case that each higher education institution is represented in the board by one or two delegates from the central level. Complaints by rectors about insufficient involvement in TEMPUS policy formation were only voiced in those countries in which the national rectors' conference is not meeting regularly and information about TEMPUS policy developments is not channeled through this body.

In addition to the representation of higher education institutions in TEMPUS advisory or supervisory boards, some of the larger CEE countries involve the central level of all higher education institutions in hearings and recommendations for national TEMPUS priorities. This is usually done by the NTOs sending a letter with the draft proposal to the rectors and asking them for comments and further proposals or suggestions. The three options for policy formation and decision-making typically available for TEMPUS key actors are also open to the rectors of higher education institutions, however, with a slight difference as regards the level which is addressed by the choice of option.

- Rectors could exercise a relatively strong programme control by using pressure to influence content and structure of national priorities and TEMPUS budget negotiations. The latter case has happened in only one of the CEE countries where the national rectors' conference is exceptionally influential. The former case, that is, participation in the establishment of national priorities, does not need a high degree of pressure as a rule because consideration of the views of institutions is usually guaranteed in one way or another.

- Rectors could exercise a stronger bureaucratic control by introducing pre-selection procedures at the institutional level of all applications for TEMPUS support before they are submitted. This is the case in some institutions in practically each of the CEE partner countries but not the rule. The respective institutions usually have an institutional development plan into which most or all TEMPUS activities are integrated.

- Rectors could opt for a bottom-up approach, that is, leaving it to the faculties and departments to initiate TEMPUS activities.

Although examples can be found for all three of the options, the most typical form of institutional involvement in TEMPUS on the national level of policy formation is through representation in the TEMPUS advisory or supervisory boards and a bottom-up approach in the institution.

A certain amount of influence must also be attributed to the *academic experts* serving in the assessment of applications. The quality criterion is predominant in the assessment exercised by the academic experts although there are additional criteria as well. In their assessment they have the opportunity of giving other criteria than quality a certain weight, and in their recommendations for support they may or may not prejudice a stronger balance in favour of weaker applications from institutions and subjects needing TEMPUS support most for renewal or in favour of geographical balance.

Striving for sensible balances is more often the result in those CEE countries in which academic experts are cooperating in the assessment and having to reach an agreement concerning their recommendations as a group. Concentration on quality regardless of possible imbalances in the chances for successful applications and distribution of funds is frequently a result in those CEE countries in which the names of the academic experts are kept secret and experts don't know each other.

Except in the case of Hungary where the legal status of the TEMPUS Steering Committee and the NTO were being disputed on the initiative of the EU Delegation during the time of our evaluation, we found well appreciated support in a number of administrative, legal and organisational matters (tax exemptions, visa, customs regulations, etc.) offered by the *EU Delegations* in several of the CEE countries. The EU Delegation in Romania is more strongly involved than delegations in other CEE countries in policy formation for the TEMPUS Programme aimed at establishing closer links between Phare and TEMPUS through pro-active participation in the development of national priorities and initiation of project activities. In the majority of CEE countries representatives of the respective EU Delegation are kept informed on national TEMPUS developments by the NTOs but are not actively involved in policy formation for or administration of TEMPUS.

The example of the EU Delegation in Romania shows that there is a certain role to play in TEMPUS for EU Delegations in the CEE partner countries which goes beyond support in legal matters, although help is needed in this respect in several countries. As long as a visible commitment to and involvement in national TEMPUS policies is offered in the form of expert advice rather than programme control or administrative controls it has possibly helped to improve links between Phare and TEMPUS and thus impacts of the TEMPUS Programme itself.

Although the involvement of the *European Commission* is not a part of our TEMPUS evaluation, it cannot be completely ignored as one of the key actors in the TEMPUS Programme on the supra-national level. The same applies to the involvement of the ETF TEMPUS Department. The role of the European Commission is of great importance with regard to programme control. It is determined by the Commission's responsibilities in setting up the TEMPUS Programme as such and introducing appropriate revisions, its measures and individual activities as well as its framework regulations. Overall, the TEMPUS Programme has been a great success and is highly appreciated in the CEE partner countries. This conclusion is supported by the fact that the vast majority of actors opt for a continuation (i.e. TEMPUS III) with basically the same measures and activities eligible for support as in TEMPUS I and TEMPUS II.

With respect to the bureaucratic (i.e. administrative) control exercised by the *ETF TEMPUS Department* as one of its major tasks, NTOs and

JEP partners from CEE institutions frequently listed three areas of problems:

- The NTOs did not always appreciate the disregard of the ETF TEMPUS Department for their growing degree of professionalisation and their ability to make independent decisions. On the one hand the ETF TEMPUS Department has transferred more and more tasks and responsibilities to the NTOs, and on the other hand the EU TEMPUS Office seems not to be prepared to offer a sufficient degree of collegial and cooperative partnership in their cooperation with the NTOs.

- A large number of CEE partners in Joint European Projects as well as beneficiaries of Individual Mobility Grants complain about serious delays in the transfer of project funds and mobility grants. This does not only cause difficulties in the organisation of the respective activities but also endangers fulfilment of contracts and the carrying out of activities as such. In case of student mobility recognition arrangements had to be cancelled when students arrived in their host countries in the middle rather than at the beginning of the term.

- Frequently, JEP partners have complained about increasing bureaucracy and paperwork required in the JEPs. In addition, low flexibility in administrative matters and disbursement of funds is seen as being detrimental to an adaptation or change of project activities once the project has started.

Our findings show that the TEMPUS Programme is highly appreciated and can be considered as successful in the CEE partner countries. Nevertheless, the role of the EU is sometimes still somewhat too prescriptive and not living up to their own promotion of moving 'from assistance to partnership'. The growing expertise which was found in several CEE partner countries in terms of acquiring the knowledge and skills necessary for successful participation in European education programmes is not always adequately recognised and taken into account by EU key actors.

4.4.3 *The Impacts of TEMPUS Policy Formation and Administration on TEMPUS Activities in Higher Education Institutions*

There are basically four areas in which national TEMPUS policy development and administration have a direct impact on TEMPUS project activities being carried out in the faculties and departments of higher education institutions:

- national priorities and preferences for TEMPUS support
- funding of activities

- changes in types of JEPs eligible for support
- information and advice.

During TEMPUS I *national TEMPUS priorities* were established in the first couple of years in such a way that applications for TEMPUS support were encouraged from certain disciplines or subject. Engineering and applied or technical sciences were strongly represented among those subjects aiming for renewal, while business administration and management studies were strongly represented among those subjects being newly established (see also pp. 224 – 228). During the second half of the TEMPUS I period law, social sciences and medical sciences as well as environmental protection were supported more often, and a broader coverage of subject areas was achieved.

Nevertheless, there were still complaints from faculties and departments and also from some specialised higher education institutions feeling excluded from opportunities to apply for TEMPUS support by the increasing number of specifications and general refinement of priorities. Attempts to balance possible disadvantages have been made by introducing a mixture of structural and subject-related priorities so that departments offering courses in 'non-priority' subjects could profit from TEMPUS as well. In some cases we also found an annual rotation among the subjects listed as eligible for support.

Some CEE countries have introduced special preferences in addition to their priorities. Most frequently, we can find preferences pertaining to the composition of partners within one JEP. Over the TEMPUS I period we saw a clear decrease of partners from several CEE countries within one JEP while at the same time there was a clear increase of several institutions from one country being partners within one JEP (see pp. 228 – 231). Preferences concerning several partner institutions from one country within a JEP may either serve to establish certain centres of excellency (concentrating and matching funds) or to enable weaker faculties or departments to profit from TEMPUS support by cooperating with a usually larger and more successful institution.

Another type of preference which can be found in the priorities of some countries introduces age or frequency limits for grant holders of Individual Mobility Grants (IMGs). Preferences concerning conditions for IMGs are often resented by academic staff members being thus excluded from the opportunity to apply. But the introduction of an age limit has served as an incentive for younger academic staff to stay at the higher education institution. Whereas brain drain to Western European countries was no major cause for concern in TEMPUS, brain drain of younger academic staff to private sector enterprises happened frequently because salaries of higher education institutions are not competitive. Offering mobility grants under the condition that staff members return to the home institution and remain in its service for a certain period of time after return from abroad has seemed to work quite well.

Frequently, regret was voiced by academic staff members about the exclusion of research cooperation in the TEMPUS Programme. Although technology transfer and cooperation between higher education institutions and industry were promoted to a certain degree in TEMPUS I, these types of activities were less frequently taken up than could be expected.

In general we can say that the process of establishing national TEMPUS priorities has been refined in most of the CEE countries during the TEMPUS I period and that priorities are widely accepted and acknowledged. Concern about the validity of published priorities for the selection of applications was only voiced strongly in those two cases in which priorities were changed by the European Commission and then published without feedback to the national actors. Attempts at redressing this change by also accepting those applications matching the original version led to confusion and irritation among applicants.

As previously stated, there are four levels on which the TEMPUS *funding arrangements* influence project activities going on at the higher education institutions.

First, the *overall TEMPUS budget* increases or decreases the number of projects which can be supported per year. This, in turn, influences the success rate of applications eligible for support. The more high quality applications are submitted, the lower might become the success rate in those cases in which the overall TEMPUS budget is not increasing proportionally. Motivation of applicants to put in the considerable time and work required to write a good application can be affected by such a development.

Second, the issue of the level of TEMPUS *support awarded to individual projects* (including mobility grants) can influence activities in several respects:

- JEP grants are usually lower than applied for although contracts demand as a rule the fulfilment of all activities originally planned in the project proposal. Frequent impacts of this are that contracts cannot be fulfilled or activities cannot be carried out properly, and in rare cases even the contractor or coordinator gave up.

- In Joint European Projects arrangements were often neglected which would enable faculties and departments to keep up the achievements accomplished in the projects after TEMPUS support stopped. With a growing awareness of this issue among JEP partners the situation has improved somewhat and the introduction of Joint European Networks (JENs) towards the end of the TEMPUS I period has eased the transition from support to non-support.

- Mobility grants for academic staff from CEE countries have turned out to be sufficient as long as low budget accommodation can be arranged in the host country. Mobility grants for students from CEE countries have proved to be somewhat on the low side. Students have sometimes regretted that they were not able to take up all opportunities that were open and offered to them.

Third, with regard to the *funding of individual activities* within a JEP the most frequent complaint was the inflexibility and strict regulation of earmarked funds. Applications to change the course or the direction of the project were usually refused by the EU. However, the most serious problem for JEP activities and mobility is caused by delays in the transfer of grants and funds.

Fourth, the regulation in the first three years of TEMPUS I that contractors and coordinators had to be institutions from the EU Member States caused some problems concerning the *distribution of funds among project partners*. Contractors forgetting or even refusing to give their CEE partners a copy of the contract and the budget breakdown were not infrequent during TEMPUS I. Although we generally found a deep appreciation for the commitment and the work of Western partners and a feeling of having highly profited from the cooperation coupled with renewed motivation and commitment to the professional tasks, we also encountered problems with regard to demands for high overheads and administrative costs by Western partners. This has led to the impression shared by quite a few of the CEE partners that in one way or another TEMPUS support finds its way back to the West. The problem could be solved in many cases as soon as CEE institutions were allowed to become coordinators and contractors.

In summarising we can say that the level of funding is mostly sufficient and satisfying. More problems are caused by delays in the transfer of grants and funds. A positive development has been the growing awareness to make arrangements for the time when TEMPUS support has ended so that achievements will not be lost.

Changes in the types of JEPs eligible for support have occurred three times since TEMPUS was established:

- the introduction of Mobility-JEPs (M-JEPs) one year after Individual Mobility Grants for students were discontinued and student mobility became only possible in the framework of JEPs

- the opportunity to form multi-CEE JEPs for the support of regional activities, which was discontinued after a couple of years in TEMPUS I but has been reintroduced in the third year of TEMPUS II

- the introduction of a special type of project called JEP+ and CME+ in the first year of TEMPUS II and their discontinuation after one year.

We noted that programme revisions of this kind usually cause some confusion among applicants and might cause disappointments when an application has been drafted by a group of partners for a project type which they then find being discontinued. Often no explanation or reason is offered for such a development.

Multi-CEE (regional) JEPs seem to have been quite successful and explanations we received for their discontinuation are not quite satisfying. It seems that Phare responsibles were not willing to share resources with other CEE countries. Mobility-JEPs were only slowly taken up, probably because student mobility during TEMPUS I was not first on the list of institutional priorities and interests of faculties and departments in the face of low budgets and other needs. However, Mobility-JEPs have acquired a different status in TEMPUS II, which is seen in many CEE countries as a period of preparation for their participation in SOCRATES.

The impacts of such programme revisions as the introduction of new JEP types and their discontinuation after a short time can disrupt the structure and the logic of the programme as such and can prevent the building up of a stable knowledge and routines in terms of planning of applications.

The provision of *information and advice* is one of the main tasks of the National TEMPUS Offices and the only task of the national TEMPUS Contact Points of the EU Member States (see also pp. 93 – 96). Information and advice to applicants and active project partners has improved considerably in quantity and quality over the period of TEMPUS I. Many NTOs introduced regular information days on TEMPUS addressed to representatives of faculties and departments. In smaller CEE countries with only few higher education institutions a complete coverage of all institutions by personal visits of NTO staff members is the rule.

When we asked JEP partners during our interviews to assess the information and advice which was available to them they rated information about the TEMPUS Programme and about the types of activities eligible for support most positively. They rated information about national TEM-PUS priorities and about the configuration of who decides what on the national level less positively. Information about the criteria of selection of applications was rated least positively (see also pp. 239 – 249).

Although the majority of applicants and JEP partners felt and still feel well informed about the TEMPUS aspects most relevant to them, information about national TEMPUS priorities often comes too late to structure applications in such a way that they are fully complying with the priorities. Since TEMPUS priorities change to a certain degree every year and applications are prepared and drafted well in advance of the deadline for submission, applicants frequently submit their applications – often without any changes – several years in a row until their proposal is accepted because it happens to match that year's priorities.

In general, the NTOs are praised for being helpful and supportive to applicants and when advice is needed by project partners. In all CEE countries the number of applications has steadily increased over the first three years of TEMPUS I. Due to the shift to multi-annual funding of JEPs the call for applications was cancelled in most of the CEE countries in the last year of TEMPUS I. Overall, the annual acceptance rates for JEP applications submitted have not been too encouraging.

4.4.4 *Institutional Policies and Support for TEMPUS Activities*

The gradual increase of TEMPUS activities at a number of higher education institutions in the CEE partner countries has led to the development of an infrastructure for services and support of TEMPUS activities in some of these institutions. In some cases a vice-rector for international cooperation, in other cases an international relations office have been assigned the tasks of dealing with matters of information and advice for TEMPUS-related issues, taking over organisational matters and acting as TEMPUS contact persons for the institution as a whole. Although in the majority of institutions the faculties and departments still prefer to provide such services and support themselves and thus be independent from the central institutional level, there are some higher education institutions in almost all CEE countries in which these service and support activities are provided by the central level.

The involvement of higher education institutions in TEMPUS can basically be distinguished according to three different dimensions:

- The central level of the higher education institutions (rectors and/or vice-rectors) is usually involved in policy decisions concerning the establishment of national TEMPUS priorities. It is also responsible for the official approvement of project applications by signing the letters of endorsement and for the possible integration of TEMPUS project activities into an institutional development plan. The central administration is frequently responsible for organisational and administrative tasks concerning TEMPUS activities with international relations offices coordinating activities as well as providing information, help and advice to applicants or project partners and finance departments sometimes being responsible for the administration and accounting of project funds.

- The faculties and departments are responsible for TEMPUS applications and actual project activities. They are the true beneficiaries of TEMPUS support and have to account for the use of funds and grants and for achieving the aims of the project.

- Apart from being partners, coordinators and/or contractors in TEMPUS projects, individual members of academic staff might serve as academic experts in the assessment of TEMPUS project applications.

With the exception of Albania where TEMPUS is organised according to a top-down approach for the whole country and with the exception of a few institutions among those we visited in each of the other countries, the majority of institutional leaders has a relatively weak position in terms of TEMPUS policy decisions on the institutional level. This is due to the high degree of autonomy enjoyed by faculties and departments. In many cases, institutional development plans have been rejected or resisted by them. Apart from the lack of a legal basis for institutional leaders to shape TEMPUS activities more strongly on the institutional level, competition among faculties and departments for TEMPUS support is still rather high and also charged with gains in prestige, so that faculties and departments prefer to go about the acquisition of grants in their own way and not have the central level involved in this process. In TEMPUS II this situation has changed to a certain degree in so far as regulations for letters of endorsement were changed and an outline of an institutional development plan must accompany the submission of an application.

This result of our interviews stands in contrast to the answers provided by the central administration and leaders of higher education institutions to our institutional survey (see pp. 232 – 239). In the survey 90 per cent of the representatives from the central level of the institutions stated that there was an institutional development plan at their institution. One explanation can be offered is that the institutional questionnaire was sent out and returned in the second year of TEMPUS II. At that time regulations had already changed and institutional developments plans were required to be included in the letters of endorsement. Furthermore, our interviews have shown that the details and refinement of such development plans are frequently more modest than might be assumed. Nevertheless, the vast majority of rectors and vice-rectors we interviewed were enthusiastic about TEMPUS and its impacts on the institution and usually provided some kind of administrative and organisational support for TEMPUS activities in the faculties and departments.

The most integrated approach to TEMPUS can be found in those institutions in which a highly professionalised international relations office has been established which closely cooperates with the rector or vice-rector on the one hand and faculties and departments on the other. In these cases coordinator and contractor functions are frequently taken over by the offices, and faculties and departments are free of administrative tasks connected to the project activities.

At the level of the faculties and departments we found much more frequently an increasingly systematic approach to acquire TEMPUS support fora the restructuring and renewal of targeted subject areas and degree courses. Here, achievements and impacts of TEMPUS activities became more visible. As could be seen in terms of the development of institutions, TEMPUS support during TEMPUS I tended to concentrate and to open a gap between the haves and the have-nots also on the level of faculties and departments and even in terms of individual academic staff members accumulating new knowledge and international contacts.

Chapter 5

The Joint European Projects

5.1 The Information Base

The TEMPUS Programme intends to promote primarily various educational activities undertaken at the units involved in the Joint European Projects (i.e. the faculties and departments of higher education institutions and other partner institutions) and the cooperation between these units. Therefore, experiences acquired within the JEPs are crucial for the overall evaluation of the TEMPUS Programme.

This evaluation study has collected information on the educational activities, their financial and administrative conditions as well as their impacts during TEMPUS I, by means of a written questionnaire. The questionnaire was sent to those administratively in charge at their respective units in CEE countries and Western countries (EU Member States and other G24-countries), that is, the 'partners' in Joint European Projects, including those who were also in charge of the overall JEP coordination ('coordinators') and of the JEP financial administration ('contractors').

The questionnaire comprised 118 questions. It addressed the profile of the JEPs and the institutions involved. It also collected basic information on the respondents themselves and their activities. Major emphasis was placed on a detailed account of the various educational activities undertaken in the respective JEPs, the way they were prepared, the processes of cooperation and the problems incurred, as well as the major achievements and drawbacks.

According to the official TEMPUS data base, about 6,100 partners have been involved in Joint European Projects during TEMPUS I. On the basis of an address survey supported by the European Training Foundation and of addresses of coordinators and contractors available from the ETF data base on JEPs, about 4,300 addresses could be collected of TEMPUS I JEP-contractors, coordinators and partners. The questionnaire was mailed in July 1995 to all partners of JEPs supported in TEMPUS I for whom addresses were available, altogether about 4,300 persons. A copy of questionnaire versions in English, French and German was sent to each person for whom none of these three languages was the home country language. A reminder letter and new copies of the questionnaire were mailed in mid-October 1995 to all partners not having responded at that time.

By the end of January 1996, 219 (4.9 per cent) of the 4,298 questionnaires were returned because the addresses were not valid. In addition, 57 respondents (1.3 per cent) indicated that they had not been involved in TEMPUS, and 179 (4.2 per cent) felt unable to fill in the questionnaire, because of insufficient information about the respective JEP.

Of the remaining 3,828 questionnaires, 1,710 were completed and returned. Because of late arrival, 14 questionnaires (0.4 per cent) could not be included in the final data base and the statistical analysis. Taking into account the vast amount of information required by the questionnaire, the return rate of 44.7 per cent shows a high degree of cooperation by both partners in JEPs from CEE and Western countries. This report is based on the responses to 1,696 questionnaires, among them 694 from Central and Eastern European countries and 1,002 from Western countries.

As Table 5.1 shows, the distribution of responses by country differed somewhat from that of all 6,146 partners actually supported during TEMPUS I. The differences are primarily caused by a variation in the availability of addresses of partners in the individual countries. However, the over-representation and under-representation can be considered low in most cases and should not cause a substantial bias of major findings.

In order to become acquainted with reasons for non-responding to the questionnaire, telephone interviews were undertaken with two to five accidentially selected partners in each individual CEE and Western country. It turned out that the main reason was a heavy workload (stated by 29 interviewees). Only a minority (2 persons out of 70) indicated that they were dissatisfied with TEMPUS as such and therefore refused to fill in the questionnaire. The latter corresponds to the degree of dissatisfaction found among partners who returned the questionnaire. Altogether, the results of the survey may provide a representative picture about the actors, processes and outcomes of Joint European Projects during the first phase of TEMPUS.

Table 5.1
Representation of Partners in Joint European Projects in the Survey and Return Rate, by Country of the Home Institution

	A All Partners[1] Number	%	B Valid addresses[2] Number	%	C Responses Number	%	Represen- tation ratio (C:A)	Return rate (C:B)
ALB	16	0.3	14	0.4	5	0.3	31.3	35.7
BG	177	2.9	131	3.4	59	3.5	33.3	45.0
CZ	237	3.9	163	4.3	88	5.1	37.1	54.0
EE	24	0.4	21	0.5	14	0.8	58.3	66.7
H	512	8.3	303	7.9	132	7.7	25.8	43.6
LT	27	0.4	20	0.5	11	0.6	40.7	55.0
LV	32	0.5	25	0.7	16	0.9	50.0	64.0
PL	514	8.4	416	10.9	233	13.6	45.3	56.0
RO	209	3.4	152	4.0	80	4.7	38.3	52.6
SK	135	2.2	65	1.7	32	1.9	23.7	49.2
SLO	74	1.2	57	1.5	34	2.0	50.0	59.7
Other *	7	1.2	–	–	–	–	–	–

	A All Partners[1] Number	%	B Valid addresses[2] Number	%	C Responses Number	%	Represen- tation ratio (C:A)	Return rate (C:B)
B	316	5.1	188	4.9	94	5.5	29.8	50.0
D	635	10.3	373	9.7	168	9.8	26.5	45.0
DK	148	2.4	90	2.4	37	2.2	25.0	41.1
E	236	3.8	142	3.7	53	3.1	22.5	37.3
F	668	10.9	388	10.1	140	8.2	21.0	36.1
GR	164	2.7	101	2.6	39	2.3	23.8	38.6
I	380	6.2	218	5.7	75	4.4	19.7	34.4
IRL	98	1.6	68	1.8	24	1.4	24.5	35.3
L	2	0.0	1	0.0	0	0.0	0.0	0.0
NL	366	6.0	219	5.7	96	5.6	26.2	43.8
P	101	1.6	63	1.6	25	1.5	24.8	39.7
UK	798	13.0	513	13.4	221	12.9	27.7	43.1

(continued)

(Table 5.1)	A All Partners[1]		B Valid addresses[2]		C Responses		Representa- tion ratio	Return rate
	Number	%	Number	%	Number	%	(C:A)	(C:B)
AT	47	0.8	24	0.6	8	0.5	17.0	33.3
AUS	4	0.1	1	0.0	0	0.0	0.0	0.0
CDN	7	0.1	2	0.1	1	0.1	14.3	50.0
CH	12	0.2	1	0.0	1	0.1	8.3	100.0
FI	39	0.6	24	0.6	10	0.6	25.6	41.7
N	16	0.3	7	0.2	2	0.1	12.5	28.6
SE	36	0.6	26	0.7	11	0.6	30.6	42.3
USA	35	0.6	12	0.3	1	0.1	2.9	8.3
Other **	7	0.1	–	–	–	–	–	–
Total	6,146	100.0	3,828	100.0	1710	100.0	27.8	44.7

1) According to the data base of the European Training Foundation
2) Excluding respondents stating no TEMPUS participation or insufficient information about the JEP
* Bosnia, Croatia, Yugoslavia, GDR
** Japan, Turkey

5.2 The Persons in Charge

Twenty-eight per cent of the respondents to the TEMPUS JEP partner survey had coordinating and/or contracting functions within their JEPs; 72 per cent were partners without any of these functions (see Table 5.2). Taking into account that the average number of partners within a JEP was about seven and that more than half of the coordinators were contractors as well, we conclude that coordinators and contractors are slightly over-represented among the respondents.

A substantial proportion of the persons in charge of the JEPs, that is, the coordinators, contractors and partners, obviously hold key positions at their respective faculties. This is notably true in the CEE countries. At the time TEMPUS support was provided, 8 per cent were rectors, 18 per cent deans or vice-deans, and 33 per cent were department heads, whereby the majority of them hold the position of full professor. A further 13 per cent were full professors without any major administrative functions, 20 per cent were in positions corresponding to that of an associate professor, 6

per cent in other academic positions, and only 2 per cent were administrative officers.

Table 5.2
Role of the Respondents within Their JEP, by Country Group (per
cent)

	CEE country	Western country	Total
Coordinator and contractor	3	18	12
Coordinator	14	8	11
Contractor	0	8	5
Solely partner	83	66	72
Total	100	100	100
(n)	(675)	(984)	(1,659)

Question 4.1: What was your role within this JEP?

Source: 'Experiences of JEP Contractors/Coordinators/Partners in the First Phase of TEM-
PUS' survey

Among the partners in Western countries, the proportions of those holding
major administrative assignments was lower (see Table 5.3). Yet the proportion of those in relatively prestigious ranks – those holding a major
administrative function and those who were full professors – was clearly
higher than the respective proportions among those in charge of ERAS-
MUS (coordinators and locals directors), as a comparison to a respective
study on the ERASMUS Programme shows.[1]

Taking into account the academic rank only, we note that 52 per cent of
the respondents were full professors at the time TEMPUS support was
provided: 57 per cent in the West as compared to 45 per cent in the CEE
partner countries. This should not be interpreted as an indicator of the
relatively low academic status of those in charge of TEMPUS in the CEE
countries. Rather, we have to take into consideration that the proportion of
full professors among all academic staff is lower on average in CEE
countries than in the West.

---

1 Maiworm F. and Teichler, U. (1995): *ERASMUS Student Mobility Pro-*
   grammes 1991/92 in the View of the Local Directors, pp. 27 - 28. Kassel.

Table 5.3
Administrative or Academic Position of the Respondents, by Country Group (per cent)

	CEE country	Western country	Total
Rector/vice-rector, etc.	8	3	5
Dean/vice-dean of faculty	18	6	11
Head of department, etc.	33	21	26
Administrative officer	2	5	4
Full professor	13	34	25
Other professorial rank	20	23	22
Other academic position	6	7	7
Total	100	100	100
(n)	(651)	(896)	(1,547)

Question 1.5: If you are working in an institution of higher education, what was your position at the time you were involved in the JEP?

Source: 'Experiences of JEP Contractors/Coordinators/Partners in the First Phase of TEMPUS' survey

The persons in charge of TEMPUS JEPs were 43 years old on average. (Actually, they reported an average age of 45 at the time the survey was conducted, but by taking into account the calendar of activities, we infer an average age of 43 at the time they were in charge of the TEMPUS-supported activities.) The average age of the partners in the CEE partner countries does not differ significantly from that of their partners in the West. They were clearly younger than the ERASMUS coordinators and local directors surveyed (48 years old on average in the academic year 1991/92). It is worth noting that neither the positions nor the age differed on average between those partners in charge of the overall coordination and those in charge of the JEP contract.

Of those in charge of TEMPUS JEPs, 18 per cent were women – 22 per cent of the respondents of the CEE countries were women as compared to only 15 per cent of the Western partners. The difference in gender composition between the JEP partners in CEE countries and in Western countries reflects the fact that the proportion of women among academics was higher in the former Communist countries than in the majority of the Western countries.

The proportion of women among JEP partners from Western countries (15 per cent) is smaller than that of women among ERASMUS ICP local directors (20 per cent). One has to bear in mind in this context that science and engineering (i.e. fields in which the proportion of women among academics is relatively low on average) are more strongly represented in TEMPUS than in ERASMUS.

The respondents spent somewhat more than 7 hours per week on average on TEMPUS-related administrative activities. As one might expect, the administrative work load was substantially higher for those from CEE countries (8.3 hours) than for those from Western countries (6.4 hours). The substantial work involved in TEMPUS might be underscored by the fact that it is more than twice as high than work involved in respective functions for the ERASMUS Programme (3.3 hours on average).

Not surprisingly, those in charge of the overall coordination or of the JEP contract spent more time on average on TEMPUS-related administration than those only serving their respective unit as JEP partners. The breakdown is as follows:
- persons in charge of JEP coordination and contracting activities spent 12 hours
- persons only in charge of the coordination spent 14 hours
- contractors spent 9 hours
- partners without coordination and contracting functions spent 5 hours.

One-eighth of the coordinators and contractors spent more than 20 hours per week on TEMPUS-related administrative functions.

As Table 5.4 shows, the amount of time spent on TEMPUS-related administrative work by partners with contracting functions differs considerably between Eastern and Western partners. Whereas Eastern and Western partners in charge of the coordination spent almost the same amount of time for administrative work, considerable differences can be observed for persons in charge of the contracting.

Respondents whose projects received TEMPUS support for one or two years reported less hours spent on TEMPUS-related activities (about 5.5 hours) than those supported three and more years (7.8 hours). This suggests that effort put into TEMPUS-related activities was successful in ensuring support for the whole period for which support could be provided.

Table 5.4
Average Hours per Week Spent on TEMPUS-Related Administrative Work, by Status of Respondent (per cent and mean)

	Coordinator and contractor		Coordinator		Contractor		Partner		Total
	CEE country	Western country	CEE country	Western country	CEE country	Western country	CEE country	Western country	
1–5	20	43	20	27	0	53	54	85	60
6–10	27	21	37	35	50	20	29	9	21
11–15	7	10	19	18	0	5	8	4	7
16–20	27	12	9	13	0	12	5	1	6
21 and more	20	15	14	15	50	9	4	1	6
Total	100	100	100	100	100	100	100	100	100
(n)	(15)	(164)	(94)	(75)	(2)	(74)	(509)	(543)	(1,476)
Mean hours	15.3	12.0	13.9	13.4	17.0	9.1	7.1	3.4	7.2

Question 4.2: Please estimate the average hours per week which you or colleagues from your department spent on administrative work related to TEMPUS.

Source: 'Experiences of JEP Contractors/Coordinators/Partners in the First Phase of TEMPUS' survey

Almost three-quarters of those in charge of the administration of TEM-PUS-related activities were supported by their institution by means of technical supplies (e.g. telephone) and more than half by means of administrative and secretarial assistance. Very few reported other kinds of support, for example additional travel funds (12 per cent), a reduction of teaching load (6 per cent), and additional remuneration (5 per cent). These figures are quite similar to those reported by ERASMUS local directors.

The respondents in charge of the JEP coordination and contracts reported only slightly more frequently than other partners that they had received the above named modes of support. Only a reduction of teaching load was clearly more often granted to JEP coordinators (12 per cent) than to other partners (5 per cent).

Almost all persons from CEE countries involved in the administration of the JEPs hoped that their activities would help them to establish teaching-related cooperation with partners in other countries and to get acquainted with other systems of higher education. About half of them each expected to become acquainted with people from other countries, to improve their foreign language proficiency and to establish research cooperation. Only 34 per cent emphasised the opportunity to travel, and 32 per cent stated hopes for career advancement. The partners from the Western countries had more moderate expectations. These matched those expressed by the partners from the CEE countries only as regards getting acquainted with people from other countries as well as research cooperation.

In the final assessment of the outcomes most of the respondents considered it worthwhile for themselves to have been involved in TEMPUS-related activities. Notably, they appreciated the establishment of (personal) contacts with staff members from partner units, the knowledge and understanding of other higher education systems, and the acquaintance with people from other countries. As regards other matters surveyed, the partners from the Western countries rated the personal outcomes substantially less favourable than their colleagues from CEE countries (see Table 5.5). The majority of partners from the CEE countries also considered exposure to new subject matter a worthwhile outcome. Only a minority of them, however, observed an improvement of their own career prospects through involvement in the TEMPUS administration (36 per cent) or appreciated the exposure to new administrative procedures (29 per cent).

Table 5.5
Positive Personal Outcomes of the JEP Activities for the Respondents, by Country Group (per cent*)

	CEE country	Western country	Total
Exposure to new subject matters	76	43	58
Exposure to new teaching methods	73	23	45
Exposure to new research methods	46	20	32
Exposure to new administrative procedures	29	15	21
Knowledge and understanding of other higher education systems	81	76	78
Establishment of personal contacts with staff members from partner institutions	92	90	90
Improvement of career prospects	36	11	23
Opportunity to travel	50	31	39
Foreign language proficiency	61	17	37
Acquaintance with people in another country	75	77	76

*) Rating 1 or 2 on a scale from 1 = 'extremely worthwhile' to 5 = 'not worthwhile at all'
Question 10.9: To what extent do you consider it worthwhile for yourself to have been involved in the activities of this JEP?
Source: 'Experiences of JEP Contractors/Coordinators/Partners in the First Phase of TEMPUS' survey

The proportion of those noting better career prospects, though, might still be viewed as remarkably high. Only 11 per cent of the Western JEP partners perceived increased career prospects. In comparison, the respective proportion among local directors of ERASMUS ICPs surveyed in the early 1990s was 14 per cent.

Altogether, the persons in charge of JEP coordination and contracting did not express higher expectations as regards their decision to participate in the JEPs. They also did not consider the outcome more worthwhile for themselves on average than the partners without coordination and contracting functions.

5.3   The Participating Institutions, Departments and Networks

Most JEP partners both in CEE and Western countries were representatives of institutions of higher education or, more correctly, of their respective units of teaching and possibly research. The TEMPUS Programme primarily addresses higher education, but also encourages an involvement of other institutions. As Table 5.6 shows, 7 per cent of partners surveyed from CEE countries and 9 per cent from Western countries were based in other institutions, for example non-profit organisations, state-owned enterprises and private enterprises. These institutions were widely spread according to economic sector and size of institution in terms of the number of employees.

Table 5.6
Type of the Respondents' Institution, by Country Group (per cent)

	CEE country	Western country	Total
Public higher education institution	91	84	87
Private higher education institution	0	5	3
Private enterprise	1	2	1
State owned enterprise	2	1	2
Non-profit organisation	2	4	3
Other types of institutions	2	2	2
Not ticked	1	3	2
Total	100	100	100
(n)	(694)	(1,002)	(1,696)

Question 1.4: Please state the type of your institution.

Source: 'Experiences of JEP Contractors/Coordinators/Partners in the First Phase of TEMPUS' survey

The respondents reported an average number of 12 partners within their JEPs. As a survey of all partners is bound to include JEPs with large numbers of partners more often than JEPs with small numbers, this number is substantially higher than the average size of JEPs. Our data suggest an average number of 7 partners per JEP (the JEP coordinators also reported an average size of 7 or 8 partners per JEP).

The JEPs varied substantially according to the number of partners involved. Of the respondents 10 per cent participated in JEPs with only three partners (i.e. the minimum required for eligibility for the TEMPUS Programme), 21 per cent in JEPs with 4–5 partners, 38 per cent in JEPs with 6–10 partners, and 31 per cent in JEPs with more than 10 partners.

In the framework of TEMPUS I, JEPs could re-apply for support up to an overall period of three years. Eventually, those supported for a period of three years were eligible for some support beyond that period. Actually, three-quarters of the partners responding participated in the respective JEP for three years or even longer in the framework of TEMPUS I, 17 per cent participated for two years, and 7 per cent only for one year. On average, the JEPs had been provided support for 2.8 years.

According to the participants, 14 per cent had received first support in the academic year 1990/91, 34 per cent in 1991/92, 41 per cent in 1992/93, and 11 per cent even later. The largest number of JEPs was supported in 1992/93 and 1993/94. The last year of support was 1992/93 or even earlier for 17 per cent, 1993/94 for 37 per cent, and 1994/95 for the remaining 46 per cent of JEPs (see Table 5.7).

Table 5.7
Years of TEMPUS Support (per cent of respondents)

Academic year	1st year	Years of participation	Last year
1990/91	14	14	1
1991/92	34	47	2
1992/93	41	86	14
1993/94	8	80	37
1994/95	3	46	46
Total	100	272	100
(n)	(1,673)	(1,673)	(1,673)

Question 3.1: In which year(s) did your department/institution participate in this JEP?
Source: 'Experiences of JEP Contractors/Coordinators/Partners in the First Phase of TEMPUS' survey

Table 5.8

Subject Area of the Joint European Projects, by Year of Start and Country Group (per cent of respondents)

	Year of start								Total
	1990/91		1991/92		1992/93		1993/94		
	CEE country	Western country	CEE country	Western country	CEE country	Western country	CEE country	Western country	
Humanities, philological sciences	0	1	1	1	1	2	3	2	1
Social sciences	3	6	5	7	9	8	5	3	7
Management and business	16	12	14	11	12	12	8	16	12
Natural sciences, mathematics	10	8	9	7	9	9	18	26	10
Medical sciences	9	9	7	9	8	8	5	13	8
Engineering, applied sciences	22	22	20	24	19	19	13	5	20
Computer sciences	10	9	6	7	8	7	16	6	8
Agricultural sciences, agrobusiness	6	5	8	8	6	5	11	16	7
Environmental protection	5	7	11	8	10	10	5	1	9
Architecture, urban and regional planning	1	1	1	1	3	4	3	0	2
Art and design	0	0	2	2	2	1	0	0	1
Language studies	11	13	7	7	2	4	3	0	6
Teacher training	1	2	4	3	5	4	11	11	4
Law	1	0	1	4	2	1	0	0	2
Other subjects	7	5	0	0	6	5	0	0	3
Total	100	100	100	100	100	100	100	100	100
(n)	(114)	(132)	(267)	(394)	(278)	(370)	(38)	(99)	(1,692)

Source: 'Experiences of JEP Contractors/Coordinators/Partners in the First Phase of TEMPUS' survey

Almost two-thirds of partners from CEE countries named science and engineering fields as the subject of their JEP. Twenty per cent named engineering, and more than a quarter named other fields in the area of engineering and applied sciences (computer sciences, environmental protection, agriculture, architecture etc.). Ten per cent named mathematics and pure sciences, and 8 per cent medical fields. In the domain of humanities and social sciences, management and business studies (13 per cent) were most strongly represented, followed by social sciences, language studies and teacher training (4–6 per cent each).

This distribution was to a large extent steered by award policies which changed to some extent over the years. As Table 5.8 suggests, engineering, business studies and language studies received more support during the first years of the TEMPUS Programme while social sciences and teacher training initially received little support, but began to play a more important role in subsequent years.

Fifty-nine per cent of the partners from CEE countries and 58 per cent of the partners from Western countries stated that their department was involved in other TEMPUS-related activities. Apart from TEMPUS, almost one-third of the partners from the CEE countries and three-quarters of the partners from the West reported that their department received EU support from other programmes. Three-quarters of those receiving other TEMPUS or other EU support noted that the various activities were linked with each other in one way or another, notably through common administrative assistance, joint use of infrastructure or the same staff being responsible for the administration and coordination.

5.4   Initiatives, Information and Administrative Cooperation

The partners received their first information on the TEMPUS Programme and its support provisions from various sources. Those in CEE countries were most often informed by colleagues from Western countries (34 per cent). In addition, the National TEMPUS Offices were the first informants for 26 per cent of the partners in the CEE countries. The partners in the West named their colleagues in CEE countries (27 per cent) and the EU TEMPUS Office in Brussels (24 per cent) as major sources of information. In both groups of countries, the central level of the home institution as well as colleagues of the home countries also played some role in initial information, as Table 5.9 shows. The EU TEMPUS Office in Brussels as well as the National TEMPUS Offices or the National Contact Point were frequently named as sources of further information. Also colleagues from various countries were often consulted.

Table 5.9
Sources of First Information about the TEMPUS Programme, by Country Group (per cent, multiple reply possible)

	CEE country	Western country	Total
EU TEMPUS Office in Brussels	10	24	18
National TEMPUS Office/Contact Point in home country	26	10	17
National ministries of education	9	4	6
Central level of the home institution	15	17	16
Persons responsible for TEMPUS in the home institution	11	15	13
Academic or other bodies in home country	4	3	4
Colleagues in the home institution	11	7	9
Colleagues of other institutions in the home country	14	8	10
Colleagues of institutions in CEE	5	27	18
Colleagues of institutions in other countries	34	17	24
Other sources	4	4	4
No first information stated	0	1	1
Not ticked	1	3	2
Total	144	139	141
(n)	(694)	(1,002)	(1,696)

Question 1.7: From whom did you or your colleagues receive information about the TEMPUS Programme?
Source: 'Experiences of JEP Contractors/Coordinators/Partners in the First Phase of TEMPUS' survey

The majority of respondents considered the information provided to them useful as far as the TEMPUS Programme as a whole is concerned as well as regarding the types of activities eligible for support. They rated the information provided less favourably as regards administration and management of TEMPUS as a whole and of the JEPs, the national priorities, the amount of support and as regards issues of application. They were least satisfied with information regarding the selection criteria among the application. Altogether, the CEE partners felt themselves better informed than the Western partners, as Table 5.10 shows.

Table 5.10
Positive Assessment of the Utility of Information Provided, by Country Group (per cent*)

	CEE country	Western country	Total
Understanding aims of TEMPUS as a whole	88	77	82
Administration/management of TEMPUS	53	37	44
Understanding of national priorities	57	40	47
Types of activity eligible for support	71	57	63
Amount of support for the various activities	55	38	45
Preparation of an application	61	41	50
Understanding the selection criteria for applications	43	25	33
Administration/management of JEP	57	32	42

* Rating 1 or 2 on a scale from 1 = 'very high' to 5 = 'very low'
Question 1.8: How would you rate on average the utility of information provided with regard to the following aspects?
Source: 'Experiences of JEP Contractors/Coordinators/Partners in the First Phase of TEMPUS' survey

According to the respondents, about half of the JEPs were initiated each by CEE partners and by Western partners. The partners from the CEE countries surveyed reported more often an initiative emerging in the CEE countries, while the partners from the Western countries perceived more frequently initiatives from the West (see Table 5.11). In science and engineering fields, the initiative came more often from the CEE countries. In humanities and social sciences, however, initiatives from the West were more frequent.

Table 5.11
Intitiator of the Joint European Project, by Country Group (per cent)

	CEE country	Western country	Total
Respondents themselves	35	24	29
CEE partner	13	36	27
West partner	38	24	30
Common initiative of JEP participants	9	10	10
Other	4	5	5
Total	100	100	100
(n)	(687)	(988)	(1,675)

Question 2.1: Who took the first initiative to start this JEP?

Source: 'Experiences of JEP Contractors/Coordinators/Partners in the First Phase of TEM-PUS' survey

About two-thirds of the coordinators stated that they themselves or their departments had taken the initiative to start this JEP. This is most true for coordinators from CEE countries.

Eighty per cent of the partners already had prior contacts with at least one of the partners involved in the respective JEP. About two-thirds each of the CEE and the Western partners already had been in touch with their partners in the other country group. In the case of most of these prior East-West contacts, the partners had met at conferences and other meetings. Prior research contacts were frequent as well, as Table 5.12 shows.

In the process of preparing the application, most respondents communicated with their partners by mail, fax or phone, while 62 per cent participated in preparatory meetings. Preparatory meetings, as a rule, were crucial for the preparation of qualified applications and for the establishment of fruitful cooparation. While two-thirds of those funded for three and more years had participated in such kinds of preparatory meetings, the respective proportion was less than one-third among those being funded only for one year.

Table 5.12
Types of Prior Contacts Between JEP Partners (per cent, multiple reply possible)

Contacts	Total	With CEE country (Western respondents)	With Western country (CEE respondents)
No response	1	1	1
No prior contacts at all	18	–	–
No prior contacts with CEE partners	–	37	–
No prior contacts with Western partners	–	–	34
Prior contacts	81	62	65
Total	100	100	100
(n)	(1,696)	(1,002)	(694)
Types of contact			
Through conferences	60	41	50
Research contacts	49	32	35
Business contacts	7	3	4
Other contacts	16	10	10

Question 2.3: What kind of prior contacts did you have with your JEP partners?

Source: 'Experiences of JEP Contractors/Coordinators/Partners in the First Phase of TEMPUS' survey

5.5 Application and Award

More than 60 per cent of the partners from CEE countries tried to get advice for the preparation of the TEMPUS application. Notably, they consulted notably colleagues from their own or from other departments, the National TEMPUS Office or the university administrators.

While 19 per cent of the partners consulted the National TEMPUS Offices, 12 per cent had been in touch with the EU TEMPUS Office in Brussels in order to get advice for the application process. A more detailed analysis of data shows that coordinators and contractors tended to address the EU TEMPUS Office more often than the National TEMPUS Offices. In contrast, twice as many partners not in charge of coordination or contract asked National TEMPUS Offices for advice than the EU TEMPUS Office in Brussels. To some extent this reflects the fact that many coordinators and most contractors were from Western countries.

Altogether, the national TEMPUS Offices played an increasing role in the preparatory process. Of the partners from CEE countries surveyed, 24 per cent of those receiving TEMPUS support for the first time in 1990/91, 30 per cent in 1991/92, 36 per cent in 1992/93 and eventually 55 per cent of those supported for the first time in 1993/94 had asked their National TEMPUS Office for advice as regards their application.

Table 5.13
Timing of Information About the Acceptance of the Application for the JEP, by Status of Respondent (per cent)

1–2 months prior	19	13	11	9	11
Within one month prior	16	28	23	15	17
Prior without detailed information	2	0	1	3	2
About the start of the academic year	37	33	42	45	42
Within one month after	10	13	5	8	8
1–2 months after	4	4	8	5	5
Two months and more after	6	5	3	4	4
After without detailed information	4	3	3	5	4
Total	100	100	100	100	100
(n)	(176)	(159)	(74)	(1,047)	(1,456)

Question 2.6: How many weeks before the start of the academic year (e.g. 1 September) were you informed about the acceptance of the application for this JEP?

Source: 'Experiences of JEP Contractors/Coordinators/Partners in the First Phase of TEMPUS' survey

The award decisions frequently were communicated to the JEP partners at a very late stage. Forty-two per cent of respondents stated that they were informed at about the beginning of the respective academic year, and 20 per cent were informed even later.

The majority of JEPs obviously were awarded lesser funds than they had applied for. The responses to the questionnaires show that a substantial proportion of the partners without coordination and contracting functions did not know the possible discrepancies between the application and award. One-third of the partners without such functions explicitly stated that they did not know, and those actually responding presented a more favourable view than the coordinators and contractors.

Of the JEP coordinators and contractors 68 per cent reported that the actual JEP budget was smaller than the amount applied for. In about one sixth of these cases of reduced award, the recipients were informed that they had not been awarded grants for certain activities they had applied for. In most cases, however, it was completely left to the recipients to decide where to reduce expenses.

According to about two-thirds of the respondents providing respective information, TEMPUS provided on average about 7,200 ECU annually per partner for the administration of the JEP. This was about 13 per cent of the total TEMPUS support provided for administrative matters. This sum includes secretarial assistance, overheads, travel and subsistence for meetings with the partners, etc. On average, partners in charge of both the coordination and contracting activities received more than 17,000 ECU, coordinators (without contracting function) more than 12,000 ECU, con tractors about 10,000 ECU and partners without those functions about 3,900 ECU for administrative activities.

The respondents, however, claimed that the TEMPUS support covered only 57 per cent on average of the actual administrative costs incurred. The respective proportion reported differed only slightly according to the functions of the partners.

Only 35 per cent of the partners expressed satisfaction with the amount of financial support provided by the TEMPUS Programme for administrative matters. Satisfaction was clearly less frequent among Western partners than among CEE partners. This holds true irrespective of the functions the partners played in their JEPs.

Altogether, the partners were not very satisfied with financial administration: 24 per cent encountered financial problems due to delay in the provision of the grant by the European Commission. Delays originating at the European Commission more frequently caused problems than delays in the provision of the grant by the respective banks (21 per cent), by the JEP contractors (14 per cent) and by their own institutions (6 per cent).

In the selected interviews conducted at higher education institutions in Central and Eastern European countries, dissatisfaction was by far most frequently expressed as regards late receipt of grants. The European Commission and the EU TEMPUS Office were often viewed as the major cause of such delays, but some of those interviewed also pointed out delays caused by contractors or by the respective National TEMPUS Office.

In addition, several JEP partners were disappointed about the inflexibility of the financial provisions. A permission to transfer funds from one of the activities to support another one or to utilise the funds at a later time than initially granted for was viewed as essential in order to react both to experiences acquired in the process about possible optimal use of the funds as well as to delays not caused by the beneficiaries.

Table 5.14
Satisfaction with Several Aspects of the Administration of the JEP, by Country Group (per cent*)

	CEE country	Western country	Total
Cooperation with the EC TEMPUS Office	81	58	68
Cooperation with national TEMPUS Office/contact point	71	48	63
Cooperation with the central administration of your institution	67	66	67
Dissemination of information within this JEP	79	69	73
Administration of the JEP grant budget by the contractor/ coordinator of the JEP	79	78	78
Amount of financial support for administrative matters	44	28	35
Involvement in JEP-relevant decisions	72	67	69
Division of tasks among partners	77	71	74
Cooperation with partners	87	79	82

* Rating 1 or 2 on a scale from 1 = 'very satisfied' to 5 = 'very dissatisfied'

Question 4.15: How satisfied are you overall regarding the following aspects related to the administration of this JEP?

Source: 'Experiences of JEP Contractors/Coordinators/Partners in the First Phase of TEMPUS' survey

The JEP partners were asked to state the degree of overall satisfaction they felt as regards the administration of the JEPs. These ratings, therefore, do not only apply to issues concerning the provision of funds awarded. Altogether, 68 per cent expressed satisfaction regarding the cooperation with the EU TEMPUS Office related to the administration of their JEP and 63 per cent correspondingly regarded positively the cooperation with the National TEMPUS Offices, respective Contact Points.

These proportions were lower than those expressed regarding administrative matters among the JEP partners. Notably, few Western partners were satisfied with the EU TEMPUS Office and the National TEMPUS Contact Points, as Table 5.14 shows.

The interviews conducted at select institutions of higher education in Central and Eastern European countries confirmed the impression that cooperation between the institutions of higher education and the National TEMPUS Offices is favourably assessed in the majority of CEE countries. However, the comments were not always favourable as regards communication between higher education institutions and the actors on the national level as far as decision-making about national priorities, the speed of information necessary for application, the role the experts are playing in the assessment of applications, and the selection among applications in general are concerned. Finally, some persons interviewed criticised the bureaucracy of the TEMPUS Programme in general, citing the workload for all involved, inflexibilities, lack of reciprocal communication, too many and overlapping reporting procedures, etc.

5.6 Cooperation Within the JEPs

According to the respondents, any JEP partner seems to cooperate closely with about three and a half partners on average. The larger the JEP, the higher was the absolute number of partners but the lower was the relative number of partners with whom the individual partners cooperated closely:

- almost all respondents of JEPs with three partners reported that they cooperated closely with the other two partners (1.9 on average)
- respondents of JEPs with 4–5 partners included on average all but one of their partners in close cooperation (2.6 on average)
- respondents of JEPs with 6–10 partners cooperated closely with slightly more than half of their partners (3.6 on average)
- respondents of JEPs with more than 10 partners cooperated closely with a minority of their partners (4.5 on average).

As one might expect, the partners from CEE countries cooperated closely with a larger number of their JEP partners (5.2 on average) than the Western partners (3.3 on average).

The JEP partners surveyed or their colleagues in the respective departments participated annually in three meetings on average with one or several of their JEP partners. This number is higher than, for example, the number of meetings attended by local directors of ERASMUS ICPs (2.3 on average). JEP coordinators as well as JEP partners without coordinating functions from CEE countries (or colleagues from their institutions) attended on average about three and a half meetings annually with their JEP partners. In contrast, partners from Western countries without coordinating functions attended almost three of those meetings annually (2.9 on average).

Table 5.15

Information on the Overall Administration of the JEP Available to Partners Without Coordinating and Contracting Functions, by Year of Operation (per cent of partners without coordinating and contracting functions)

	Year of operation			In comparison:
	First	Second	Third	ERASMUS local directors
Copies of the original applications and completed update forms	87	80	80	86
Notification of JEP selection results	61	58	58	53
Copies of the JEP contract	86	80	80	65
Details of the JEP budget breakdown among partner institutions	69	76	76	38
Copies of the JEP final (annual) report and statement of expenditures	68	73	73	34
Total	371	367	367	274
(n)	(1,050)	(1,029)	(935)	(1,784)

Question 4.4 What kind of information related to the overall administration of the JEP was available to you?

Source: 'Experiences of JEP Contractors/Coordinators/Partners in the First Phase of TEM-PUS' survey

Exchange of information within JEPs about the application and award decisions was by no means perfect. As Table 5.15 shows, more 13 per cent of the partners neither in charge of the coordination nor of the financial administration of the JEP did not receive copies of the application and of the JEP contracts in the first year of cooperation. The respective proportions increased even up to 20 per cent in the second and third year of cooperation. As regards details of the budget breakdown among the partner institutions of the JEP, about one-third of the partners not in charge of coordination and contracts did not receive copies in the first year of cooperation. About the same proportion did not receive copies of the annual reports and statements of expenditures.

It should be noted that this kind of information availability to partners was higher within the TEMPUS JEPs than within ERASMUS ICPs, as Table 5.15 shows. However, as TEMPUS support is very high and very crucial for the development of the departments involved, these information gaps within the JEPs are obviously more grave.

Asked about the basis on which the JEP grant budget was administered:

- 25 per cent of the partners reported that the budget was centrally administered and that funds for partners were not earmarked
- 58 per cent stated that the budget was centrally administered but funds for partners were earmarked
- 18 per cent reported a sub-allocation of funds to the respective partners.

As Table 5.16 shows, a sub-allocation was most common within JEPs comprising few partners.

It might be added at this point that the central administration of the respective institutions of higher education administered the funds for about two-thirds of the JEP contractors. In most of the remaining cases, the central administration received the funds and passed them on. Naturally, the central administration was less often involved in the administration of funds for partners not in the contractor role.

Problems regarding the financial administration within the JEPs were less often perceived than problems due to a delay in the provision of grants by the European Commission. Yet, the former were not negligible, as Table 5.17 shows. Notably, 25 per cent of JEP contractors who were not coordinators stated considerable difficulties with the administration of the grant at their institution. The respective proportion is 14 per cent among those who were in charge both of the JEP coordination and contracting issues.

Table 5.16

Mode of Grant Budget Administration Within the JEP, by Number of Partners Within the JEP (per cent)

	Number of partners within the JEP				Total
	3	4-5	6-10	11 and more	
Centrally administered, funds for partners not earmarked	22	17	26	30	25
Centrally administered, funds for partners earmarked	53	63	57	57	58
Sub-allocated	25	20	18	14	18
Total	100	100	100	100	100
(n)	(155)	(325)	(592)	(474)	(1,546)

Question 4.9: On what basis was your JEP grant budget administered?

Source: 'Experiences of JEP Contractors/Coordinators/Partners in the First Phase of TEMPUS' survey

Eight per cent of the JEP partners not involved in coordinating functions stated considerable problems in terms of an unbalanced distribution of funds. As one might expect, the respective proportion was lower among partners with coordinating and contracting function (4 per cent). Again, we note that a similar proportion of ERASMUS ICP local directors not in charge of the ICP coordination complained about an unbalanced distribution of funds (10 per cent) but, again, we must state that such an imbalance is a more serious issue for the participating partners in TEMPUS because of the amount of support involved.

The survey also addressed a few additional aspects concerning communication within the JEPs. As their language of communication, 93 per cent used English, 28 per cent French, and 24 per cent German, while other official languages of the countries were used by at most 5 (Italian) or 6 per cent (Polish) of the partners surveyed. This indicates a higher concentration on English than within ERASMUS ICPs where 79 per cent of the local directors named English, 48 per cent named French and 23 per cent named German as a language of communication.

Table 5.17
Financial Problems Encountered by the Departments Participating in JEPs, by Status of Respondent (per cent*)

	Coordinator and contractor	Coordinator	Contractor	Partner	Total
Delay in provision of the grant by the European Commission	31	27	19	23	24
Delay in provision of the grant by the bank	18	24	17	20	20
Delay in provision of the grant by the JEP Contractor	1	12	2	16	14
Delay in provision of the grant by your institution	7	6	18	5	6
Difficulties with the institutional administration of the grant	14	10	25	10	11
Difficulties with the administration of the grant within the JEP	8	8	12	7	8
Unbalanced distribution of funds among partners	4	4	5	8	7

* Rating 1 or 2 on a scale from 1 = 'very considerable' to 5 = 'not at all'

Question 4.14: Please state the extent to which your department encountered financial problems regarding the following aspects.

Source: 'Experiences of JEP Contractors/Coordinators/Partners in the First Phase of TEMPUS' survey

Among the partners from CEE countries, 96 per cent used English, 26 per cent German (considerably above average were Slovenians, Hungarians and Czechs), 25 per cent French (notably Romanians), 10 per cent Polish and 6 per cent each Czech and Hungarian. Of the partners from Western countries, 92 per cent used English, 30 per cent French (notably French and above average Spanish, Belgian, and Italian partners), and 23 per cent German (notably German, Austrian and Swiss partners). Any other language was used 5 per cent at most.

Asked about the proportion of the respective languages used, TEMPUS JEP partners stated that 72 per cent used English, 13 per cent French, and 8 per cent German (notably in the humanities and social sciences, i.e. 12 per cent), while 9 per cent used any other European language (2 per cent Polish).

Most respondents were informed about the academic curriculum and the time-table of the academic year of the partners. About two-thirds were informed about the teaching methods and technical equipment at their partner institutions, and approximately half about other facilities as well as about examinations and degrees at their partner institutions. Only about one-third were informed about recognition arrangements. As Table 5.18 shows, more respondents from CEE countries were informed about characteristics of their higher education partners than respondents from Western countries.

Table 5.18
Characteristics of the Partner Departments the Respondents were Informed About, by Country Group (per cent, multiple reply possible)

	CEE country	Western country	Total
Academic curriculum and academic year	85	76	80
Academic recognition arrangements	37	33	34
Teaching methods	80	57	66
Examination procedures and final degrees	56	42	48
Kinds of technical equipment used for teaching and research	74	55	63
Institutional facilities	71	47	56
Other	5	5	5
Not ticked	4	14	10
Total	411	328	362
(n)	(694)	(1,002)	(1,696)

Question 4.5: About which characteristics of your higher education partner departments in this JEP were you informed?

Source: 'Experiences of JEP Contractors/Coordinators/Partners in the First Phase of TEMPUS' survey

Altogether, four out of five respondents were satisfied with the cooperation among the partners as regards the JEP administration. The proportion of those satisfied with three single aspects of the JEP administration addressed in the questionnaire ranged from 73 to 78 per cent. Partners from CEE countries were more satisfied with the JEP administration than partners from Western countries (see Table 5.14). For example, 87 per cent of the former were satisfied with the cooperation regarding administrative matters in general as compared to 79 per cent of the latter.

In science and engineering fields, JEP partners tended to spend slightly less time, effort and money on administrative cooperation than in humanities and social science. The partners from science and engineering fields, however, stated on average similar outcomes and the same degree of satisfaction as regards administrative matters of their JEPs.

In the framework of interviews conducted at select institutions of higher education in Central and Eastern European countries, dissatisfaction with Western partners was somewhat more strongly voiced than one would expect on the basis of the responses given to the questionnaire survey. Two points were often raised. First, some Western partners were criticised for demanding and possibly keeping sizeable proportions of the overall funds for their administration and the services they provided within the Joint European Programmes. Second, several Western partners were criticised for advocating certain priorities, certain major curricular thrusts, etc., without full empathy and appreciation of the needs felt by their partners in Central and Eastern European countries.

As one might expect, the interviews also provided ample opportunity for reporting most unfortunate incidences in the West–East cooperation: some Western partners seem to sell or franchise their courses rather than to cooperate in the development of new curricula, some Western partners were viewed as sending guest lecturers and experts who were academically too weak to play the expected advisory role, some seemed to have unreasonable demands concerning their treatment by the hosts during visits in CEE countries and some blocked support for incoming students and staff, if funds were not made available in time. These experiences, however, do not call into question the general finding that most Central and Eastern partners considered cooperation with their Western partners as a valuable contribution to educational activities at their departments and faculties.

5.7 Objectives and Activities

Most of the respondents considered all the four major areas of activities supported in the framework of TEMPUS I, namely curriculum development measures, structural development, staff exchange and student exchange, as important for their respective JEP.

As regards curricular measures, about three-quarters each of the respondents from CEE countries considered as important goals:

- the offer of new course contents and new paradigms (80 per cent)
- the establishment of new course programmes (78 per cent)
- the provision of staff development and continuous education programmes
- the introduction of new teaching methods (72 per cent each).

Only a minority viewed changes in the degree structure (30 per cent) and the establishment of new faculties and departments (25 per cent) as essential for their JEP. Also administrative objectives, which play some role in the framework of TEMPUS II, were viewed by only a few partners as a major objective of their JEP activities while being supported in the framework of TEMPUS I. Of the partners 27 per cent from CEE countries, emphasised the improvement of higher education management and 13 per cent the reorganisation of administrative structures and procedures as important goals.

The goals differed substantially according to field of study. The establishment of new departments and new course programmes was a concern of fields newly emerging or following other paradigms than in the past, for example management and business studies. Also, staff and student exchange was less emphasised in some fields, as Table 5.19 shows. Finally, contact to industry was most strongly appreciated by partners of management and business studies.

Most of the JEPs actually were involved in all the four areas of activities for which TEMPUS I provided support. According to the partners surveyed, almost all were active in staff mobility (95 per cent) and in cooperative educational measures (93 per cent), while about three-quarters each were involved in structural development (77 per cent) and student exchange (75 per cent).

We note some differences according to subject area in the latter activities, which reflect the differences in objectives named above (see Table 5.20).

Table 5.19
Important Goals within the JEP with Regard to the Development of the Targeted Department/Institution, by Subject Area of the JEP (per cent*)

	Subject area															Total
	Hum	Soc	Man	Nat	Med	Eng	Com	Agr	Env	Arc	Art	Lan	Tea	Law	Oth	
Establishment of new faculties/departments	24	51	41	9	27	23	22	27	27	12	6	23	16	12	32	26
Changes of degree structures	28	38	35	26	22	37	33	38	26	22	28	33	25	35	34	32
Offer new course programmes	72	78	80	65	65	78	81	71	72	62	75	67	62	62	65	73
Offer new course contents/paradigms	89	79	81	77	73	85	80	81	83	79	67	79	81	59	67	80
Establishment of staff development and continuous education programmes	84	68	68	58	70	65	66	66	68	62	41	66	69	53	63	66
Introduction of new teaching methods	65	65	73	61	75	66	60	76	68	79	75	79	79	33	63	69
Reorganisations of administrative structures and procedures	20	19	17	8	22	14	14	13	11	31	22	20	14	18	27	16

(continued)

(Table 5.19)	Hum	Soc	Man	Nat	Med	Eng	Com	Agr	Env	Arc	Art	Lan	Tea	Law	Oth	Total
Improvement of equipment e.g. computer centres, laboratories, libraries etc.	80	80	70	78	72	85	91	85	86	86	86	79	64	64	66	80
Promotion of student exchange	95	66	52	83	60	75	66	78	81	83	100	78	70	75	82	72
Promotion of staff exchange	95	77	68	82	81	80	80	85	89	77	85	82	79	71	86	80
Improvement of higher education management	24	25	27	30	29	24	18	25	19	27	17	16	31	24	30	25
Establishment of cooperation between the targeted institution and industry	6	23	50	23	22	42	33	40	36	33	32	9	8	18	36	33

* Rating 1 or 2 on a scale from 1 = 'very important ' to 5 = 'no goal at all'

Hum = Humanities, philological sciences
Soc = Social sciences
Man = Management and business
Nat = Natural sciences
Med = Medical sciences

Eng = Engineering, applied sciences
Com = Computer sciences
Agr = Agricultural sciences, agrobusiness
Env = Environmental protection
Arc = Architecture, urban and regional planning

Art = Art and design
Lan = Language studies
Tea = Teacher training
Law = Law
Oth = Other subjects

Question 2.2: From your point of view, how important were the following aspects concerning the development of the targeted department/institution within this JEP?

Source: 'Experiences of JEP Contractors/Coordinators/Partners in the First Phase of TEMPUS' survey

Table 5.20
Participation of the Respondents' Department/Institution in the TEMPUS Activities of Their JEP, by Subject Area of the JEP (per cent, multiple reply possible)

	Hum	Soc	Man	Nat	Med	Eng	Com	Agr	Env	Arc	Art	Lan	Tea	Law	Oth	Total
Cooperation measures in teaching/learning	100	95	95	87	87	97	98	92	97	97	91	96	89	86	81	93
Structural development	95	79	80	68	68	81	86	78	80	76	82	87	77	32	58	77
Staff mobility	100	100	95	90	85	98	96	97	99	100	100	100	90	86	92	95
Student mobility	90	64	56	87	63	79	70	82	77	76	100	86	73	79	90	75
Total	385	338	327	332	303	355	350	348	353	348	373	368	329	282	321	340
(n)	(20)	(112)	(209)	(165)	(142)	(333)	(127)	(121)	(145)	(33)	(22)	(98)	(73)	(28)	(52)	(1,680)

Hum = Humanities, philological sciences
Soc = Social sciences
Man = Management and business
Nat = Natural sciences
Med = Medical sciences

Eng = Engineering, applied sciences
Com = Computer sciences
Agr = Agricultural sciences, agrobusiness
Env = Environmental protection
Arc = Architecture, urban and regional planning

Art = Art and design
Lan = Language studies
Tea = Teacher training
Law = Law
Oth = Other subjects

Question 5.1: In which of the following activities was your department/institution involved within the JEP?

Source: 'Experiences of JEP Contractors/Coordinators/Partners in the First Phase of TEMPUS' survey

Table 5.21
Average Number of Staff Members Sent Abroad per Partner Department, by Year of Start of the Joint European Project and by Country Group (mean)

| | 1990/91 | | 1991/92 | | 1992/93 | | 1993/94 | | Total | |
| | Department from | | Department from | | Department from | | Department from | | Department from | |
Year abroad	CEE country	Western country	CEE country	Western country	CEE country	Western country	CEE country	Western country	CEE country	Western country
1990/91	5.4	3.4	–	–	–	–	–	–	5.4	3.4
1991/92	6.0	3.3	7.4	3.1	–	–	–	–	7.0	3.2
1992/93	6.9	4.0	8.2	3.3	6.6	2.8	–	–	7.3	3.2
1993/94	3.2	2.2	8.4	3.6	8.2	2.9	6.3	2.4	8.1	3.1
1994/95	4.4	1.5	3.2	2.4	9.5	3.1	8.8	2.5	9.0	2.9
Total	14.9	9.2	21.4	8.2	21.1	7.5	12.9	4.2	19.8	7.8
(n)	(103)	(307)	(239)	(307)	(252)	(324)	(30)	(46)	(624)	(780)

Year of start

Question 3.5: How many staff members from your department went abroad in each TEMPUS–supported year and how many staff members did you receive from your partner departments/institutions?

Source: 'Experiences of JEP Contractors/Coordinators/Partners in the First Phase of TEMPUS' survey

Besides, almost all partners from CEE countries emphasised that they were involved in structural development (90 per cent), while the respective proportion was considerably smaller for partners from Western countries (67 per cent). This clearly shows that structural development activities are less based on cooperation than the other major activities supported by TEMPUS I.

Almost all departments from CEE countries involved in JEPs participated in staff exchange and almost all of them used all opportunities to send their staff abroad, that is, did so in more or less all the academic years they were provided TEMPUS support. They sent on average seven staff members abroad during an academic year. During the years they received TEMPUS support, they sent on average altogether 20 staff members abroad. As Table 5.21 shows, the number of staff sent by departments from CEE countries increased over the years the respective JEP was supported by TEMPUS. Also, the later the partner department started being involved in TEMPUS, the more staff they sent abroad annually.

Some of the departments from Western countries involved in staff mobility either only sent or only received staff from their partners. Those actually sending staff abroad also made use of more or less the whole period they were awarded TEMPUS support. They sent, however, only about three staff members annually (3.2 on average). During the years they were involved in a TEMPUS JEP, they sent slightly less than eight staff members abroad on average. Altogether, more staff was mobile from CEE countries to Western countries (67 per cent according to these survey data) than from Western countries to the CEE countries.

As already reported, only about three-quarters of the partners reported that their department was involved in student exchange. But most of those partners from CEE actually involved in student mobility sent students abroad, and if they did, they sent students more or less continuously over the whole period they were awarded TEMPUS support. They sent abroad between 7 and 8 students on average annually (7.8), and altogether 19 students over the maximum of three years of regular TEMPUS support. Less than half of them, though, received students from their partner departments. As in the case of staff mobility, the number of students sent by departments from CEE countries increased over the years the respective JEP was supported by TEMPUS. Also, the later the partner department started being involved in TEMPUS, the more students they sent abroad annually (see Table 5.22).

Most departments from Western countries involved in TEMPUS-supported student mobility only received students from the CEE countries. Only 29 per cent of partners from the West provided data on the

Table 5.22

Average Number of Students Sent Abroad per Partner Department, by Year of Start of the Joint European Project and by Country Group (mean)

	Year of start										
	1990/91		1991/92		1992/93		1993/94		Total	
	Department from		Department from		Department from		Department from		Department from	
Year abroad	CEE country	Western country	CEE country	Western country	CEE country	Western country	CEE country	Western country	CEE country	Western country
1990/91	6.2	2.8	–	–	–	–	–	–	6.2	2.8
1991/92	6.5	3.4	6.6	3.6	–	–	–	–	6.5	3.5
1992/93	7.5	3.8	8.1	5.6	9.0	4.0	–	–	8.3	4.7
1993/94	5.2	2.2	8.2	5.6	9.1	4.0	9.9	3.2	8.7	4.7
1994/95	7.0	2.3	6.7	6.2	9.3	4.1	7.9	2.3	9.1	3.8
Total	15.8	6.9	18.7	9.2	21.6	7.9	14.1	3.9	19.1	7.9
(n)	(81)	(34)	(179)	(79)	(187)	(84)	(28)	(19)	(475)	(216)

Question 3.6: How many students from your own department did you send abroad in each TEMPUS-supported year and how many students did you receive from your partner departments?

Source: 'Experiences of JEP Contractors/Coordinators/Partners in the First Phase of TEMPUS' survey

number of students they sent, while 87 per cent provided data on the number of students received. Those departments from Western countries sending students in the framework of TEMPUS actually did so more or less during the whole TEMPUS-supported period. They sent on average 3.9 students annually. As Table 5.22 shows, altogether they sent about eight students on average during the regular TEMPUS-supported period of up to three years.

According to the JEP partners responding to this survey, about 80 per cent of the mobile students supported by TEMPUS went from CEE countries to Western countries. The dominance of student mobility from the CEE countries to the Western countries envisaged initially was thus realised by and large.

5.8   Cooperation Measures in Teaching and Education

5.8.1   Frequency of Activities

Altogether, 97 per cent of JEP partners from CEE countries surveyed participated in cooperation measures in the field of teaching and education. Among them, most were involved in staff development and about three-quarters each undertook the production of teaching material, participated in curriculum development and arranged short intensive courses in the framework of their JEP.

Table 5.23
Type of Activities in the Field of Teaching and Education, by Country Group (per cent, multiple reply possible)

	CEE country	Western country	Total
Staff training/staff development	88	72	79
Production of teaching material	73	57	64
Curriculum development	73	57	64
Short intensive courses	74	59	65
Other measures	6	5	6
Not ticked	4	11	8
Total	319	261	286
(n)	(659)	(874)	(1,533)

Question 6.1.1: Please state for each year this JEP was in operation the type of activities in the field of teaching and education in which your department was involved.

Source: 'Experiences of JEP Contractors/Coordinators/Partners in the First Phase of TEMPUS' survey

The proportion of partners from Western countries involved in these co-operation measures was lower, as Table 5.23 shows. In part, they shared the responsibilities of cooperation with their respective JEP partners from Western countries.

5.8.2 Staff Development

Partners involved in staff development had a broad range of objectives in mind. Of the respective partners from CEE countries:
- almost all wanted to promote new teaching methods,
- about two-thirds emphasised the handling of modern equipment,
- about half each wanted to foster a change of theories and paradigms as well as an improvement of foreign language proficiency
- about two-fifths hoped to contribute to new research methods as well.

Table 5.24
Problems Regarding Staff Training/Staff Development as Perceived by the Respondents, by Country Group (per cent*)

	CEE country	Western country	Total
Language problems	13	22	18
Content of training not suitable to the needs of trainees	3	5	4
Level of training too high	2	4	3
Level of training too low	4	2	3
Trainer/teacher too dominant	1	3	2
Trainer/teacher too passive	1	3	2
Group of trainees too heterogeneous	7	11	9
Group of trainees too homogeneous	2	1	2
Duration of training too short	15	22	18
Duration of training too long	2	3	2

* Rating 1 or 2 on a scale from 1 = 'serious problem' to 5 = 'no problem at all'
Question 6.2.5: To what extent did you perceive problems in any of the following areas?
Source: 'Experiences of JEP Contractors/Coordinators/Partners in the First Phase of TEM-PUS' survey

Staff development was most frequently undertaken with the help of special courses, but training on the job as well as provision of written and audio-visual material played a role as well. Of the partners from CEE countries involved in special courses for staff development:

- 47 per cent reported that they were undertaken both in Western and CEE countries
- 32 per cent that they were undertaken solely in CEE countries
- 21 per cent that the courses were undertaken exclusively in Western countries.

According to the respective respondents from CEE countries, the staff development activities made use of 7 persons on average in training and supervisory functions and addressed 15 persons on average in learning functions. Of the respective JEPs involved in staff development (again according to the respondents from CEE countries):

- 81 per cent made use of staff members of the JEP partners from Western countries
- 27 per cent of other experts from Western countries
- 2 per cent of experts from international organisations
- 50 per cent of staff members of the JEP partners from CEE countries
- 10 per cent of other experts from CEE countries.

As Table 5.24 shows, the partners from Western countries involved in staff development stated more often serious problems (1 or 2 on a scale from 1 = 'very serious problem' to 5 = 'no problem at all') than the partners from CEE countries. Three problems were most frequently observed by both sides:

- The duration of the training period was viewed as too short in some instances.
- Problems of language proficiency occurred.
- The group of trainees was too heterogeneous.

Most of the respondents, when asked to rate the outcomes, came to the conclusion that the staff development activities were successful:

- 84 per cent of the respective respondents from CEE countries and 82 per cent from Western countries observed a high improvement of the respective knowledge on the part of the trainees.
- 83 per cent and 73 per cent respectively stated that staff development has contributed to the quality of teaching in the targeted departments.

In addition, about half of the respondents believed that the staff development activities have also contributed to the quality of research. About one-fifth had the impression that the staff development measures have served the improvement of administrative procedures as well.

5.8.3   Development of Teaching Material

Of the about 70 per cent JEP partners from CEE countries involved in the production of teaching material in the framework of the TEMPUS Programme:

- about three-quarters developed hand-outs and other unpublished documents
- more than half prepared textbooks
- about one-third each developed audio-visual material and computer software.

Most partners from CEE countries involved in the production of teaching material reported that staff members from their (or from their CEE partners') departments (93 per cent) as well as from Western partners' departments (72 per cent) actually undertook the development of material. Only in a few cases were experts from other CEE institutions (14 per cent) or other Western institutions (17 per cent) involved.

According to the respective partners from CEE countries, half of them were involved in the development of completely new material. Three quarters participated in the production of material partly based on existing material. Finally, 13 per cent were involved in the translation of existing material. Nine per cent of the respective partners from CEE countries developed this material solely for use in distance teaching and learning. A further 34 per cent also took distance teaching and learning into consideration.

About 40 per cent addressed both first-degree and doctoral students, and a similar percentage addressed first-degree students only (among them a quarter were students of the first years and a similar number were students in the later years of first degree programmes). Finally, about 10 per cent each addressed only students in advanced and doctoral studies as well as professionally active persons.

Various problems were named each by 10 per cent at most of those involved in the production of material. Again, as Table 5.25 suggests, partners from Western countries voiced more criticism than partners from CEE countries.

More than 80 per cent of the partners involved rated the major outcomes of the production of teaching material positively. Most partners considered its academic level as appropriate for their respective target groups (90 per cent). Almost as many came to the conclusion that it reflected the current state of academic knowledge well (83 per cent) and that it was well structured (81 per cent). The ratings by Western partners were slightly more critical than those by the partners from CEE countries.

Table 5.25
Difficulties Encountered in the Development of the Teaching Material, by Subject Area of the JEP (per cent*)

	Hum	Soc	Man	Nat	Med	Eng	Com	Agr	Env	Arc	Art	Lan	Tea	Law	Oth	Total
Diverging views among partners	0	8	5	2	9	4	4	5	3	13	8	5	10	0	0	5
Inaccurate definition of work-sharing among partners	10	19	7	3	8	5	5	5	3	5	8	4	6	0	7	5
Language problems among partners	0	9	9	1	7	2	2	8	2	9	8	2	16	0	11	5
Imperfect translation of existing or newly developed teaching material	0	7	4	0	4	2	1	0	2	0	8	0	0	0	8	2
Late provision of contributions from partners	11	19	9	3	8	9	4	8	7	5	8	11	13	22	8	9
Lack of access to resources and facilities necessary for the development	0	6	6	2	9	4	1	11	8	15	8	5	9	11	4	6

* Rating 1 or 2 on a scale from 1 = 'very serious difficulties' to 5 = 'no difficulties at all'

** Explanation see Table 5.20

Question 6.3.6: To what extent did you encounter difficulties in the development of the teaching material?

Source: 'Experiences of JEP Contractors/Coordinators/Partners in the First Phase of TEMPUS' survey

Very few problems emerged in adopting the developed material, as far as acceptance by colleagues and by the targeted institution is concerned (2 per cent each). However, one-quarter of the respective respondents from CEE countries pointed out that they faced serious problems due to lack of funds for the production and distribution of the material.

5.8.4 Curriculum Development

About three-quarters of the JEP partners from CEE countries were involved in curriculum development. Among them, about 60 per cent stated that they created a new course programme. Most of the others had more moderate goals: a partial revision of a course programme or the development of single courses. Seven per cent stated that they wanted to change the degree structure. In addition, about 19 per cent wanted to create a new department or faculty accommodating the respective course programme.

The characteristics of the curricular structure were manifold. About half of the respective partners from CEE countries stated that they developed courses introducing new concepts and paradigms, courses introducing a European dimension, interdisciplinary courses, specialised courses, courses promoting general knowledge, courses which can easily be transferred to other faculties or institutions, courses making use of new teaching and learning methods and courses making use of new technologies. Forty per cent even stated that the courses are offered at least partly in a foreign language. As one might expect, some of these thrusts of curriculum development varied substantially according to subject area (see Table 5.26).

About half of the curriculum development activities addressed first-degree studies, while two-fifths addressed both first-degree and doctoral studies. Less than 10 per cent were developed solely for doctoral studies.

According to the partners from CEE countries, persons from almost all of their partner departments were involved in curriculum development. In two-thirds of the activities of curriculum development, representatives from the Western partners were involved as well. In almost one-third of the cases, students – mostly from the CEE countries – also participated. External experts from CEE countries as well as from Western countries participated each in about one-tenth of the cases.

More than 10 per cent each of the respective respondents from CEE countries observed problems of curriculum development in terms of convincing the central administration and in terms of convincing colleagues in the targeted departments. Again, the Western partners perceived more problems than their partners from CEE countries, as Table 5.27 shows.

Table 5.26
Characteristic Curricular Changes at the Targeted Department, by Subject Area of the JEP (per cent, multiple reply possible)

	Hum	Soc	Man	Nat	Med	Eng	Com	Agr	Env	Arc	Art	Lan	Tea	Law	Oth	Total
Courses are offered at least partly in a foreign language	70	41	37	46	44	38	31	31	44	33	28	45	39	82	33	39
Courses provide a high degree of specialisation	50	48	46	53	51	62	62	48	51	57	56	38	35	64	48	52
Courses provide broad and general knowledge	40	50	55	40	44	50	49	47	44	62	50	45	50	64	48	48
Courses introduce new theories and paradigms in the respective field	100	65	62	51	50	50	51	59	47	52	78	41	70	55	37	54
Courses provide comparative perspectives	20	73	67	29	42	35	17	50	53	48	67	62	69	91	52	48
Courses aim at interdisciplinarity	80	48	39	31	45	44	25	57	63	57	67	32	57	45	41	45
Courses aim at introducing a European dimension	50	68	66	33	55	54	27	58	50	71	67	54	65	100	56	54
Courses introduce new methods of teaching and learning	70	54	66	44	63	54	56	66	45	62	72	72	83	27	52	58

(continued)

(Table 5.26)	Hum	Soc	Man	Nat	Med	Eng	Com	Agr	Env	Arc	Art	Lan	Tea	Law	Oth	Total
Mandatory or optional period abroad	0	16	16	16	15	17	6	13	15	5	11	18	9	18	15	14
Courses can be easily transferred to other faculties/institutions	30	36	36	35	35	43	48	51	48	29	28	39	43	64	37	41
Course contents provide a high degree of praxis relevance	20	41	48	23	40	34	20	34	32	33	33	32	56	0	41	35
Courses integrate use of new technologies	70	39	50	50	53	70	72	59	56	76	61	45	39	0	48	56
Students carry out a period in practical placement	0	25	27	11	26	28	15	33	20	0	17	8	33	9	37	23
Other	0	3	1	1	1	2	0	2	0	5	0	0	0	0	7	1
Not ticked	0	3	4	2	3	2	3	5	3	0	0	1	2	0	0	3
Total	600	608	619	466	567	581	482	611	570	590	633	534	650	618	552	571
(n)	(10)	(80)	(147)	(96)	(86)	(250)	(95)	(88)	(110)	(21)	(18)	(71)	(54)	(11)	(27)	(1,164)

Question 6.4.3: Which of the following aspects could be considered as characteristic for the curricular changes?

Source: 'Experiences of JEP Contractors/Coordinators/Partners in the First Phase of TEMPUS' survey

As regards the implementation of the curricula developed, 23 per cent of the respective partners from CEE countries emphasised a lack of resources. Thirteen per cent noted problems as regards recognition of the developed courses or course programmes.

By and large, the results of curriculum development were highly regarded by the respondents. About 80 per cent came to the conclusion that the newly developed courses or course programmes enhanced scientific knowledge to a considerable extent.

Table 5.27
Difficulties Encountered in the Development of the New Courses/ Course Programmes in the Targeted Department/Institution, by Country Group (per cent*)

	CEE country	Western country	Total
Convincing colleagues in the targeted department about the advantages	13	13	13
Convincing the central administration of the targeted institution	15	19	17
Defining the content and structure of new course among partners in the JEP	3	10	7
Language problems	4	8	6
Late provision of contributions from partners	3	8	6
Lack of quality of contributions from partners	2	3	2
Lack of access to resources and facilities necessary for the development	10	8	9

* Rating 1 or 2 on a scale from 1 = 'very serious difficulties' to 5 = 'no difficulties at all'

Question 6.4.6: To what extent did you encounter difficulties in the development of the new courses/course programmes in the targeted department/institution?

Source: 'Experiences of JEP Contractors/Coordinators/Partners in the First Phase of TEMPUS' survey

5.8.5 Short Intensive Courses

About three-quarters of the JEP partners from CEE countries were involved in short intensive courses supported by TEMPUS. Of the respective partners 86 per cent took part in courses with subject-related content, 31 per cent in language training courses, and 7 per cent in courses with other content.

The respective partner units in the CEE countries were involved in almost 6 short intensive courses on average with a mean duration of 11 days. About three-quarters of them reported that those courses were offered at their institution, about half at the Western partner institutions, and one-third reported that these courses were offered at another institution in CEE countries.

Most partners from CEE countries were involved in short intensive courses addressing staff of their institution (82 per cent) and students of their institution (68 per cent) as trainees. Also some students from Western countries (21 per cent), some staff members from Western countries (6 per cent) and some other experts from CEE countries (18 per cent) were addressed. Of the partners from CEE countries, the majority each reported that staff from Western countries (69 per cent) and staff of their own institution (60 per cent) served as teachers in these courses, followed by other experts from Western countries (23 per cent) and other experts from CEE countries (21 per cent).

Altogether, about half of the respective partner departments in CEE countries played a role both in teaching and learning in these intensive courses, while 12 per cent played a role only in teaching. In contrast, about 80 per cent of Western partners were involved only in teaching functions, about 19 per cent both in teaching and learning and only 1 per cent solely in learning functions.

The respective partners from the CEE countries reported that the average participation of their own staff members in short intensive courses was about 10, and that of their own students 18. The respective figures, as one might expect, were substantially lower for partners from Western countries (4 and 5 respectively).

Problems occurred most frequently in short intensive programmes due to insufficient language proficiency and due to a heterogeneous composition of trainees. Altogether, the proportion of partners stating problems was low, with the Western partners – again – were more critical than their partners from CEE countries (see Table 5.28).

Altogether, most CEE partners appreciated the outcomes of the short intensive courses – 84 per cent rated the level of courses as high – 84 per cent praised their didactic quality and 81 perceived a substantial improvement of the participants' knowledge. The partners from Western countries rated the respective outcomes almost as highly as their partners from CEE countries.

Table 5.28
Problems Perceived Regarding the Short Intensive Courses, by Country Group (per cent*)

	CEE country	Western country	Total
Language problems	10	17	14
Content of training not suitable for the needs of participants	2	5	4
Level of training too high	2	5	4
Level of training too low	1	3	2
Trainer/teacher too dominant	0	2	1
Trainer/teacher too passive	1	3	2
Group of trainees too heterogeneous	6	11	9
Group of trainees too homogeneous	0	1	1

* Rating 1 or 2 on a scale from 1 = 'very serious difficulties' to 5 = 'no difficulties at all'
Question 6.5.6: To what extent did you perceive problems in any of the following areas?
Source: 'Experiences of JEP Contractors/Coordinators/Partners in the First Phase of TEMPUS' survey

5.9   Structural Development and Provision of Equipment

TEMPUS funds were used for structural development and provision of equipment by almost all partners from CEE countries in more or less all the years they were awarded support. The new equipment was used for:

- teaching by 95 per cent of the respective partners from CEE countries
- research by 57 per cent
- administration by 45 per cent
- services by 14 per cent
- other activities by 1 per cent.

The areas of utilisation varied to some extent, as one might expect, according to subject area. In most subject areas, the funds were frequently used for classroom equipment and computer centres, as Table 5.29 shows.

Table 5.29
Utilisation of New Equipment, by Subject Area* of the JEP (per cent, multiple reply possible)

Areas of utilisation	Hum	Soc	Man	Nat	Med	Eng	Com	Agr	Env	Arc	Art	Lan	Tea	Law	Oth	Total
Classroom	41	61	62	53	49	56	55	53	60	61	72	60	64	25	68	57
Science laboratory	65	22	21	67	48	72	61	71	64	57	28	9	17	13	36	49
Administrative offices	18	42	53	22	33	23	18	35	26	35	39	37	53	75	61	33
Library	65	65	63	41	58	29	20	38	42	30	78	63	64	100	54	46
Language laboratory	6	10	19	1	7	6	2	7	1	0	11	52	32	13	21	12
Computer centre	65	49	65	41	51	45	55	40	51	70	50	48	40	63	57	50
Other areas	6	4	6	9	10	10	8	10	9	13	17	6	13	0	4	9
No area indicated	6	9	2	3	2	4	1	7	3	4	6	6	8	0	4	4
Not ticked	6	4	1	0	2	1	0	2	2	4	0	1	2	0	4	2
Total	276	266	291	237	260	246	221	264	258	274	300	283	292	288	307	262
(n)	(17)	(77)	(150)	(97)	(88)	(254)	(96)	(86)	(106)	(23)	(18)	(81)	(53)	(8)	(28)	(1,182)

Question 7.2: For which activities and in which area is the new equipment utilised?

* Explanation see Table 5.20

Source: 'Experiences of JEP Contractors/Coordinators/Partners in the First Phase of TEMPUS' survey

Table 5.30
Type of Equipment Acquired Within Targeted Department, by Subject Area* of the JEP (per cent, multiple reply possible)

	Hum	Soc	Man	Nat	Med	Eng	Com	Agr	Env	Arc	Art	Lan	Tea	Law	Oth	Total
Computer hardware and/or software	82	87	95	84	77	92	97	78	86	96	89	80	91	75	93	88
Laboratory equipment	24	16	21	61	45	68	36	66	65	35	17	33	30	13	36	46
Office machines and/or special furniture	24	47	57	28	44	41	36	43	44	48	39	46	62	50	46	44
Books, periodicals, scientific literature, etc.	76	83	85	75	72	74	76	74	78	70	94	81	91	100	61	78
Other	6	14	11	5	17	4	2	9	5	0	39	10	13	0	4	8
Not ticked	12	5	1	2	5	2	1	5	5	14	0	6	2	0	7	3
Total	224	252	271	255	260	280	249	276	283	252	278	257	289	238	246	267
(n)	(17)	(77)	(150)	(97)	(88)	(254)	(96)	(86)	(106)	(23)	(18)	(81)	(53)	(8)	(28)	(1,182)

Question 7.3: What type of equipment was acquired and who has access to the equipment within the targeted institution?
* Explanation see Table 5.20.

Source: 'Experiences of JEP Contractors/Coordinators/Partners in the First Phase of TEMPUS' survey

While they were used most frequently in science and engineering fields for laboratory equipment, the humanities and social sciences often used this support for libraries and offices.

Most JEP partners from CEE countries used TEMPUS funds for the purchase of computer hardware and/or software as well as for academic literature. Almost half of them purchased laboratory equipment as well as office machines and furniture. Again, the major thrusts differed according to subject area, as Table 5.30 shows.

As one might expect, academic literature served in more than half of the cases the institutions of higher education in general. In contrast, the office equipment served in the majority of cases only the respective JEP unit. Most noteworthy, however, might be the fact that the computer as well as the laboratory equipment in almost half of the cases served only the unit involved in the respective JEP (see Table 5.31).

According to the JEP partners in the CEE countries their Western partners were involved in almost half of the JEPs in the identification of needs and the process of selection and ordering equipment. In most of those cases they did this in cooperation with their partners from CEE countries. Only in 2 per cent of the JEPs did the Western partners solely undertake the identification of needs, and in 9 per cent of the JEPs the Western partners solely undertook the selection and ordering of equipment, as Table 5.32 shows.

Table 5.31

Accessibility of Equipment Acquired with TEMPUS Support (per cent of JEP partners from CEE countries purchasing respective equipment)

Accessibility	Computer	Literature	Lab equ.	Office equ.
Only for JEP department	44	21	46	59
Other departments	31	20	31	21
All depts. of institution	23	56	20	19
Accessibility not specified	2	3	3	1
Total	100	100	100	100
(n)	(537)	(491)	(287)	(278)

Question 7.3: What type of equipment was acquired and who has access to the equipment within the targeted institution?

Source: 'Experiences of JEP Contractors/Coordinators/Partners in the First Phase of TEMPUS' survey

While the Western partners frequently played a role in the identification of needs and in the selection and ordering, they were little involved in the implementation of the equipment as well as its maintenance. The respective proportions were 16 per cent and 5 per cent.

Table 5.32
Involvement in the Acquisition of Equipment (per cent of JEP partners from CEE countries purchasing equipment)

Involved units	Need identification	Selection/ ordering	Imple- mentation	Mainten- ance
Solely own unit	47	40	73	83
Add./solely other CEE Unit	1	8	7	5
Own and West partner	34	37	13	4
West partner solely	2	9	2	1
Own, CEE and West partner	9	5	1	0
No answer	2	1	5	7
Total	100	100	100	100
(n)	(599)	(599)	(599)	(599)

Question 7.4: Who was involved and in which way in the structural development at the targeted institution?

Maintenance was cared for notably (at 19 per cent of the partners in CEE countries) through long-term contracts with the manufacturer or supplier, or a fixed amount was annually provided by the targeted institution (24 per cent). However, 13 per cent did not know at all whether any provisions for maintenance were made, and 38 per cent stated that no provisions were made.

The partners from the CEE countries named some problems encountered in the structural development activities quite frequently – 23 per cent stated problems due to a shortage of funds allocated, 17 per cent pointed out problems in terms of delays in the provision of equipment and 9 per cent experienced difficulties regarding COCOM licensing rules. As Table 5.33 shows, their Western partners reported problems more frequently – notably, regarding the transportation of equipment (22 per cent) as well as difficulties due to interventions by administration.

At the time the survey was undertaken:

- 15 per cent of the partners from CEE countries rated the computer hardware or software purchased with TEMPUS means as deficient (some do not work, some are out-dated or even all are outdated)
- 7 per cent rated the respective laboratory equipment as deficient
- 13 per cent noted similar problems as far as office machines and other equipment are concerned.

Interviews suggest that the discontinuation of funding for structural development is seen as a serious problem. This also holds true for the lack of continuity in the purchase of academic literature.

Table 5.33
Difficulties the Respondents' Departments Encountered Within the Structural Development/Acquisition of Equipment, by Country Group (per cent*)

	CEE country	Western country	Total
Delays in the provision of equipment	17	23	19
Transport of equipment	10	22	15
Functioning of the equipment after implementation	4	6	5
Guarantee conditions	6	7	6
Intervention by administration	5	11	7
Disagreement regarding the type of equipment required	5	5	5
Identification and selection of appropriate equipment	6	8	7
Shortage of funds allocated for the equipment	23	21	22
COCOM licensing rules	9	9	9

* Rating 1 or 2 on a scale from 1 = 'very serious difficulties' to 5 = 'no difficulties at all'

Question 7.5: To what extent did your department encounter difficulties with regard to the following aspects?

Source: 'Experiences of JEP Contractors/Coordinators/Partners in the First Phase of TEMPUS' survey

5.10   Staff Mobility

Replies to a question regarding the involvement in staff mobility in the framework of the respective JEP show that 98 per cent of the JEP partners from CEE countries sent their own staff and 88 per cent received staff from their partner institutions, while 82 per cent of the partners from Western countries sent their own staff and 97 per cent received staff from their partner institutions. As already shown above (see pp. 179 – 186), more staff members mobile in the framework of JEPs went from CEE to Western countries than from Western to CEE countries.

Considerable difficulties were encountered in sending staff abroad. These differed substantially between the CEE and the Western partners, as Table 5.34 indicates.

Table 5.34
Difficulties Encountered by Sending Staff to the JEP-Partner Departments, by Country Group (per cent, multiple reply possible)

	CEE country	Western country	Total
Finding staff members for a period abroad	16	38	27
Replacement of staff members during their period abroad	23	28	25
Administrative problems with your institution	7	6	7
Administrative problems with your local/national authorities	5	2	3
Getting the necessary documents from the host country	15	5	10
Language competence of staff members	21	11	16
Preparation of cooperation with the partner prior to the visit	10	15	13
Other difficulties	3	3	3
Not ticked	39	35	37
Total	138	143	141
(n)	(632)	(678)	(1,310)

Question 8.2.1: Did you encounter any of the following difficulties while sending staff to the partner department/ institution?

Source: 'Experiences of JEP Contractors/Coordinators/Partners in the First Phase of TEMPUS' survey

Table 5.35
Staff Activities Abroad According to the Hosts, by Country Group of Respondent (per cent, multiple reply possible)

	Activities of staff from Western countries as perceived by CEE hosts	Activities of staff from CEE countries as perceived by Western hosts
Lecturing/teaching/training at your department/institution	60	46
Participating in re-training courses/ programmes	28	36
Updating of knowledge/gathering of new knowledge	33	81
Establishing research contacts/working on research projects	26	53
Developing teaching material	41	56
Developing curricula	39	48
Upgrading facilities	19	22
Preparing student/staff mobility	40	49
Working on matters related to the management of the JEP	42	40
Establishing university/industry cooperation	17	21
Participating in conference, seminar, workshop	41	51
Gathering work experience outside higher education	12	18
Other activities	2	2
No CEE visitors	28	1
Not ticked	2	3
Total	427	528
(n)	(694)	(815)

Question 8.3.1: What were the activities of staff members from partner departments/institutions who visited you and where did they come from?

Source: 'Experiences of JEP Contractors/Coordinators/Partners in the First Phase of TEMPUS' survey

- Western partners most often faced difficulties in finding staff willing to spend some period at their partner institutions (38 per cent). This difficulty was named more than twice as often by respondents from Western countries than by those from CEE countries (16 per cent).

- Western partners also faced more problems as regards the replacement of their staff (28 per cent) than their CEE partners (23 per cent).

- Finally, Western partners pointed out difficulties more often in preparing the exchange with their partners (15 per cent as compared to 10 per cent).

- In contrast, partners from CEE countries more often observed problems as regards the foreign language proficiency of their staff (21 per cent as compared to 11 per cent) as well as obtaining visa and other documents from the host country (15 per cent as compared to 5 per cent).

Partners from CEE countries few stated problems in hosting staff from other countries. In contrast, partners from Western countries notably had problems in finding accommodation for their guests (25 per cent). Besides, some of them (almost ten per cent each) noted problems related to the cultural differences, varying styles of teaching, and personal attitudes of their guests.

Mobility from the CEE to Western countries in the framework of TEMPUS is expected to be in part a learning process. This is pointed out by the fact that 81 per cent of the Western hosts perceived their guests from CEE countries as being active in gathering new knowledge and updating their knowledge. The proportion of hosts from CEE countries stating this with regard to their guests from Western countries was only 33 per cent, that is, less than half as high. Besides, staff members from CEE countries have to play a more goal-directed role during their visits in contributing to the various objectives of the TEMPUS Programme. A higher proportion of them than of staff from Western countries was engaged in curriculum development, upgrading facilities, participation in retraining and many other activities, as Table 5.35 shows.

In contrast, Western staff lectured at the CEE partner departments more often (60 per cent) than staff from CEE countries did at their partner institutions in Western countries (46 per cent). In addition, CEE country staff more frequently made use of the visit at the partner institution for the preparation of student and staff mobility.

The teaching activities of visiting staff at the host institutions were on a moderate scale:

- Visiting staff at partner departments in CEE countries teaching there during their visit actually taught 23 hours on average, thereby addressing on average slightly more than 90 students.
- Visiting staff at institutions in Western countries teaching there actually taught 21 hours on average and addressed altogether less than 60 students on average.

Responses to the questions regarding the target groups of those courses suggest that most of these lectures and courses were open to a broad audience.

Table 5.36
Positive Outcomes of Staff Mobility Perceived by JEP Partners, by Country Group (per cent*)

Outcome	East-West mobility Respondents from:		West-East mobility Respondents from:	
	CEE country	Western country	CEE country	Western country
Improvement of professional knowledge of mobile staff	89	79	65	46
Contribution to quality of teaching in CEE departments	84	67	78	73
Contribution to quality of research in CEE departments	50	51	48	47
Contribution to administrative procedures at CEE departments	20	13	19	13

Questions 8.2.2/8.3.8: How would you rate the outcome of the staff mobility with regard to the following aspects?

* 1 or 2 on a scale from 1 = 'very high' to 5 = 'very low'

Source: 'Experiences of JEP Contractors/Coordinators/Partners in the First Phase of TEM-PUS' survey

As one might expect, only about 5 per cent of the staff visiting Central and Eastern European countries taught in the language of the host country.

The most significant outcome of staff mobility, according to the JEP partners, is the improvement of professional knowledge of staff from CEE countries. Eighty-nine per cent of the respondents from CEE countries perceived a high degree of improvement, as did their hosts in Western countries (79 per cent). About 80 per cent of partners from CEE countries believed that the quality of teaching at their departments increased both due to sending staff to Western countries and due to hosting staff from Western countries. Western partners considered the outcomes more moderately both regarding the knowledge improvement of their staff as well as regarding the quality of teaching both in the CEE countries and at their home institution.

Half of the JEP partners from CEE countries believe that both sending staff abroad and receiving staff from abroad also contributed significantly to the quality of research at their departments. Similarly, half of partners from Western countries believe that this staff exchange serves the quality of research in the CEE countries (see Table 5.36).

5.11 Student Mobility

According to the partners responding to the respective question:
- 97 per cent of the departments from CEE countries sent students abroad in the framework of their JEP, and 41 per cent received students from their partner departments.
- 30 per cent of the departments from Western countries involved in JEPs sent students to their partners, while 98 per cent received students from their partner departments.

JEP partners from CEE countries stated that on average 30 per cent of their mobile students participated in a work placement abroad. In contrast, only 18 per cent of the mobile students from the West, according to the mean of the partners' responses, participated in a work placement in the host country. Similarly, more mobile students from CEE countries (26 per cent) than from Western countries (11 per cent) worked on their thesis during their study period abroad.

According to their respective hosts, many students from Western countries mobile in the framework of TEMPUS spent their study period abroad in predominantly or exclusively undertaking individual study, as 50 per cent of the hosts from CEE countries reported. The respective proportion is smaller in the case of students from CEE countries spending some period abroad (stated by 38 per cent of hosts in Western countries), but this proportion was considerably higher than in the framework of ERASMUS student mobility, as shown in Table 5.37. Obviously, TEMPUS students were not expected as much as ERASMUS students to be highly integrated into the regular study processes abroad, but rather to experience various contrasts of study at the host institution to that at their home institution.

Table 5.37

Differences between Incoming and own TEMPUS Students in Course Participation, by Country Group (per cent, multiple reply possible)

	Country group			In comparison: ERASMUS students according to ICP local directors*
	CEE country	Western country	Total	
More or less the same course load as own students	28	43	40	52
Restricted choice of courses	14	19	18	20
Fewer courses	7	14	12	20
More courses	2	3	3	4
Attendance in courses provided for own students of earlier study year	1	5	4	11
Special courses offered to incoming students	27	23	24	17
Predominantly or exclusively individual study	50	38	41	26
Other	10	8	8	10
Not ticked	7	5	5	5
Total	145	159	156	164
(n)	(196)	(695)	(891)	(2,428)

* Survey addressing ERASMUS ICP local directors 1991/92[1]

Question 9.3.1: In what way, if any, did the incoming students' participation in the course programme at your institution differ from that of your students at your department/institution?

Source: 'Experiences of JEP Contractors/Coordinators/Partners in the First Phase of TEMPUS' survey

An emphasis on individual study might be based on various sound rationales. In the framework of TEMPUS, one certainly also has to take into account the existing language barriers. According to the respective host partners, 88 per cent of the learning which was undertaken by mobile TEMPUS students in CEE countries was not based on the host country language, and also 38 per cent of the learning abroad by TEMPUS students in Western countries was not based on the host country language (as

---

1   See Maiworm, F. and Teichler, U. (1995) *ERASMUS Student Mobility Programmes 1991/92 in the View of the Local Directors*. Kassel.

compared to 21 per cent in the ERASMUS Programme according to the local directors 1991/92).

Table 5.38
Degree to which the Incoming Students were provided with Assistance/Guidance/Advice, by Country Group (per cent*)

	Country group			In comparison:
	CEE country	Western country	Total	ERASMUS students according to ICP local directors*
Information regarding recognition matters	53	49	50	–
Registration, course selection	58	72	69	82
Accommodation	89	92	91	83
Matters regarding students' financial support	45	66	61	29
Academic matters	67	71	70	77
Work placement matters	65	58	60	59
Information about your institution and the higher education system	82	69	72	60
Language training	23	51	45	57
Visa, registration in your country	30	57	52	–
Your country in general	56	51	52	41
The local community in which the host institution is situated	54	57	57	47
Personal matters	54	53	53	46

*   1 or 2 on a scale from 1 = 'very considerable' to 5 = 'none'
**   Survey addressing ERASMUS ICP local directors 1991/92 (Maiworm/Teichler 1995, loc. cit.)
Question 9.3.2: To what extent did your department/institution provide assistance/guidance/advice to incoming students in any of the following areas?
Source: 'Experiences of JEP Contractors/Coordinators/Partners in the First Phase of TEMPUS' survey

TEMPUS students were provided with substantial support by their host departments and institutions. For example, most of them were provided help as regards accommodation and received information about the host institution and the higher education system of the host country, as Table 5.38 shows. Both TEMPUS students going to CEE and to Western countries more often received support than ERASMUS students except in areas which are relevant for curricular integration, for example course selection, language training and recognition matters.

The proportion of partners in TEMPUS JEPs observing serious academic problems of incoming students – both from CEE and from Western countries – turned out to be substantially higher than the respective proportion of ERASMUS local directors observing serious academic problems of incoming ERASMUS students. In both the TEMPUS and in the ERASMUS Programme, we note a higher proportion of critical voices in observing incoming students from partner institutions than in observing one's own outgoing students.

TEMPUS students from Western countries most frequently faced problems in the CEE countries due to a lack of proficiency in the language of the host country. TEMPUS students from CEE countries also faced more problems in terms of foreign language proficiency in the host country than ERASMUS students do. In addition, some of those in charge of sending or hosting students observed considerable problems due to differences in teaching and learning methods as well as regarding matters of recognition, while discrepancies of academic quality are seldom voiced as problems (see Table 5.39).

On the contrary, both the partners from CEE countries and from Western countries rated the academic performance of the incoming TEMPUS students favourably. On average, CEE partners rated their incoming TEMPUS students 2.8 and Western partners rated their incoming students 2.9 on average on a scale from 1 = 'incoming students much better' to 5 = 'incoming students much worse', that is, they rated incoming students slightly more favourably than their own students, while ERASMUS local directors rated the incoming students slightly worse on average than their own students (3.1). These findings suggest that the mutual respect for academic competence within the TEMPUS Programme is quite high. Also, selection according to merit plays a substantial role in providing TEMPUS student mobility grants. However, the ratings of incoming students vary considerably by subject area.

In contrast to widespread rumours, the partners from CEE countries stated that on average only about 6 per cent of their TEMPUS students did not return to the home country but continued study in the host or another country or got employed in the host country or another country. This is even a slightly smaller proportion than that among TEMPUS students from Western countries (7 per cent) not returning to their home country, and a much smaller proportion than among ERASMUS students, of whom almost 20 per cent lived abroad after the completion of the degree programme.

Table 5.39

Academic Problems Encountered by TEMPUS Students According to the Respondents from Sending and Hosting Departments, by Country Group of Respondents (per cent* of partners responding)

Academic problems faced abroad	Students from Western countries		Students from CEE Countries		In comparison ERASMUS students	
	Viewed by sending W. partners	Viewed by hosting CEE partners	Viewed by sending CEE partners	Viewed by hosting W. partners	Viewed by sending local director	Viewed by hosting local director
Matters of recognition, award of credits and credit transfer	7	9	17	11	5	6
Taking courses in a foreign language	14	26	11	17	7	14
Taking examination in a foreign language	10	20	14	15	9	15
Academic level of courses too high	1	2	2	8	4	10
Academic level of courses too low	6	2	1	1	5	2
Differences in teaching/learning methods (between home and host institution)	13	8	9	15	10	12
Differences in class or student project size	5	8	5	6	6	9

* Rating 1 or 2 on a scale from 1 = 'serious problem' to 5 = 'no problem'

Question 9.2.2: To what extent did your students encounter major academic problems in any of the following areas during their study period abroad?

Question 9.3.3: To what extent did the incoming students encounter major academic problems in any of the following areas during their study period abroad?

Source: 'Experiences of JEP Contractors/Coordinators/Partners in the First Phase of TEMPUS' survey

5.12   Overall Assessment

Most JEP partners considered TEMPUS important in its specific target areas, that is, improvement of educational activities, structural development and academic mobility. Asked about the importance of TEMPUS support and JEP cooperation for the development in those areas, between three-quarters and nine-tenth responded affirmatively.

Some activities were singled out as most important: specifically, provision of equipment and academic staff exchange. Staff development and student mobility were rated almost as favourably, but curriculum development, production of teaching material and short intensive courses met with a few more dissenting voices. Only mobility of administrative staff was assessed by a smaller proportion of the partners (one-third) as an important activity in the context of the development of the targeted department and institution.

As a matter of course, TEMPUS is not viewed as especially powerful as far as institutional reorganisation is concerned. About half of the respondents noted a considerable contribution to departmental reorganisation and a quarter to university reorganisation. Thus, it is also not surprising to note that the JEP partners considered their departmental colleagues' attitudes more often supportive (stated by 90 per cent of the partners from CEE countries and by 71 per cent of those from Western countries) than those of persons in charge of the university (stated by 73 per cent and 63 per cent respectively).

When asked more specifically about the impact on the departments involved from CEE countries, the improvement of equipment is named most frequently as successful. Promotion of staff exchange as well as offer of new course content are named almost as often. In comparing the ratings between partners from CEE countries and those from Western countries, the highest discrepancies occur with respect to the establishment of staff development and continuous education programmes (favourable rating: 59 per cent by CEE partners, 39 per cent by Western partners) and the introduction of new teaching methods. this kind of impact on the departments in the CEE countries is noted by 65 per cent of respondents from that area, but only by 50 per cent from Western countries.

The impacts of TEMPUS on the departments involved in JEPs are viewed as varying considerably by subject area, as Table 5.40 suggests. The impacts are rated slightly higher on average by respondents from humanities and from social sciences and more negatively by respondents from medicine and from teacher training.

Table 5.40
Impacts of the JEP Activities on the Targeted Department/Institution, by Subject Area of the JEP (per cent*)

	Hum	Soc	Man	Nat	Med	Eng	Com	Agr	Env	Arc	Art	Lan	Tea	Law	Oth	Total
Establishment of new faculties/departments	25	46	39	13	30	32	27	30	28	30	22	29	16	10	24	29
Foster international research cooperation	67	49	39	56	48	56	52	54	39	50	69	48	30	54	40	49
Changes of degree structures	40	30	35	15	17	31	26	25	17	28	35	35	18	5	23	26
Offer new course programmes	56	69	71	43	48	67	68	64	67	46	60	61	56	39	53	61
Offer new course contents/paradigms	79	72	72	58	61	77	77	73	74	70	65	74	73	59	58	71
Establishment of staff development and continuous education programmes	60	48	54	43	52	49	45	45	51	28	33	41	57	19	50	48
Introduction of new teaching methods	59	57	59	45	62	55	57	60	52	64	60	72	71	14	52	57
Reorganisation of administrative structures and procedures	21	13	9	5	12	7	13	13	3	17	22	16	15	5	18	10
Improvement of equipment e.g. computer centres, laboratories, libraries etc.	78	74	66	71	67	81	86	75	86	81	86	79	63	64	47	75

(continued)

(Table 5.40)

	Hum	Soc	Man	Nat	Med	Eng	Com	Agr	Env	Arc	Art	Lan	Tea	Law	Oth	Total
Promotion of student exchange	88	61	49	78	58	67	57	63	73	82	90	74	65	86	78	66
Promotion of staff exchange	89	67	67	70	61	73	73	65	80	83	81	71	74	74	76	71
Improvement of higher education management	14	20	21	13	16	18	15	20	14	16	15	11	23	15	33	18
Improvement of foreign language proficiency	60	44	58	48	49	56	44	65	48	50	60	67	56	67	52	54
Improvement of career prospects of students	31	50	65	53	50	57	46	56	49	73	62	64	41	70	76	56
Establishment/ improvement of cooperation with industry/commerce	15	23	46	10	21	39	31	29	24	20	26	14	8	10	20	28
Improvement of career prospects of staff	27	35	46	27	38	45	49	39	35	46	25	38	34	35	46	40

* Rating 1 or 2 on a scale from 1 = 'very high impact' to 5 = 'no impact at all'

Question 10.1: Please assess the JEPs impact on the targeted department/institution regarding the following academic and administrative aspects.

Source: 'Experiences of JEP Contractors/Coordinators/Partners in the First Phase of TEMPUS' survey

It is obvious that the TEMPUS Programme concentrates a relatively high amount of money on relatively few beneficiaries. Yet, the beneficiaries do not only observe a broad range of opportunities provided, but also experience the remaining constraints as far as a complete innovation and restructuring of higher education is concerned. The majority of partners from the East consider the TEMPUS support provided as generous. But proportions of 56 per cent considering the overall support for the JEP as generous and of 49 per cent similarly rating the support to their own unit also indicate some reservation.

The partners from Western countries assessed the overall financial support from their JEP with more caution. Only 33 per cent conceived it as generous. The overall rating is 2.9 on average on a scale from 1 = 'very generous' to 5 = 'very limited'. By far more negative were the Western partners' ratings of the TEMPUS support for their own institution. The mean rating was 3.6, and only 13 per cent observed a 'generous' support. Though they know that TEMPUS is primarily understood as support for CEE countries, many Western partners still think they should be eligible for higher support in the framework of the TEMPUS Programme.

A substantial proportion of JEP partners from CEE countries noted spin-off activities following the operation of the JEP, that is, impacts beyond the immediate target areas of the TEMPUS-supported activities undertaken within the respective JEP. For example:

- 40 per cent observed subsequent research cooperation which was neither undertaken before the JEP cooperation nor envisaged at the beginning of the cooperation.
  35 per cent reported cooperation in the area of teaching and education which was not envisaged initially. Various partners also reported that other activities promoted by TEMPUS, such as staff and student exchange, expanded beyond the scale initially striven for.
- 35 per cent reported as well that the teaching material developed in the framework of their JEP became standard in the JEP subject in the targeted country and/or was used by other institutions or departments in that country.

Thus, it does not come as a surprise to find that 32 per cent of the institutions from the CEE countries established formal partnerships with their partner institutions. In more than a quarter of the cases, additional departments were included in subsequent cooperation.

More than half of the partners from the Central and Eastern European countries expressed in summary that they were very satisfied and a further third that they were satisfied with the achievements which were gained in their Joint European Project. Only 1 per cent expressed dissatisfaction. Of the partners from Western countries, 7 per cent expressed dissatisfaction. In general, the Western partners expressed a considerably more cautious view about the achievements of TEMPUS, as Table 5.41 shows. More than half of the dissatisfied partners from the CEE countries and Western countries were involved in JEPs supported for less than three years. Those who were dissatisfied clustered somewhat in JEPs with a larger number of partners, as well as in three CEE countries.

Table 5.41
Overall Assessment of the Achievements of the JEP, by Country Group (per cent)

	CEE country	Western country	Total
Very satisfied	59	32	43
2	33	45	40
3	7	15	12
4	1	5	4
Very dissatisfied	0	2	1
Total	100	100	100
(n)	(685)	(963)	(1,648)

Question 10.10: How satisfied are you overall with the achievements which were accomplished with this JEP?
Source: 'Experiences of JEP Contractors/Coordinators/Partners in the First Phase of TEMPUS' survey

5.13 Variations of Problems and Achievements

Aiming to identify possible causes for the range and gravity of problems or for the extent to which successes were achieved with the TEMPUS support, we began looking at various parameters: how do the activities, the problems encountered and the achievements differ according to the duration of the support provided, the number and composition of the partners involved, the subject areas of the JEPs and, finally, according to the eligible countries?

5.13.1 Duration of TEMPUS Support

In the framework of TEMPUS I, the JEPs could annually re-apply for support up to three years. Actually, three-quarters of the respondents reported that their departments participated in the respective JEP for three years (or even longer), while 17 per cent participated for two years and 7 per cent only for one year. On average, the JEPs had been provided support for 2.8 years. More than two-thirds of those supported for only one or two years could have been provided support for a longer period in TEMPUS I than they were actually supported, while less than one-third had their year of first support close to the end of TEMPUS I.

It is fair to assume that more or less all of the partners liked to be awarded TEMPUS support for a period of three years, if the project worked well. Therefore, we can assume that those being supported for a shorter period, though a longer period was still part of TEMPUS I, had more problems and less achievements than those supported for three years – irrespective of, whether or not they decided to re-apply or whether their re-application was rejected. If they were as successful on average as the others, something would have been wrong with the process of self-selection or of selection for continuous support.

The data actually show that, first, those supported for a short period by TEMPUS funds participated in larger JEPs in terms of the total number of partners. The numbers of partners they actually cooperated with, however, was about average. The average number of staff and students sent abroad and received was clearly lower among the JEPs supported only for a shorter period than those supported for three or more years.

Second, the responses clearly indicate that cooperation among the partners was less intensive among those supported only for a shorter period. They had by far less often arranged prior meetings for the preparation of the first application, and a smaller proportion of them had informed their partners thoroughly about their departments, about the application and award, etc.

Third, those supported for a shorter period reported somewhat more moderate goals, fewer activities and somewhat more moderate achievements in various respects. One should bear in mind, though, that the scope of activities increased beyond those initially striven for among many of the JEPs supported for three or more years. Thus, this difference might be in part the cause of being supported for only a short period.

Fourth, we note that the proportion of respondents of JEPs supported for a shorter period observing problems in the process of pursuing the various activities promoted by TEMPUS was not higher, by and large, than among those supported for three or more years. Those supported for a shorter period were active on a smaller scale and with less ambitions, and in this framework they did not run into more serious problems, according to their own view, than others.

Altogether we note that those supported for a shorter period, not surprisingly, were less satisfied on average than those supported for three years. While of the latter 84 per cent expressed a high level of overall satisfaction (1 or 2 on a scale from 1 = 'very satisfied' to 5 = 'very dissatisfied), the respective proportion for those supported for two years was 70 per cent, and for those supported for one year 63 per cent. This shows, however, that even the majority of those not applying for or not being awarded continuous support were to some extent satisfied with the achievements and accomplishments of their TEMPUS activities.

5.13.2 Structure of Partnerships and Their Impacts

As already reported, the JEPs varied substantially according to the number of partners involved. At least three partners had to cooperate, but a substantial number of JEPs comprised more than ten partners. Actually, we noted trends towards a moderate growth of the average number of partners in the course of TEMPUS I.

The majority of JEPs comprised only one of several organisations from a single CEE country. 'Multi CEE JEPs', that is, those comprising partners from more than one CEE country, were a minority from the beginning, and their proportion declined somewhat over the years.

Our survey shows that cooperation within small departmental networks is closer than in larger ones. For example, partners involved in JEPs comprising three partners report a close cooperation with 63 per cent of the their partners on average, while those involved in JEPs comprising more than 10 partners cooperate closely only with 28 per cent of their partners. It might be added here that smaller networks in the framework of the ERASMUS Programme also tend to cooperate more closely than large ones.

By and large, we note that large JEPs harbour slightly less ambitious goals, cooperate less closely with their partners and eventually report slightly more moderate achievements. However, problems reported in pursuing the respective TEMPUS-supported activities hardly differ according to the size of the JEPs. Altogether, the data are not encouraging for the establishment of large networks.

Multi CEE JEPs, thus, could be expected to be less successful than JEPs including only a single CEE country because they are bound to be larger than three partners. In controlling for size, however, we do not note any drawbacks of regional JEPs as far as the ambitions, the processes and the perceived achievements are concerned. On the contrary, multi CEE JEPs are more favourably assessed than mono-CEE JEPs of the same size, as, for example, the overall assessment shows (see Table 5.42).

Table 5.42
Overall Assessment of the Achievements of the JEP, by Size and Configuration of the JEP (per cent)

	Size and configuration of the JEP					
	4-5 partners, mono CEE	4-5 partners, multi CEE	6-10 partners, mono CEE	6-10 partners, multi CEE	11 and more partners, mono CEE	11 and more partners, multi CEE
Very satisfied	48	60	38	44	40	42
2	38	29	43	43	40	40
3	9	10	13	8	14	14
4	3	2	4	4	5	4
Very dissatisfied	1	0	2	1	2	0
Total	100	100	100	100	100	100
(n)	(292)	(42)	(432)	(196)	(265)	(250)

Question 10.10: How satisfied are you overall with the achievements which were accomplished with this JEP?

Source: 'Experiences of JEP Contractors/Coordinators/Partners in the First Phase of TEMPUS' survey

5.13.3   Subject Area

Problems encountered and outcomes achieved do not vary consistently by subject area in all areas analysed. We tried to reduce the bewildering variety of findings by establishing an index of outcomes based on responses to 17 aspects rated by the respondents.

On average, 58 per cent of the respondents rated the various aspects positively. Thereby, the mean ratings varied only from 56 per cent to 61 per cent in most of the subjects supported in the framework of TEMPUS I. Partners of JEPs in humanities rated the achievements slightly more positively (62 per cent). For example, they reported most often that the course programmes were completely restructured, that the department was restructured in the course of reorganisation and that agreements for continuous cooperation with their partner departments were signed.

In contrast, natural science partners rated the outcomes more negatively than partners of almost all other subject areas (53 per cent). They rated the improvement of professional knowledge through staff mobility least positively, and they reported least often that a new course programme was introduced in the framework of their TEMPUS-supported cooperation. The average rating of outcomes was even lower in law (52 per cent). For example, the partners of this discipline least often reported that staff development programmes were established.

5.13.4 Variation by Eligible Country

In analysing the differences according to the CEE countries, we compared the statements made by the respondents from the CEE countries and their respective partners both regarding the problems encountered (index based on 27 items) and the outcomes (the above named index based on 17 items) they perceived. As already noted, the Western partners reported problems somewhat more frequently and rated the outcomes somewhat more cautiously.

We note that partners from most CEE countries reported between 13 and 20 per cent serious problems on average in 27 areas of potential problems analysed. Similarly, the Western partners of most of the CEE countries reported between 16 and 22 per cent serious problems. Less problems were consistently reported by respondents from Latvia (12 per cent) and their partners (14 per cent), and more problems from respondents from Lithuania and their partners (27 per cent). Bulgarian respondents reported few problems (13 per cent on average), but their respective partners did not confirm this view. The few respondents from Yugoslavia reported exceptionally few problems, while their partners from Western countries observed frequent problems.

As regards outcomes of the TEMPUS support, respondents from Estonia, Lithuania and Slovakia, and their Western partners, conceived them as quite positive. Thus, Slovakian TEMPUS-related activities are viewed as positive and as not encountering above-average problems in the process, while the problems encountered by partners from Estonia and Lithuania are viewed as more serious than those encountered in most other CEE countries.

In respect to some CEE countries, the views held by respondents from these countries and their partners from Western countries diverge. Romanian respondents consider the outcomes of their TEMPUS-related activities as clearly above average, while their Western partners view them as below average. The problems encountered in the process differ not much from the average. In the case of the view rating regarding Yugoslavia, the ratings are most divergent between the respondents from these countries on the one hand, who view both the problems encountered as small and the outcomes as positive, and, on the other, their partners, who observed many problems in the JEP-related processes and below-average outcomes. Finally, the outcomes of TEMPUS-related activities in Latvia were viewed both by the respondents from that countries and their Western partners as around-average, though both noted exceptionally few problems in the JEP-related process undertaken.

Below-average outcomes were stated both by respondents from the respective countries and their Western partners in the case of Albania, the Czech Republic, Hungary, Poland and Slovenia. In all these countries, problems encountered in the framework of TEMPUS-related activities and processes were close to average, both according to respondents from these countries and their Western partners.

Below-average outcomes in most countries already supported in the early years of TEMPUS Programmes call for explanation. We might conclude that the outcomes of TEMPUS look less striking in countries which did not face the most serious problems at the outset.

Chapter 6

The Central and Eastern European Institutions of Higher Education Participating in TEMPUS

6.1 Aims and Methods of the Survey

During its first phase, TEMPUS was a primarily department-based programme. With only a few exceptions, activities supported by TEMPUS – for example, cooperative measures in the field of education, structural development and student and staff mobility – were undertaken in the framework of networks of departments. This does not mean, however, that TEMPUS is solely linked to the departmental level of higher education. The central level, that is, decision-making, administration and infrastructural services of the higher education institution as a whole, came into play since the inauguration of the TEMPUS Programme and is intended to play an increasing role in TEMPUS II.

To become acquainted with the role the institutional management plays in the process of development and restructuring of higher education institutions in general and the links of these efforts to TEMPUS in particular, a survey was undertaken. It comprised all higher education institutions in Central and Eastern Europe represented in Joint European Projects supported during the first phase of TEMPUS. The major themes addressed in the 'Survey on the Development and Restructuring of Institutions Participating in TEMPUS' were:

- the profile of the institutions: type of institution, legal status, number of students and academic staff, number of faculties and degree programmes, subject areas offered, changes in the profile since 1990, etc.
- the managerial, administrative and infrastructural support for international contacts: respective activities at the central level, kinds of administrative or service units for international cooperation, etc.

- the involvement in TEMPUS: kind and quality of available information about the TEMPUS Programme, years of participation, TEMPUS-supported activities, knowledge about national priorities, assistance of the central level for TEMPUS activities, difficulties encountered, etc.
- impacts of the TEMPUS Programme: contribution of TEMPUS to the changes at the institution, spin-off activities from TEMPUS at the higher education institutions
- involvement in TEMPUS II: activities supported under TEMPUS II, type and degree of future educational and structural changes at the institution, intended use of TEMPUS support.

The predominantly structured questionnaire comprised 43 questions with altogether about 500 variables. As in the case of the survey on JEP coordinators, contractors and partners, the original questionnaire was developed in English and subsequently translated into German and French.

All three language versions of the questionnaire were sent to each rector (presidents, vice-chancellors, principals, etc.) of the targeted institutions in the CEE countries. The rectors were expected to contact the units and persons most suitable to answer the respective questions, since some of the questions could best be answered by persons in charge of regular administrative tasks, others by staff specialised in international relations and others by the rectors themselves.

All institutions awarded support for Joint European Projects in the framework of the TEMPUS Programme were asked to respond to the questionnaire. The first questionnaire was sent in October 1995. A reminder letter was sent in December 1995 to all institutions of higher education which had not returned the questionnaire within eight weeks.

Altogether 265 institutions were identified as possible candidates according to the award decisions and were sent a copy of each of the three language versions of the questionnaire. Actually, 6 questionnaires were returned because the addresses were invalid or the envisaged TEMPUS activities did not take place. Thus, the number of valid addresses (i.e. the population of the survey) was reduced to 259. Within 16 weeks after the first mailing, altogether 113 institutions of higher education had responded to the questionnaire. The return rate was, thus, about 44 per cent. Because of their late return, 3 questionnaires were excluded from the statistical analysis which is based on the responses of 110 institutions. Taking into account the relatively short time available for sending and collecting the questionnaires, the return rate might be considered satisfactory.

Table 6.1
Return Rate of the Survey on TEMPUS-Supported Institutions in CEE Countries

	All Institutions		Valid addresses		Respondents provided		Return rate
Country	Number	%	Number	%	Number	%	
ALB	5	1.9	5	1.9	1	0.0	20.0
BG	26	9.8	26	10.0	12	10.6	46.2
CZ	22	8.3	22	8.5	8	7.1	36.4
EE	5	1.9	5	1.9	4	3.5	80.0
H	74	27.9	71	27.4	33	29.2	46.5
LT	9	3.4	9	3.5	4	3.5	44.4
LV	10	3.8	10	3.9	7	6.2	70.0
PL	70	26.4	68	26.3	28	24.8	41.2
RO	26	9.8	26	10.0	7	6.2	26.9
SK	14	5.3	14	5.4	8	7.1	57.1
SLO	4	1.5	3	1.2	1	0.9	33.3
Total	265	100.0	259	100.0	113	100.0	43.6

As Table 6.1 shows, the distribution of respondents by country differed considerably from that of all TEMPUS-supported higher education institutions in Central and Eastern Europe. The return rates ranged from 80 per cent of Estonian institutions to 20 per cent (one out of five) of Albanian institutions.

It should be noted that the tables do not provide distinct information on responding institutions from Albania and Slovenia because information on individual institutions would neither be justifiable in respect to data protection nor allow any statistical analysis. The two respective institutions, however, are included in the data set.

6.2   The Profile of the Participating Institutions

All TEMPUS-supported institutions of higher education in the Central and Eastern European countries responding to the survey are public institutions. As shown in Chapter 5, all respondents to the JEP partner survey from CEE countries were also from public institutions of higher education (or from institutions outside the higher education sector which is not addressed in this survey).

Most institutions of higher education included in the survey are supervised by a Ministry of Education, a Ministry of Higher Education, etc. Only 12 per cent are under the legal authority of specialised ministries (for agriculture, health, etc.), while 2 per cent are linked to other authorities.

Of the institutions included in the institutional survey, 46 per cent are universities and 34 per cent are specialised institutions of higher education on university level. Non-university institutions of higher education – 20 per cent of the institutions included in this survey – were strongly represented among respondents from Hungary.

Fifty-seven per cent of the institutions provided study opportunities both in the humanities and social sciences as well as in science and engineering. Sixteen per cent were specialised in humanities and social science areas, while 27 per cent provided study opportunities only in science and engineering fields. In all countries, the majority of university-level institutions were active in both major disciplinary areas, as Table 6.2 shows.

More than half of the TEMPUS-supported institutions of higher education in the Central and Eastern European countries responding to this survey provided study opportunities in business and management sciences (53 per cent). Teacher training (45 per cent), computer sciences (44 per cent) and engineering (39 per cent) were represented at many institutions as well. Other major disciplinary groups ranged from 13 per cent (law) to 30 per cent (natural sciences).

Twenty-eight per cent of the institutions of higher education were located in the capital of the respective country; also, the majority of higher education institutions located outside the capitals were not the only institutions of higher education in their respective town – 76 per cent of the respondents had other higher education institutions (on average nine) in their respective town.

The average size of the higher education institutions in the Central and Eastern European Countries has grown over the last few years. With an

Table 6.2
Subject Areas of Course Programmes Offered, by CEE Countries (absolute numbers of institutions)

Objectives of JEPs	BG	CZ	EE	H	LT	LV	PL	RO	SK	Other	Total
Humanities/social sc./ natural sc./engineering	7	5	4	11	2	3	14	3	4	2	55
Only human./social sc.	1	1	0	8	0	2	3	0	1	0	16
Only natural sc./engineering	2	1	0	11	2	0	8	1	1	0	26
Total	10	7	4	30	4	5	25	4	6	2	97

Question 1.9: Please state the actual number of degree programmes (excluding advanced/doctoral programmes) at your higher education institution within the disciplines mentioned below.

Source: Survey on the development and restructuring of institutions participating in TEMPUS

average number of almost 5,800 students in the TEMPUS-supported institutions responding in 1995, their size was not as much lower than the
average number of ERASMUS and LINGUA-supported institutions of
higher education in Western Europe (almost 6,900 students according to a
survey undertaken in 1994) .[1] As Table 6.3 shows:

- TEMPUS-supported universities comprised on average seven faculties
  in 1995, and they offered more than 30 degree programmes. The mean
  number of academic staff was close to 700, and they served on average
  about 7,900 students (including part-time and distance students).

- Specialised university-level institutions of higher education had on
  average almost five faculties and more than 15 degree programmes.
  The average number of academic staff was about 600 and the number
  of students about 4,500.

- The non-university higher education institutions comprised on average
  about five faculties and about 10 degree programmes. The average
  number of academic staff was about 140 and that of students about
  2,800.

Table 6.3
Size of TEMPUS-Supported Institutions of Higher Education 1995,
by Type of Institution (per cent and mean)

	Type of higher education institution			Total
	University	Specialised university-type institution	Other higher education institution	
Number of faculties				
1	4	8	16	8
2	8	19	11	13
3	10	14	21	13
4-5	19	32	37	27
6-10	38	16	5	24
11 and more	21	11	11	15
Total	100	100	100	100
(n)	(48)	(37)	(19)	(104)
Mean	7.0	4.9	5.0	5.9

(continued)

1   See Maiworm, F.; Sosa, W. and Teichler, U. (1996) *The Context of ERAS-
MUS: A Survey of Institutional Management and Infrastructure in Support of
Mobility and Cooperation.* Kassel.

(Table 6.3)	Type of higher education institution			Total
	University	Specialised university-type institution	Other higher education institution	
Number of academic staff				
Up to 100	6	18	55	20
101 - 250	13	18	30	18
251 - 500	28	26	15	25
501 - 1000	32	24	0	23
1001 and more	21	15	0	15
Total	100	100	100	100
(n)	(47)	(34)	(20)	(101)
Mean	694	606	137	554
Overall number of students in 1995				
Up to 1,000	10	19	42	19
1,001 - 2,500	21	38	16	26
2,501 - 5,000	21	19	37	24
5,001 - 10,000	38	19	0	24
More than 10,000	10	6	5	8
Total	100	100	100	100
(n)	(42)	(32)	(19)	(93)
Mean	5,489	3,939	2,392	4,323
Mean number of students in 1995				
Full-time students	6,489	3,607	1,291	4,518
Part-time/evening students	1,074	504	1,292	927
Distance students	337	383	263	338
(n)	(51)	(36)	(21)	(108)

Question 1.8: What was the number of faculties existing at your higher education institution in 1990 and how many faculties does your institution have currently?

Question 1.7: Could you please state (estimate) the number of students and academic staff at your higher education institution in the year 1990 and currently.

Source: Survey on the development and restructuring of institutions participating in TEMPUS

In 1990/91 and 1991/92, many relatively large institutions of higher education were recipients of TEMPUS grants. In contrast, the size of most institutions receiving TEMPUS support for the first time in 1992/93 or later was considerably smaller on average.

6.3 Recent Changes and Reforms

Most TEMPUS-supported institutions of higher education in the CEE countries experienced a considerable growth between 1990 and 1995. The number of full-time students increased by more than 50 per cent and the number of part-time students and of distance students even more. Similarly, the number of faculties increased by almost 50 per cent, while the increase of academic staff was only moderate, with somewhat more than 20 per cent. The growth was most pronounced in universities and only moderate at other university-level institutions as well as at non-university institutions of higher education.

At almost all institutions, the faculty and departmental structure was revised (see Table 6.4):

- Faculties were newly founded at 73 per cent and departments at 89 per cent of the institutions of higher education included in the survey. About half of the restructuring undertaken aimed at accommodating new fields, but divisions and mergers were almost as frequent. Only 5 per cent of institutions took over faculties from other institutions through re-allocation or institutional merger.

- Faculties were abolished at 20 per cent and departments at 48 per cent of the institutions of higher education surveyed. However, only a single institution of higher education reported a closure of a whole faculty and 15 per cent a closure of departments. A re-allocation of individual fields within departments or within faculties, however, had been undertaken at more than a third of the institutions surveyed.

Among the degree programmes existing at TEMPUS-supported institutions of higher education in 1995, about 40 per cent had been newly established during the last five years. As demonstrated in Table 6.5, almost 30 per cent changed substantially during that period, and only slightly more than 30 per cent remained unchanged.

As regards fields of study, we note that about three-quarters of the degree programmes in business studies (75 per cent) and law (74 per cent) had been newly established. The same holds true for more than half of the degree programmes in social sciences, computer sciences and humanities,

Table 6.4
Type of Structural Change at Institutions of Higher Education, by CEE Countries (per cent, multiple reply possible)

	BG	CZ	EE	H	LT	LV	PL	RO	SK	Other	Total
Establishment of new faculties	75	75	100	67	100	83	59	100	86	50	73
Abolition of existing faculties	17	0	50	9	50	50	26	14	29	0	20
Establishment of new departments	92	88	100	82	100	100	85	100	100	100	89
Abolition of existing departments	58	75	50	36	100	50	33	43	71	100	48
Not ticked	0	0	0	9	0	0	4	0	0	0	4
Total	242	238	300	203	350	283	207	257	286	250	234
(n)	(12)	(8)	(4)	(33)	(4)	(6)	(27)	(7)	(7)	(2)	(110)

Question 1.10: Which of the following structural changes have taken place at your higher education institution since 1990?

Source: Survey on the development and restructuring of institutions participating in TEMPUS

Table 6.5
Change of Degree Programmes at TEMPUS-Supported Institutions of Higher Education in CEE since 1990

	Subjects offered		Proportion of institutions providing programmes in the respective field			Proportion of degree programmes		
	Prop. of institutions providing respective field	Average number of degree progr. per institution	Proportion of institutions establishing new progr. since 1990	Proportion of institutions changing programmes substantially	Proportion of institutions keeping progr. without subst. changes	Proportion of degree progr. newly established since 1990	Proportion of degree programmes subst. changed since 1990	Proportion of degree progr. not subst. changed since 1990
Agricultural sciences	23.5	8.5	78.3	39.1	43.5	49.1	25.6	25.3
Architecture, urban and regional planning	18.4	1.8	50.0	33.3	38.9	38.6	30.6	30.8
Art and design/music	19.4	6.1	73.7	26.3	42.1	48.9	22.1	29.0
Business studies/ management sciences	53.1	4.9	84.6	19.2	17.3	74.7	16.1	9.1
Education/teacher training	44.9	8.5	56.8	31.8	47.7	36.0	26.2	37.8
Engineering, technology	38.8	10.1	73.7	36.8	55.3	38.4	26.8	34.7
Humanities, philological sc.	23.5	7.1	73.9	26.1	34.8	54.8	22.1	23.1
Informatics, computer sc.	43.9	2.0	62.8	23.3	30.2	56.6	19.8	23.6
Languages	24.5	6.3	70.8	20.8	45.8	48.5	15.6	35.8
Law	13.3	2.0	84.6	23.1	15.4	74.4	17.9	7.7
Medical sciences	19.4	12.9	47.4	31.6	57.9	26.4	28.2	45.4
Natural sciences, mathematics	29.6	6.2	72.4	31.0	44.8	48.0	21.9	30.1
Social sciences	20.4	7.3	75.0	30.0	25.0	61.1	25.7	13.3
Other areas of studies	17.3	3.0	58.8	17.6	41.2	49.8	15.3	34.9

Question 1.9: Please state the actual number of degree programmes (excluding advanced/doctoral programmes) at your higher education institution within the disciplines mentioned below. Please state also how many of these programmes are newly established since 1990 and how many programmes are still being offered without substantial changes in terms of structure and content.

as well as for about half of the degree programmes in agriculture, fine arts, languages and natural sciences. A mixture of new establishment, substantial change and continuation without substantial change was characteristic for architecture, education and teacher training as well as for engineering. Continuation of degree programmes without substantial curricular change was most frequent in medical sciences. But even in medicine, we note that 47 per cent of the institutions of higher education providing medical education established of at least one new programme, and 32 per cent introduced substantial curricular change of at least one medical degree programme.

6.4 Involvement in TEMPUS

Of the institutions included in the survey 39 per cent received TEMPUS support in 1990/91 (i.e. in the first year of the TEMPUS Programme). 34 per cent were granted support for the first time in the second year of TEMPUS (i.e. 1991/92), 19 per cent received a first grant in 1992/93 and 8 per cent even later. Actually, more than half of the institutions were granted support in the first year of their eligibility for TEMPUS support.

On average the responding institutions were involved in seven JEPs. However, 42 per cent were involved in five JEPs at most, 31 per cent in six to ten projects, and 27 per cent in more than ten projects.

Of the institutions of higher education from the Central and Eastern European Countries responding to this survey, 98 per cent were beneficiaries of TEMPUS grants in the framework of Joint European Projects; 83 per cent sent or received persons supported in the framework of Individual Mobility Grants, and 30 per cent were involved in Complementary Measures.

A substantial proportion of the institutions of higher education in Central and Eastern Europe were recipients of TEMPUS grants in more than one JEP or other activities. This also explains why most institutions report TEMPUS support for a longer period than that typically granted to JEPs (see Table 6.6).

It is worth noting that 86 per cent of the institutions surveyed reported that they cooperated with other institutions of higher education of their respective country in TEMPUS projects. In fact, all institutions reporting an enrolment of more than 5,000 full-time students were involved in such cooperation within their country.

Table 6.6
Years of Involvement in TEMPUS, by First Year of Participation in TEMPUS (per cent and mean)

		Year of first participation					Total
	1990/91	1991/92		1992/93		1993/94	
		Previously eligible	Newly eligible	Previously eligible	Newly eligible	and later	
1	13	19	6	10	0	44	14
2	0	5	6	0	0	22	4
3	3	19	0	40	0	33	11
4	5	5	6	50	100	0	19
5	5	52	82	0	0	0	25
6	74	0	0	0	0	0	27
Total	100	100	100	100	100	100	100
(n)	(39)	(21)	(17)	(10)	(11)	(9)	(107)
Mean	5.1	3.7	4.5	3.3	4.0	1.9	4.2

Question 3.1: In which academic years did/does your higher education institution participate in the TEMPUS Programme?

Source: Survey on the development and restructuring of institutions participating in TEMPUS

6.5 Perceived Contribution of TEMPUS to Innovation

Almost all respondents of the institutional survey were convinced that TEMPUS has significantly contributed to changes at their institution since 1990. As Table 6.7 shows, more than two-thirds noted a substantial contribution of the TEMPUS to the establishment of international contacts, and to the increase of staff exchange.

More than half of the respondents each perceived a substantial contribution of TEMPUS to change in its other prime target areas:

• the improvement of equipment
• the introduction of new teaching methods
• the establishment of new course programmes

- the increase of student exchange
- the introduction of new course contents and paradigms.

Staff development was named as a substantial contribution by only about one-third of the respondents (i.e. not more frequently than the establishment of international research cooperation). A substantial contribution to the reorganisation of course programmes or of the faculty and departmental structure was only noted by about a quarter of the respondents each, and very few stated a substantial impact of TEMPUS on administrative procedures, the management of the higher education institutions or on links between higher education and industry.

As readiness for change and barriers to change might differ in the various areas directly or indirectly addressed by the TEMPUS Programme, the questionnaire also referred to the degree of change actually realised in those areas. The respective responses confirm, as Table 6.7 shows, that TEMPUS contributed substantially in most cases to change occurring in international cooperation and exchange and improvement of equipment, as well as content and methods of teaching. It played a substantial role less frequently, though, in structural and administrative changes.

Table 6.7 also indicates that substantial changes of various kinds were more often reported by institutions involved in a large number of Joint European Programmes. Similarly, spin-offs (i.e. effects beyond the targeted areas) were more impressive at institutions involved in a substantial number of JEPs. On the basis of these finding, one could not exclude the assumption that the ratings of 'substantial change' just reflect the visibility of large absolute numbers of staff exchange, student exchange, cooperation contracts, etc., but do not really indicate a larger extent of change of the overall institution. However, in response to another question referred to below, the respondents from institutions involved in large numbers of JEPs in fact perceived on average a stronger TEMPUS impact on the overall changes at their institutions than the respondents from institutions involved in smaller numbers of JEPs.

Most respondents came to the conclusion that faculties and departments at institutions of higher education in the Central and Eastern European countries involved in TEMPUS were not only more active than others in staff and student exchange as well as in improving their equipment, but also in the introduction of new course contents and of new teaching methods. About two-thirds regarded them also as more active in changes of the degree structure, staff development and research cooperation. In

Table 6.7
Perceived Contribution of TEMPUS to the Change at Institutions of Higher Education in Central and Eastern Europe, by Number of JEPs (per cent of institutions)

	Substantial contribution of TEMPUS to change* Number of JEPs					Substantial changes occurring** Number of JEPs				
	1-2	3-5	6-10	11 and more	Total	1-2	3-5	6-10	11 and more	Total
Establishment of international academic contacts	56	64	71	82	70	76	76	88	86	83
Increase of staff exchange	63	52	68	90	69	67	44	82	72	68
Improvement of equipment e.g. computer centres, laboratories, libraries etc.	61	63	62	69	64	76	72	82	79	78
Introduction of new teaching methods	56	44	55	82	60	53	48	45	59	51
Establishment of new course programmes	50	43	70	64	59	75	68	76	67	71
Increase of student exchange	47	44	53	83	58	63	44	55	83	61
Introduction of new contents/paradigms	57	60	52	61	57	62	72	55	74	66
Establishment of international research cooperation	33	29	30	43	34	50	38	43	64	49

(continued)

(Table 6.7)

	Substantial contribution of TEMPUS to change* Number of JEPs					Substantial changes occurring** Number of JEPs				
	1-2	3-5	6-10	11 and more	Total	1-2	3-5	6-10	11 and more	Total
Reorganisation of staff development and continuous education programmes	38	26	27	42	33	38	42	23	35	33
Establishment of new faculties/departments	29	17	29	35	27	56	52	57	59	56
Changes of the degree structures	18	29	25	24	25	43	57	30	42	42
Reorganisation of higher education management	0	15	9	17	11	13	14	25	38	24
Establishment of cooperation between institution and industry/commerce	8	16	10	8	10	21	11	16	16	16
Establishment of technology transfer units or centres	9	0	11	14	9	29	5	29	13	19
Reorganisation of administrative structures and procedures	8	9	0	14	7	7	26	27	22	23

* Percentage of respondents stating 1 or 2 on a scale from 1 = 'very substantial changes' to 5 = 'no changes at all' among all responding to the respective area

** Percentage of respondents stating 1 or 2 on a scale from 1 = 'very substantial contribution' to 5 = 'no changes at all' among all responding to the respective area

Question 3.5: Please rate the extent to which changes occurred since about 1990 at your higher education institution in the following areas and the extent to which TEMPUS activities contributed to these changes:

Source: Survey on the development and restructuring of institutions participating in TEMPUS

Table 6.8
Proportion of Institutions of Higher Education in CEE Countries Experiencing more Change-Oriented Activities at TEMPUS-supported than at other Faculties and Departments, by First Year of Participation in TEMPUS (per cent)

		Year of first participation					Total
	1990/91	1991/92		1992/93		1993/94 and later	
		Previously eligible	Newly eligible	Previously eligible	Newly eligible		
Introduction of new course contents/paradigms	94	82	100	78	91	100	92
Establishment of new course programmes	91	82	100	89	91	100	92
Establishment of international academic contacts	97	85	88	89	91	80	91
Improvement of equipment e.g. computer centres, laboratories, libraries etc.	94	92	88	89	91	60	90
Increase of staff exchange	94	75	88	78	82	100	87
Increase of student exchange	91	100	75	50	64	60	80
Introduction of new teaching methods	82	92	86	78	64	40	79
Establishment of staff development and continuous education programmes	65	50	67	67	91	75	67
Changes of the degree structure	67	64	67	43	73	60	64
Establishment of international research cooperation	69	73	63	44	55	75	64
Reorganisation of administrative structures/procedures	40	50	36	33	20	50	38
Reorganisation of cooperation with industry	26	33	55	14	38	60	34
Total	100	100	100	100	100	100	100
(n)	(27)	(9)	(11)	(7)	(8)	(5)	(67)

Question 3.6: Do you think that faculties/departments involved in TEMPUS activities are more active than those without TEMPUS activities regarding the following aspects?

Source: Survey on the development and restructuring of institutions participating in TEMPUS

contrast, as Table 6.8 shows, only a minority of respondents considered TEMPUS-supported departments as active above average in administrative reorganisation and in cooperation with industry.

Innovations may surpass the areas and the institutional frame directly addressed by a support programme. In a response to a question regarding the 'spin-off' activities (i.e. effects of TEMPUS beyond its immediate target areas), 60 per cent of the respondents pointed out that formal partnership agreements were signed with partner institutions. At 18 per cent of the institutions, a unit for international activities was established as a consequence of involvement in TEMPUS, and foreign language training was introduced at 34 per cent of the institutions. As one might expect, involvement in TEMPUS also stimulated the introduction of systems aimed to ensure recognition of study periods abroad as well as staff training for departments not directly involved in TEMPUS.

The educational spin-offs beyond the respective institution of higher education were most impressive, as Table 6.9 shows: 51 per cent reported that teaching material developed in TEMPUS projects had become standard in the respective country, and 33 per cent stated that course programmes developed at their institution were adopted by other institutions in the respective country.

The overall impact of TEMPUS on the changes that took place at the institutions of higher education was rated more cautiously. Actually, 50 per cent stating a strong general impact of TEMPUS (ratings of 1 or 2 on a scale from 1 = 'very strong impact' to 5 = 'very limited impact'; see Table 6.10).

The larger the institution in terms of student enrolment, the more spin-offs were reported and the higher the impact of TEMPUS was rated on the overall changes of the institution. This finding is extraordinarily surprising. For a programme directed primarily towards departmental cooperation and providing support for only a small proportion of the overall number of departments, it is more likely to make a strong difference to small institutions, because any support at a small institution affects by definition a relatively larger proportion of its units and activities. In a corresponding survey of institutions of higher education involved in ERASMUS, for example, we note in fact that the proportion of small institutions involved in ERASMUS is limited, but those involved are more strongly affected by this involvement.[2]

---

2 See Maiworm, F.; Sosa, W. and Teichler, U. (1996) *The Context of ERASMUS: A Survey of Institutional Management and Infrastructure in Support of Mobility and Cooperation.* Kassel. pp. 130 – 131.

Table 6.9
Spin-off Activities from the TEMPUS Activities at the Higher Education Institution, by Number of Full-Time Students (per cent, multiple reply possible)

	Full time students 1995				Total
	Up to 1000	1001 - 2500	2501 - 5000	more than 5000	
Formal partnership agreements with the partner institution(s)	46	59	48	83	60
Teaching material developed in TEMPUS projects became a standard in the country	46	55	48	57	51
Establishment of special units/ courses for language training	27	23	31	50	34
Courses/course programmes developed were adopted by other institution(s) in the country	38	32	38	27	34
Introduction of a system for recognition of study periods abroad	27	23	38	37	32
Provision of training courses for staff members from departments/ institutions not involved in TEMPUS	23	36	28	33	30
Establishment of special unit/office responsible for international activities	8	23	21	43	24
Membership of department/ institution in international networks	12	9	17	33	19
Establishment of inter-library loans services	12	14	14	7	11
Other	0	0	3	3	2
Not ticked	12	5	3	3	6
Total	250	277	290	377	302
(n)	(26)	(22)	(29)	(30)	(107)

Question 3.17: Are there any spin-off activities from the TEMPUS activities at your higher education institution?

Source: Survey on the development and restructuring of institutions participating in TEMPUS

Table 6.10

Impact of TEMPUS Activities on the Changes at the Higher Education Institutions, by Number of Full-Time Students (per cent and mean)

	Full time students 1995				Total
	Up to 1000	1001 - 2500	2501 - 5000	more than 5000	
Very strong impact	8	14	25	33	21
2	24	32	29	37	30
3	44	41	36	23	35
4	12	14	11	7	10
Very limited impact	12	0	0	0	3
Total	100	100	100	100	100
(n)	(25)	(22)	(28)	(30)	(105)
Mean	3.0	2.5	2.3	2.0	2.4

Question 3.18: How do you rate in general the impact of TEMPUS activities in the framework of the changes that have taken place in your higher education institution during the last years?

Source: Survey on the development and restructuring of institutions participating in TEMPUS

The finding that stronger impacts of TEMPUS are noted at institutions of higher education comprising large numbers of students than at those comprising small numbers of students can be in part explained by the fact that many of the large institutions were already supported by TEMPUS in its year of inauguration, and the initial effects seem to have been the most impressive ones. In addition, however, institutions with large numbers of students are more likely to be involved in a larger number of JEPs, and the cumulation of JEPs, in the view of the respondents from the central level of the higher education institutions, seems to contribute to stronger impacts.

6.6 The Role of the Central Level of the Institutions

Higher education experts agree that faculties and departments at institutions of higher education in Central and Eastern Europe tend to have more formal competencies and actually more power in shaping the inner life of higher education institutions than their counterparts in Western Europe. Respondents, therefore, were asked to rate the role of the central level of the institution in contrast to the role of faculties and department in general, as far as introduction of change is concerned, before specific questions addressed TEMPUS-related activities.

As Table 6.11 shows, the respondents, possibly rectors and their staff, perceived the role of the central level quite similarly to how central level actors are likely to do in Western Europe. At TEMPUS-supported institutions, the central level of the institutions seems to have, both formally and in practice, a major say in the management structure and the administrative procedures of the institution, in the establishment of faculties and in changes of the degree structures. On average, there is neither a clear dominance of the central level nor of the faculty level in technology transfer, the establishment of international academic contacts and in the reorganisation of staff development. As one might expect, the faculties and departments dominate the scene as far as the establishment of course programmes, changes of curricula and teaching methods as well as research activities are concerned.

The roles played by the central level and the faculties might be influenced by many factors, among others by the size of the institution and specific institutional cultures of the individual institutions. It is obvious, as well, that different practices have been cultivated in the various Central and Eastern European countries over the years – practices which did not change overnight during the 1990s. The most centralised approaches could be observed in the Baltic States, while a strong role of the faculties was most obvious in Poland and Romania.

The central level might play a substantial role in TEMPUS because most international offices and other units specifically in charge of support for international activities tend to be located at this level. As Table 6.12 shows, 76 per cent of the respondents reported that their institution has established one or more units specifically in charge of international activities. In fact:

- 64 per cent of the institutions included in the survey had an international office at the central level of the institution
- 22 per cent had specialised units at the central level (mostly language centres, additionally a few centres for the support of international networks)
- 16 per cent had units in charge of international activities at faculty level (mostly for the support of mobile staff and students)

Table 6.11
Formal Involvement and Role of the Central and Departmental Level and Role of the Central and Departmental Level in Development and Restructuring of the Institution of Higher Education (per cent)

	Formally involved		Dominant role			Total
	Central level	Departm. level	Central level*	Balanced	Departm. level**	
Establishment of new faculties/departments	85	35	71	11	18	100
Changes of the degree structure	65	36	48	24	28	100
Establishment of new course programmes	41	72	14	20	66	100
Introduction of new course contents/paradigms	14	84	4	10	86	100
Introduction of new teaching methods	12	87	4	11	85	100
Reorganisation of staff development and cont. education programmes	51	55	27	27	47	100
Establishment of international academic contacts	71	65	27	30	43	100
Establishment of international research cooperation	45	75	16	19	65	100
Participation in international exchange programmes	56	72	23	24	52	100
Reorganisation of administrative structures/procedures at institution	82	25	69	16	14	100
Improvement of equipment, e.g. computers, labs, libraries etc.	53	75	24	33	42	100
Organisation of regular cooperation with industry	36	66	14	29	57	100
Establishment of technology transfer units/centres	49	36	46	17	37	100

*   Percentage of respondents stating 1 or 2 on a scale from 1 = 'central level dominant' to 5 = 'departmental/faculty level dominant' among all responding to the respective area

** Percentage of respondents stating 4 or 5 on a scale from 1 = 'central level dominant' to 5 = 'departmental/faculty level dominant' among all responding to the respective area

Question 1.11: Are the central level (i.e. rector, senate, central administration etc.), the faculties/departments or both officially involved in decisions regarding the following activities? Which institutional level is currently playing the dominant role in introducing change in the respective areas?

Source: Survey on the development and restructuring of institutions participating in TEMPUS

- 7 per cent had joint international offices with other institutions of higher education
- 4 per cent had other arrangements.

The respondents estimated that the international offices at the central level spend more than a quarter of their time on TEMPUS-related activities. The respective proportion at the international offices at faculty-level is about half of the time.

International offices at the institutions surveyed typically comprise two or three professional and one or two secretarial staff. The few units at faculty level are somewhat larger on average. The language centres report an average of more than 20 professional and about 5 secretarial staff.

Asked about activities undertaken by the central level of the TEMPUS-supported higher education institutions in Central and Eastern Europe to build up international contacts:

- 82 per cent reported that the central level encourages and possibly supports the participation of staff members in international meetings
- at 79 per cent of the institutions surveyed, conferences with international participation were initiated by the central level
- at 79 per cent of the institutions, one or several persons were appointed to initiate and foster international contacts at the central level
- at 63 per cent of the institutions surveyed representatives of the central level themselves participated in international meetings.

Asked about the kind of assistance the central level of the institutions of higher education in CEE countries provided for TEMPUS-related activities, the majority, though by far not all of the representatives of the institutions surveyed, named various kinds of procedural support for the participation in the TEMPUS Programme:

- 67 per cent named support regarding the preparation of applications for TEMPUS projects
- 56 per cent regarding administrative assistance
- 53 per cent financial administration of TEMPUS money.

The central level less frequently provided considerable resources for carrying out TEMPUS-related activities:

- 36 per cent reported the assignment of special staff for managing TEMPUS activities
- 23 per cent financial contributions to TEMPUS activities
- 8 per cent a reduction of the teaching load of staff involved in TEMPUS activities.

Table 6.12
Type of Units Specifically in Charge of International Activities, by CEE Countries (per cent, multiple reply possible)

	BG	CZ	EE	H	LT	LV	PL	RO	SK	Other	Total
Central unit for international affairs	83	50	75	52	100	50	77	57	57	0	64
Specialised central units	17	13	75	10	0	33	38	14	29	0	22
Units on faculty/departmental level	17	50	25	13	25	17	8	0	29	0	16
Joint units with other HEI	0	25	0	3	0	17	12	0	0	0	7
Other units in charge of international activities	0	0	25	10	0	0	0	0	0	0	4
No unit established	0	13	25	35	0	33	12	43	43	100	24
Not specified	17	25	0	3	0	0	8	0	0	0	7
Total	133	175	225	126	125	150	154	114	157	100	143
(n)	(12)	(8)	(4)	(31)	(4)	(6)	(26)	(7)	(7)	(2)	(107)

Question 1.14: Please describe the units specifically in charge of international activities.

Source: Survey on the development and restructuring of institutions participating in TEMPUS

Table 6.13

Assistance Provided by the Central Level to TEMPUS-Related Activities, by Centralisation of Change (per cent, multiple reply possible)

	Dominant role			Total
	Central level	Balanced	Departm. level	
Support regarding the preparation of applications for TEMPUS projects	70	68	67	68
Use of prestige/contacts of the institution	63	45	23	44
Assignment of special staff for managing TEMPUS activities	50	30	33	37
Administrative/secretarial assistance	63	65	40	57
Reduction of teaching load for staff involved in TEMPUS activities	13	5	7	8
Financial administration of TEMPUS money	57	55	47	53
Financial contributions for TEMPUS activities	20	30	17	23
Acquisition of additional financial resources from external national sources	10	20	13	15
Acquisition of additional financial resources from international sources	10	10	0	7
Acting as mediator between JEP partners and higher level authorities	57	43	30	43
Administrative support concerning staff/student exchanges	80	73	60	71
Providing incoming staff/students with accommodation	77	65	47	63
Organisation of TEMPUS related meetings/conferences	57	45	53	51
Other forms of support	0	0	3	1
No assistance provided	0	0	7	2
Not ticked	0	0	0	0
Total	627	553	447	543
(n)	(30)	(40)	(30)	(100)

Question 3.7: What kind of assistance does the central level of your higher education institution offer to the various TEMPUS activities within the institution?

Source: Survey on the development and restructuring of institutions participating in TEMPUS

Some respondents also noted a role of the central level of the institution in supra-institutional contacts and negotiations:

- 43 per cent noted the use of the institutional prestige and contacts
- 41 per cent acted as mediators between JEP partners and higher level authorities
- 14 per cent helped with the acquisition of additional financial means from external national sources
- 7 per cent assisted with the acquisition of additional financial means from international sources.

Finally, the central level of many of the institutions was active in providing services linked to specific TEMPUS-related activities:

- 71 per cent provided administrative support concerning staff and student exchange
- 63 per cent provided accommodation to incoming staff and students
- 50 per cent organised TEMPUS-related meetings.

As one might expect, a higher proportion of the institutions of higher education located in the capital played a role in establishing and supporting supra-institutional contacts. In contrast, the central level of institutions located at other places was more often ready to provide personal and financial resources to support the TEMPUS-related activities.

Table 6.13 suggests that in institutions of higher education at which the central level plays a relatively strong role in introducing change (the index measure is based on the findings presented in Table 6.11), the central level also provides more assistance to TEMPUS-related activities than institutions at which the faculties and departments are regarded by the respondents as the major agents of change. This relationship, which does not come as a surprise, does not hold true for all activities: Institutions with a strong change-stimulating central level are not more likely to provide financial assistance for TEMPUS-related activities than the more decentralised ones.

The strong importance the institutions of higher education also placed on TEMPUS-related activities at the central institutional level was clearly expressed in responses to a question related to overall development strategies of the institutions: 45 per cent stated that all TEMPUS projects, and 40 per cent that some TEMPUS projects were integrated into an overall institutional development strategy. Only at 6 per cent of the institutions, did TEMPUS activities not play any role in the institutional development strategy, and 9 per cent stated that they did not have any overall development strategy.

Table 6.14

Integration of the TEMPUS Projects into the Overall Institutional Development Strategy, by CEE Countries
(per cent)

	BG	CZ	EE	H	LT	LV	PL	RO	SK	Other	Total
All TEMPUS projects	42	29	50	36	75	67	38	86	43	50	44
Some TEMPUS projects	50	57	0	48	0	0	46	14	43	0	39
None	8	14	50	15	25	33	15	0	14	50	17
Total	100	100	100	100	100	100	100	100	100	100	100
(n)	(12)	(7)	(4)	(33)	(4)	(6)	(26)	(7)	(7)	(2)	(108)

Question 3.14: Are the TEMPUS projects at your higher education institution integrated into the overall institutional development strategy?

Source: Survey on the development and restructuring of institutions participating in TEMPUS

At more than half of the institutions of higher education, the central level – according to the responses – made suggestions regarding the objectives of TEMPUS-related activities. At more than one-third of the institutions, the central level initiated applications for TEMPUS projects. At some institutions, the central level played a stronger role in the actual TEMPUS activities: at one-seventh of the institutions, the objectives were determined by the central level, and at one-tenth of the institutions confirmation of some applications for TEMPUS projects by means of endorsement letters was refused by the central level. By and large, the central level of higher education institutions claimed to play more often a pro-active or determining role in those countries which became TEMPUS partner countries at a later stage than in countries becoming partners in the first and second year of the TEMPUS Programme (see Table 6.14).

According to the respondents at the central level, TEMPUS-related activities rarely encountered difficulties as far the decision-making at the central level of the higher education institution is concerned. Actually, only 3 per cent reported difficulties regarding the allocation and use of TEMPUS-supported equipment; 5 per cent noted difficulties of the central level regarding the adoption of developed teaching material, and 8 per cent regarding the adoption of new courses or even whole course programmes. A somewhat higher proportion (15 per cent) noted difficulties at the central level when decisions were at stake regarding the provision of institutional resources for the support of TEMPUS activities.

In general, a substantial number of the respondents noted difficulties as far as the provision of resources for TEMPUS activities on the part of the higher education institutions were concerned:

- 53 per cent in terms of covering costs not borne by TEMPUS funds,
- 30 per cent in terms of prefinancing TEMPUS activities because the receipt of TEMPUS funds was delayed,
- 22 per cent regarding costs for maintenance, spare parts, etc. of the equipment, and
- 22 per cent covering the workload of staff involved in TEMPUS activities or mobile staff.

Most of these difficulties were named slightly less often by representatives from institutions of higher education which were beneficiaries of TEMPUS grants for the first time in 1992/93 or later (see Table 6.15). Again, we have to bear in mind that those underscoring the above named difficulties are over-proportionally from relatively large institutions with a relatively large number of JEPs. We cannot exclude the possibility that the absolute number of cases to be dealt with might increase the awareness both regarding the achievements on the one hand and the problems experienced on the other.

Table 6.15
Difficulties Regarding Decisions at The Central Level, by Year of First Participation in TEMPUS (per cent*)

		Year of first participation					Total
	1990/91	1991/92		1992/93		1993/94 and later	
		Previously eligible	Newly eligible	Previously eligible	Newly eligible		
Adoption of new courses/course programmes	7	11	13	0	0	17	8
Adoption of newly developed teaching material	9	6	0	0	0	20	6
Allocation and use of equipment acquired with TEMPUS funds	6	0	0	0	0	17	3
Decision-making regarding the provision of institutional resources	17	13	8	0	25	33	15
(n)	(24)	(15)	(13)	(8)	(8)	(6)	(74)

* Percentage of respondents stating 1 or 2 on a scale from 1 = 'serious difficulties' to 5 = 'no difficulties at all'

Question 3.8: To what extent did you perceive difficulties regarding decisions at the central level of your higher education institution on the following aspects of TEMPUS activities?

Source: Survey on the development and restructuring of institutions participating in TEMPUS

An analysis of the relationships between the role played by the central level of the higher education institutions and the impacts of TEMPUS activities calls for some caution. A strong involvement of the central level, strategic planning emphasising TEMPUS and support for the daily affairs of TEMPUS-related activities might be helpful in various respects here and there. On average, however, the perceived success of TEMPUS activities in the faculties and departments does not seem to differ strikingly according to the extent the central institutional level is involved.

6.7 The Supra-Institutional Setting: Perception and Links

The majority of higher education institutions in Central and Eastern European countries were informed for the first time about the TEMPUS Programme by their National TEMPUS Office. Between one and two first informants were stated on average, among them the national educational authorities (37 per cent) were named second most frequently. In addition, colleagues from other countries (20 per cent), colleagues of their own country (12 per cent), and the EU TEMPUS Office (15 per cent) were mentioned more than occasionally as the or one of the major initial sources of information. A similar pattern in many respects emerged in response to a question about subsequent information; the EU TEMPUS Office, however, was named twice as often as an additional source of information (31 per cent).

Altogether, ratings of the availability and the quality of information provided were positive, though not enthusiastic. They were both 2.2 on average on a scale from 1 = 'very good' to 5 = 'very limited'. The ratings, as Table 6.16 shows, were most positive by representatives from the central level of higher education institutions in Bulgaria and least positive from those in Hungary.

In response to the question 'If you asked any of the bodies mentioned below for help regarding administrative matters of TEMPUS activities at your higher education institution, how cooperative were they?', almost all respondents expressed a favourable view about their National TEMPUS Office. Actually, as Table 6.17 shows, 90 per cent referred to their National TEMPUS Offices, and 80 per cent rated them as cooperative.

More than three-quarters referred to their partners at higher education institutions in Western countries, and more than three-quarters rated them as cooperative. Slightly more than half of the respondents referred to the EU TEMPUS Office; among them, about three quarters considered it as cooperative. Fewer references were made to the national Ministry of Edu cation or national academic bodies, and these reference were less positive on average.

Table 6.16
Availability and Quality of Information Regarding the TEMPUS Programme in General, by CEE Countries (mean*)

	Availability of information	Quality of available information	(n)
Bulgaria	1.8	1.8	12
Czech Republic	1.5	1.6	8
Estonia	1.5	2.0	4
Hungary	2.2	2.0	33
Latvia	2.2	2.0	6
Lithuania	1.5	1.8	4
Poland	1.9	1.9	26
Romania	2.7	2.7	7
Slovak Republic	1.4	1.7	7
Other	2.0	3.5	2
Total	2.0	1.9	109

*Percentage of respondents stating 1 or 2 on a scale from 1 = 'very good' to 5 = 'very limited'

Question 2.4: How would you rate the availability and quality of information regarding the TEMPUS Programme in general?

Source: Survey on the development and restructuring of institutions participating in TEMPUS

Few respondents reported difficulties as regards the recognition of curricular innovation on the part of responsible authorities or bodies in their country: 2 per cent noted difficulties as far as recognition or accreditation of teaching material was concerned, and 9 per cent stated difficul-ties as regards the recognition of course programmes newly developed or revised in the framework of TEMPUS activities.

In contrast, administrative difficulties caused externally were mentioned by a substantial proportion of the representatives of higher education institutions in Central and Eastern Europe involved in TEMPUS:

- 37 per cent encountered difficulties due to delayed provision of TEMPUS funds by the Commission

Table 6.17
Cooperation and Assistance Provided for the Administration of TEMPUS Activities by External Bodies, by CEE Countries (per cent*)

	BG	CZ	EE	H	LT	LV	PL	RO	SK	Other	Total
Availability of information	1.8	1.5	1.5	2.2	1.5	2.2	1.9	2.7	1.4	2.0	2.0
National (Higher) Education Ministry	63	75	100	0	0	33	71	50	50	50	58
National academic bodies	100	50	67	33	50	50	63	50	50	0	53
National TEMPUS Office	91	100	100	83	75	80	96	83	100	0	89
TEMPUS partner higher education institutions in EC Member States	89	100	75	74	75	75	75	100	67	50	79
EC TEMPUS Office in Brussels/Torino	80	80	100	65	100	100	75	80	80	100	76

* Percentage of respondents stating 1 or 2 on a scale from 1 = 'very cooperative' to 5 = 'not cooperative at all'

Question 3.12: If you asked any of the bodies mentioned below for help regarding administrative matters of TEMPUS activities at your higher education institution, how cooperative were they?

Source: Survey on the development and restructuring of institutions participating in TEMPUS

Table 6.18
Difficulties Encountered in the Administration of TEMPUS Funds, by CEE Countries (per cent*)

	BG	CZ	EE	H	LT	LV	PL	RO	SK	Other	Total
Delay in provision of TEMPUS funds by the European Commission	27	17	75	48	0	0	52	0	43	100	38
Delay in provision of TEMPUS funds by the JEP contractor	40	0	0	14	25	20	43	0	40	0	24
Missing rules for book-keeping	22	0	0	29	25	0	41	0	20	0	23
Required rules for book-keeping not compatible with regularly used rules	11	17	0	30	33	0	29	0	20	0	21
Delay in the provision of receipts and pieces of evidence by TEMPUS participants	0	0	33	18	0	0	0	0	0	0	7

* Percentage of respondents stating 1 or 2 on a scale from 1 = 'very considerable' to 5 = 'not at all' among all responding to the respective area.

Question 3.10: To what extent did your higher education institution encounter difficulties in the administration of TEMPUS funds regarding the following aspects?

Source: Survey on the development and restructuring of institutions participating in TEMPUS

- 24 per cent encountered similar difficulties as regards delay of the provision of TEMPUS funds by JEP contractors from another institution of higher education
- 24 per cent referred in this context to missing rules for book-keeping
- 21 per cent reported an incompatibility of rules for TEMPUS book-keeping and those regularly used at their institution.

As Table 6.18 shows, these difficulties were named more often by respondents from institutions which are involved in a large number of Joint European Projects. As already stated above, the involvement in a substantial number of JEPs seems to sharpen problem awareness but, again, one has to take into account that a substantial proportion of the institutions have been beneficiaries of support in the inauguration year of TEMPUS and, thus, experienced problems inflated both by the early stages of political transformation and of the rapid start of the TEMPUS scheme.

Finally, the central level of the higher education institutions might have an influence on the provision of TEMPUS grants. This might not only affect the encouragement or discouragement as well as a pre-selection of applications within the respective institution of higher education, but also the supra-institutional consultations and decisions in the respective country. In response to a targeted question, only 23 per cent of the respondents stated that the central level of the institution of higher education had a strong influence regarding the pre-selection of applications for TEMPUS projects. A larger proportion noted a supra-institutional influence: 33 per cent stated that their institution had a strong influence regarding the setting of national priorities for TEMPUS projects, and 23 per cent said the same regarding the selection of TEMPUS projects.

Such supra-institutional influence was most pronounced, according to the respondents, in the Baltic states.

Chapter 7

Changes of Activities in the Second Phase of TEMPUS

7.1 Development and Revisions of Major Programme Measures

TEMPUS tends to be a very dynamic programme because of a constant need to adapt to the changing situation and needs in the various CEE partner countries. In this and the following sections of this chapter an overview will be given about major programme developments and revisions on the national and on the supra-national level. Their impacts on activities, policy formation and administration in the second phase of TEMPUS (TEMPUS II) in the CEE partner countries and their higher education institutions will be discussed. Some results of the 'Survey on the Development and Restructuring of Institutions Participating in TEMPUS' are included in order to provide a context for the impact assessment.

Since the beginning of TEMPUS in 1990/91, there have been altogether seven areas concerning the structure of the TEMPUS Programme, its measures and activities as well as overall regulations for participation in which major programme changes and revisions were initiated by the EU. Not all of these programme revisions and changes were greeted with equal enthusiasm in the CEE partner countries. Frequently, the changes became known quite late and created a problem concerning the timely information about new opportunities or stricter regulations to be taken into account when applying for TEMPUS support.

7.1.1 The number of countries participating in TEMPUS

The first area to be pointed out is the rapid increase in the number of countries participating in TEMPUS. Already in the first year of TEMPUS operations the number of CEE partner countries increased from originally two (Poland and Hungary) to four (Hungary, Poland, the German Democratic Republic and Czechoslovakia). In the second year of TEMPUS I there were already six CEE partner countries: because of the German unification the former GDR was not counted among the CEE partner countries any longer, but Romania, Bulgaria and Yugoslavia joined TEMPUS. With the addition of Albania and the three Baltic States in 1992/93, the number of CEE partner countries increased to ten in the third year of TEMPUS. In the same year, participation of Yugoslavia was suspended because of the ongoing civil war. Slovenia, however became a TEMPUS partner country in its own right. There were eleven CEE partner countries in the last year of TEMPUS I because former Czechoslovakia separated into two independent states, the Czech and the Slovak Republic.

The number of EU Member States participating in TEMPUS increased as well, from 12 to 15, when Austria, Finland and Sweden joined the EU in 1994. Before that, these three countries could participate in TEMPUS in the status of G24 countries. Since the first year of TEMPUS II (1994/95) Cyprus and Malta can also participate in TEMPUS under the same conditions as the other G24 countries that are not EU Member States.

Concerning the country participation in TEMPUS, we still note an unequal distribution in various respects (cf. pp. 51 – 65) which was already visible during TEMPUS I. Some of the EU Member States are clearly under-represented in TEMPUS, while others are over-represented. Some CEE partner countries complained about not being sufficiently attractive to those Western partners they would like to cooperate with while other CEE partner countries have moved to a stage in which they do not find themselves purely on the receiving side any longer but also having something to offer. This development reflects the differences in speed and in level of progress achieved by the various CEE partner countries and confirms a trend towards 'Socratisation' on the one hand and 'residualisation' on the other (cf. Chapter 9). This can be pointed out as one of the major possible developments for the TEMPUS Programme. It means that the stronger CEE countries are aiming at participation in SOCRATES and the weaker CEE countries would form the rest of the CEE partner countries in TEMPUS. The trend is also reflected by the fact that some of the CEE partner countries are actively using TEMPUS as an instrument of preparation to participate in SOCRATES, frequently coupled with the expectation that TEMPUS funds will diminish in their country.

7.1.2 Joint European Projects

The second area in which major programme revisions took place are the Joint European Projects (JEPs). Since 1990/91, regional activities were an option for structural JEPs involving partner institutions from more than one CEE partner country. These multi-CEE JEPs were discontinued in 1994/95 and again re-introduced as an option for structural JEPs in 1996/97.

In 1993/94, the last year of TEMPUS I, a second JEP-type – called Mobility JEPs – was introduced into the TEMPUS activities addressing organised student mobility. The structure of TEMPUS Mobility JEPs is modelled according to the organisation of student mobility in ERASMUS within the framework of ICPs.

A third change concerning the Joint European Projects in TEMPUS occurred in 1994/95, the first year of TEMPUS II, with the introduction of the JEP+ projects. This JEP-type was designed to serve particular needs concerning the development of higher education institutions as a whole and their management and administrative structures. One year later it was discontinued.

It remains to be seen whether the re-introduction of the option for multi-CEE JEPs will be taken up. Multi-CEE JEPs tended to be more successful than regular structural JEPs but their potential was not quite used to its full extent. Successful applications for multi-CEE JEPs will be difficult to achieve because they have to comply with the national TEMPUS priorities of two or more CEE partner countries.

While Mobility JEPs during TEMPUS I were not initiated as often as could be expected and student mobility in general was less integrated into the other JEP activities, this seems to have changed in TEMPUS II. Many of the CEE partner countries expecting to participate soon in SOCRATES are using the organisation of Mobility JEPs as a preparation for this participation. Student mobility is clearly more often defined as one of the national priorities in TEMPUS II than it was in TEMPUS I (cf. also pp. 269 – 274). It is also used to achieve recognition and to prove that a European standard has been reached in higher education. The European Course Credit Transfer Scheme (ECTS) as applied in ERASMUS is seen as the lever for this. It seems, however, that two aspects in this context tend to be overlooked by higher education institutions in the CEE partner countries. In the face of existing diversity of higher education systems and higher education institutions in the European Union, it is quite unclear what is meant by achieving a 'European standard' in higher education institutions of the CEE countries and – as is frequently formulated in the national priorities – 'compatibility with EU higher education'.

The second aspect derives from the first. As long as higher education is something still profoundly national having to do with traditions and identity, it might not be wise for CEE partner countries to simply adopt Western European models and adapt to Western European requirements without reflecting traditions and positive features of their own systems. Nevertheless, the fact should not be dismissed that achieving recognition and being acknowledged as partners on equal terms, receiving as well as offering and giving, sending students abroad as well as hosting students from Western partner institutions, contributes considerably to CEE self-confidence.

The introduction and discontinuation of JEP+ projects after one year has cut off some of the plans to work out respective projects since they needed a longer time for preparation because of their scope and the expectations connected with this JEP-type. Meanwhile, however, activities similar to those supported in JEP+ projects can be supported in the framework of regular structural JEPs.

7.1.3 Individual Mobility Grants

The third area in which changes and programme revisions took place are the Individual Mobility Grants (IMGs). In 1992/93, the possibility for students to obtain an IMG was discontinued. Thereafter, student mobility was solely organised in the framework of JEPs. As mentioned above, a special JEP-type to organise student mobility was introduced in 1993/94. In 1995/96, the second year of TEMPUS II, IMGs were restricted to academic staff members from CEE partner countries only. In addition, a number of selection pre-conditions and preferences for IMG applications were set up in most of the CEE partner countries. From 1996/97 on, IMGs are available again for academic staff from EU Member States.

Individual Mobility Grants (IMGs) have always been considered an important opportunity to become familiar with new teaching methods, to up-date and exchange knowledge and establish personal contacts in the international community of scholars. The gradual introduction of pre-selection criteria and preferences for IMGs by most of the CEE partner countries has led to some disappointment of those staff members, who feel excluded, be it because of age limits or frequency limits.

However, it can be noted that IMGs have more and more been used as an incentive measure to attract and keep junior academic staff. The stricter selection criteria were intended to prevent 'academic tourism' and provide for better outcomes by being more goal-directed. During interviews with JEP partners at CEE partner institutions it was often mentioned that short visits of two to three days by Western partners were considered to be a waste of time and money because the outcomes could not compare to the costs incurred. A minimum of one week for short visits by

Western partners was stated most frequently as a sufficient length to guarantee an adequate outcome.

7.1.4 Complementary Measures

The fourth area of programme change are activities in the framework of Complementary Measures (CMEs). Parallel to the introduction of JEP+ projects CME+ projects were also introduced in the first year of TEMPUS II and discontinued in the second year of TEMPUS II. CME+ projects were designed to give national authorities in the CEE partner countries the means to reach practical objectives in accordance with their policy for the development of the higher education system in their country. The projects could only be proposed by the national authorities in the CEE partner countries. CME+ projects were designed as feasibility studies, development of directories on special issues of the higher education system, the establishment of national data bases or the development of recommendations for special schemes based on surveys and analyses.

CME+ projects were supported only in 1994/95. However, from 1995/96 onwards the range of activities eligible under CMEs was completely re-defined. Instead of grants to facilitate the integration of CEE institutions and associations into European university associations, grants for the preparation of publications and other information activities and grants for surveys and studies, Complementary Measures since 1995/96 comprise three new strands of activities eligible for TEMPUS support:

- to develop and strengthen capacities for strategic planning and institutional development at the level of the higher education institution(s) or faculty(ies)
- for the dissemination of TEMPUS results and achievements within particular subject areas or sectors and dissemination of innovative outcomes of programmes other than TEMPUS
- for projects contributing to the elaboration of a national strategy in a CEE partner country for the development of a specific aspect of higher education which has been identified by the national authorities of the respective country.

While the second strand of the new CME activities is still closely related to some of the CME activities eligible until 1994/95, it becomes clearly visible that the first new strand is closely related to activities previously supported in JEP+ projects and that the third new strand is closely related to activities previously supported in CME+ projects.

Complementary Measures (CMEs) so far have not been very much in the foreground of available options. The possibility to improve the dissemination of results of TEMPUS activities or introduce more strategic approaches to reform and renewal on the macro-level by carrying out respective surveys and studies was not as frequently taken up during TEMPUS I as one could have expected. Possibly the introduction of CME+ projects has moved these opportunities and possibilities more into the foreground. It remains to be seen whether the re-definition of three new strands of activities eligible for CME grants as well as a considerably higher amount of TEMPUS funds allocated to CME activities in 1995/96 will improve the situation.

7.1.5 Joint European Networks

A fifth area of programme revisions in TEMPUS concerns the introduction of Joint European Networks. In 1993/94, there was a pilot phase of support for Joint European Networks (JENs), a form of support which was officially introduced in 1994/95. JENs are defined in the Guide for Applicants as a form of support which may be given for the maintenance of Joint European Project achievements to a limited number of projects which have completed their maximum three-year period of TEMPUS support. The JEN grants are awarded for a maximum of two years and serve to achieve self-sustainability of project activities and to disseminate the results beyond the faculty or department in the CEE partner country.

The introduction of Joint European Networks (JENs) has been highly and almost unanimously appreciated in the CEE partner countries. JENs are seen as a good opportunity to finish project activities, especially when partners had to cope continuously with various delays (for example, delivery of equipment or finishing off publications, text books and other written material developed in the framework of the JEP). JENs also offer the opportunity to make further arrangements for cooperation, look for different funding of activities, improve the dissemination of results and/or stabilise achievements of the JEP activities.

7.1.6 Changes in funding and objectives for JEPs

The sixth area of programme revisions in TEMPUS concerns changes in funding and objectives for JEPs. As in other areas of overall programme revisions, these measures were introduced by the EU as well.

- In 1994/95, together with the shift from annual to multi-annual funding of JEPs, the necessity for a strict compliance of JEP proposals with national TEMPUS priorities was introduced into the selection process. This was not the rule in TEMPUS I.

- In 1995/96, five overall objectives were introduced on top of the national priorities representing a new classification system for activities eligible for support in the framework of JEPs. Each JEP application was supposed to fit into at least one of these overall objectives of which four related to structural JEPs and one to mobility JEPs. A number of eligible activities was sub-ordinated under each of the objectives. A new aspect among these objectives was the emphasis on a review and improvement of university management.

- Since 1995/96, higher education institutions in the CEE countries had to submit institutional development plans together with the letter of endorsement. The respective statements attached to the project proposals before submission should not only declare that the project was endorsed by the relevant authority representing the institution involved in the JEP but also describe the development of the recipient higher education institution or faculty and the project's coherence with this plan.

The shift towards multi-annual funding of JEPs introduced at the beginning of TEMPUS II has also been highly and almost unanimously appreciated in the CEE partner countries. The multi-annual funding of JEPs offers a better planning perspective for all partners involved and allows a certain degree of flexibility to adapt activities to the dynamics of ongoing project work. Nevertheless, JEP partners in CEE countries commented quite frequently on the lack of flexibility in the utilisation of project funds.

The introduction of five overall objectives was accompanied by a new emphasis on the review and improvement of university management and central administrative structures of the institutions. Together with the requirement of the project's coherence with an institutional development plan, this new emphasis certainly triggered a new awareness of the possibilities and potentials contained in a more strategic and integrated approach towards TEMPUS activities at the higher education institutions in the CEE countries.

While eligible activities for JEPs listed in the Guidelines for Applicants up to 1994/95 were explicitly intended to be only examples, overall objectives and their specifications in the form of eligible activities since 1995/96 were introduced as a limited number (five) of options from which a choice has to be made. Although the overall objectives take up most of the former eligible activities given as examples, their structure and hierarchy has changed to a considerable degree.

7.1.7 Contractor and coordinator functions for JEPs

The last area of programme revisions and changes to be mentioned here concerns the management functions within individual JEPs, that is, contractor and coordinator functions. Whereas in 1990/91, the first year of TEMPUS I, contractor and coordinator functions could only be taken over by institutions in EU Member States, the coordinator and contractor function was separated in the following year and from then on any institution involved in a JEP was allowed to take over the coordinator function. This included also institutions from the G24 countries. The contractor function remained with institutions from EU Member States in that year. In the third year of TEMPUS I (1992/93) institutions from Czechoslovakia and Hungary were allowed to take over contractor functions as well. The number of CEE partner countries in which institutions involved in JEPs took over contractor functions gradually increased each year after that. In the last year of TEMPUS I (1993/94) Slovenian institutions could become contractors; in 1994/95, the first year of TEMPUS II, Polish institutions were added, in the second year of TEMPUS II Romanian institutions could also become contractors and, from 1996/97 on, Bulgarian institutions will be added. This gradual increase in the number of countries in which higher education institutions could take over the contractor function is a reflection not only of the development of the banking system but also of the growing skills in terms of administrative tasks in the higher education institutions themselves.

As soon as partners from various CEE countries became eligible for coordinator and contractor functions, preferences for JEPs being coordinated or contracted by CEE institutions were added to the national priorities of the respective countries. Although JEP partners from CEE countries in coordinator and or contractor functions have frequently complained about the amount of administrative work connected with these functions and also about not being properly re-imbursed for this work, these functions were nevertheless seen as an opportunity to gain insider knowledge and experience in the administration of international projects and the acquisition of external funding on a competitive base. To take over these functions is also deemed to ease certain problems which occurred quite frequently in the cooperation with Western partners at the beginning of TEMPUS, namely to define one's needs oneself rather than having them defined; to participate more actively in the allocation of JEP funds among partners and determine according budget breakdowns; to have a better control of project activities and administrative costs incurred; and to be more selective with regard to the choice of Western partners for cooperation within a JEP. Becoming coordinator and/or contractor was a further step in the direction of establishing a feeling of being a partner on equal terms.

7.2 Major Patterns of TEMPUS Policy Formation

Structures and processes of TEMPUS policy formation in the CEE partner countries were established during TEMPUS I and have not changed significantly during TEMPUS II. Policy decisions take place in three areas:
- budget negotiations between Phare responsibles and TEMPUS actors concerning the annual establishment of the TEMPUS budget as a proportion of the national Phare budget
- annual establishment of national TEMPUS priorities
- annual organisation of the various assessment procedures of TEMPUS project applications.

7.2.1 The role of the TEMPUS advisory boards

The role of the TEMPUS advisory or supervisory boards has not changed in TEMPUS II (cf. pp. 98 – 104). Such a board has been established in all CEE partner countries to provide an arena in which all key actors involved in the TEMPUS policy decisions can discuss their views and reach a consensus or agree on proposals. The mandate of these boards as well as the composition of their members vary to a certain degree from country to country although their function is quite similar. They either play a more advisory and consultative role or have been accorded decision-making powers. In general, their most important task is the discussion and proposal of the national TEMPUS priorities. In some countries they are consulted on further issues related to policy decisions and administrative processes of the TEMPUS Programme. As a body they serve to balance the interests of all authorities and interest groups involved in TEMPUS. Frequently, the National TEMPUS Offices (NTOs) are their executive body or secretariat. With the exception of Hungary, the chairperson of these boards is a representative of the Ministry of Education.

It is, in principle, an optimal model to give the responsibilities for the steering of the TEMPUS Programme to such a board representing all interest groups. In practice the functioning of this model depends on a number of further factors. One of them is the size of the board: a large number of members tends to lead to the situation that not all representatives participate in the meetings or that decisions are made in exclusive and smaller groups, the legitimacy of which is questionable. In contrast to this, a very limited number of members tends to lead to criticism of the board's decisions and/or proposals by those groups and authorities involved in TEMPUS but excluded from representation in the board.

7.2.2 Key actors

Key actors in TEMPUS policy formation on the national level in the CEE partner countries are the Ministry of Education, the Phare responsibles or national Phare Coordinator, the NTOs and representatives of higher education institutions. Concerning the role of these actors in the various processes of policy formation and decision-making a continuing development can be noted. In almost all CEE partner countries there is a routinisation and stabilisation of policy formation for TEMPUS. The decision-making procedures of the national key actors play a more important role and show a more integrated approach to TEMPUS. This seems to be reinforced to quite an extent by the insistence of the Europen Commission that national TEMPUS priorities should reflect a more strategic approach towards higher education reform and renewal on the national as well as on the institutional level and that links between TEMPUS and Phare should be more clearly established.

The opportunity of a more pro-active involvement of the Ministries of Education responsible for TEMPUS and the integration of TEMPUS into an overall higher education development strategy being targeted towards further integration into European activities has become an issue of awareness in several of the CEE countries and was supported by CME+ and CME projects in TEMPUS II. In three CEE partner countries Ministries have initiated studies or strategic statements concerning the role and place of TEMPUS for the reform and development of the national higher education system. The interest of Phare responsibles to play a pro-active role in TEMPUS policy formation continues and is more pronounced in several CEE countries. The focus of Phare activities has also extended to a certain degree by including strategies for European integration, a development having started already towards the end of TEMPUS I. Some Phare responsibles promote the view that TEMPUS support should be concentrated on such areas and disciplines which the former regimes did not allow to develop properly. Thus, not only better links of TEMPUS activities in higher education with industry and consideration of labour market needs are promoted by Phare but also, for example, a European dimension in legal education, the development of European studies and foreign language learning. It should, however, be stated here that the promotion of these activities is not always reflected in actual projects (cf. Table 3.5).

Thus, for example, JEPs concerned with law education constitute an average proportion among all JEPs of not more than two per cent and there is no increase in their number in TEMPUS II. Similarly, teacher education constitutes an average proportion of four per cent among all JEPs in the first six years of TEMPUS and humanities are covered by only one per cent of the JEPs on average. Nevertheless, these foci on certain subjects form an area in which consensus among the key actors can easily be established. Areas of dispute and resentment from higher education institutions, NTOs and Ministries of Education emerge partly in those cases in which Phare responsibles attempt to influence project selection (i.e. preferential selection of a certain number of JEPs in a specified subject) or actively promote the exclusion of some subjects from TEMPUS support.

7.2.3 The TEMPUS budget

In the majority of the CEE partner countries the TEMPUS budget is expected to decrease. Four reasons for this expectation were frequently stated as an explanation. One of them is the introduction of further educational activities into the human resources development part of Phare. In the overall framework of the Phare budget TEMPUS will have to share its proportion with these additional activities also directed towards the field of higher education. Another reason is the necessity to provide funds for participation in SOCRATES. In some of the CEE partner countries negotiations have been going on with Phare to provide at least a transitional budget for this purpose since national education budgets are still rather low. Third, we can note a shift in role of TEMPUS as a support programme for higher education in some of the CEE partner countries which is closely connected to a stabilisation of higher education budgets on the one hand and emphasis on participation in SOCRATES on the other. The necessity for TEMPUS support then seems to remain only for those institutions and subjects which have tended to be losers in the competition for TEMPUS support during the first years of the programme. Finally, attention has shifted in some of the stronger CEE countries to an increasing multitude of other international programmes offering support (e.g. World Bank, Soros Foundation, bilateral programmes, etc.), many of them also including grants for research cooperation.

7.3 Development of TEMPUS Administration

The transfer of administrative tasks and responsibilities from the ETF TEMPUS Department to the National TEMPUS Offices (NTOs) in most of the CEE partner countries has continued in TEMPUS II. Meanwhile, most of the NTOs are carrying out the technical assessment of applications and the assessment concerning the compliance of applications with national priorities themselves with only occasional parallel checks by the ETF TEMPUS Department. The majority of NTOs are handling the assessment of applications for Individual Mobility Grants (IMGs), the distribution of contracts to successful applications and payment of grants which they receive as a lump sum transfer from the ETF TEMPUS Department. Together with the ETF TEMPUS Department NTOs are also involved in the selection of JEPs for a Joint European Network (JEN) grant.

In 1995, a discussion among NTO directors was taking place aiming at a redistribution of tasks between the NTOs and the ETF TEMPUS Department. The growing professionalisation of NTO staff and a stabilisation and routinisation of tasks together with increased responsibilities have led to a higher degree of self-confidence of the NTOs. The different state of development and differences in the speed of progress in the various CEE partner countries tend to support the view of the NTOs that a further decentralisation of TEMPUS administration coupled with a stronger focus on individual national developments would take existing differences more appropriately into account. This issue gives rise to the question to what degree overall objectives and aims can be or should be achieved with TEMPUS beyond a regional diversification and whether a shift from administrative control to 'programme leadership' might constitute a new function for the ETF TEMPUS Department in the face of the professionalisation of the NTOs (cf. also Chapter 9).

A few issues of TEMPUS administration should be mentioned as needing further improvement: information and dissemination of results of TEMPUS activities. The annual changes in national priorities as well as frequent programme revisions require intensive information activities. These are usually organised by the NTOs in the form of regional or – in smaller countries – country-wide information days, apart from continuous individual advice and support for applicants. However, the increase of regulations, objectives, preferences, selection criteria, etc. which have to be considered by applicants together with a higher degree of competition and the limited availability of TEMPUS funds so that not even all applications with positive ratings from the various assessment procedures can be supported has led many applicants to invest considerable time into their project proposal in order to submit a competitive application. This means that project ideas are being developed well in advance of submission deadlines. Programme revisions and national priorities become known at a time in the year when many applicants are already quite advanced in their project proposal and an exact match of the proposed project with priorities and possibly new regulations is difficult to achieve. In TEMPUS II it has become somewhat of a problem to inform applicants about changes at a time which gives them sufficient leeway to match their proposals with the priorities and to take into account other possible changes and still meet the deadline for the submission of the application. More attention to the timing of information may be needed.

The frequent complaints by TEMPUS actors as well as JEP partners about the intransparency of selection criteria for application seems to have been redressed to a certain extent by including a rather detailed explanation in the guidelines for applicants.

Except for the one occasion which has been quoted as the only model of good practice ever since it had taken place, the dissemination of results of activities supported by TEMPUS has remained a somewhat neglected issue in TEMPUS II. The model of good practice referred to here was a conference organised by the Polish TEMPUS Office bringing together partners from various JEPs in one discipline with academic staff members from the same discipline who had never been involved in TEMPUS activities. In the meantime analyses of TEMPUS impacts and outcomes have been given more attention also on the side of the European Commission. This is reflected in the re-definition of activities eligible for a CME grant and several studies have been commissioned to focus on TEMPUS output promotion. Only very recently a more targeted approach towards dissemination of results of TEMPUS activities can be noted. Thus, it still remains to be seen whether dissemination will improve in the second half of TEMPUS II and what its effects might be. Expectations of impacts or spin-offs from TEMPUS output promotion on institutional development and strategic management which are currently strongly promoted by the EU will be discussed later in the chapter.

Just as in TEMPUS I, the following administrative issues give rise to widespread criticism from applicants and partners involved in JEPs in TEMPUS II:

- late information of TEMPUS priorities and programme revisions
- delays of funds, late contracts
- inflexibility of JEP budget utilisation, not allowing sufficient adaptation to project dynamics
- increased bureaucracy and paper work.

Most institutions of higher education in Central and Eastern Europe tend to be more or less satisfied with the communication with their National

TEMPUS Offices and with the information flow in general. If problems of information are expressed, they are likely to imply criticism as far as the acceptance of decisions and their transparency are concerned. Asked about the changes in the availability and quality of information about the TEMPUS Programme since the start of TEMPUS II, the majority of institutions stated a better availability (59 per cent) and a better quality (57 per cent). Most of the remaining institutions saw no change and only very few institutions (3 per cent each) stated that availability and quality of information has become worse during TEMPUS II.

Notably, the actors on the central level of higher education institutions advocated increased flexibility of the funding arrangements, further continuation and increase of TEMPUS support and a decrease of bureaucracy as far as details of book-keeping and reporting are concerned. Some changes of the overall administrative procedures are called for, and some suggest a reconsideration of priorities mostly in favour of increased student mobility.

Two administrative issues in TEMPUS should be pointed out and put into a context in this report. On the one hand, the transfer of responsibilities and tasks can be noted from the ETF TEMPUS Department to the NTOs in the CEE partner countries. On the other hand, management functions (i.e. contractor and coordinator functions) within JEPs have also gradually been transferred and taken over by JEP partners from CEE countries. The proportion of newly established JEPs coordinated by CEE partners was 67 per cent in the first year of TEMPUS II and 80 per cent in the second year of TEMPUS II. The proportion of newly established JEPs in both years of TEMPUS II contracted by CEE partners was 39 per cent, having increased from 4 per cent in TEMPUS I (cf. Tables 3.8 and 3.9). These developments lead to the conclusion that administrative functions in TEMPUS and management functions within JEPs are gradually being transferred from the EU and the Western partners into the hands of the CEE partner countries. It cannot be ignored any longer that, in terms of administrative matters, the relationships between the EU and Western partners on the one hand and CEE countries and partners on the other have become more asymmetrical and that it might be worthwhile to think about the following questions:

- Will reduced opportunities for Western partners to take over coordinator and contractor functions lead to a loss of interest in participating in the TEMPUS Programme?

- Should the controlling and management functions within TEMPUS projects be left to the recipients of the support?

- What is the future role of the ETF TEMPUS Department? Is there still a need for an overall administrative bracket?
- Which administrative tasks for TEMPUS should be decentralised and nationalised and which tasks should remain the responsibility of a central supra-national unit?

7.4 National Priorities and Selection Criteria for TEMPUS Applications

An analysis of the changes in national TEMPUS priorities shows a gradual development from predominantly subject area oriented priorities to predominantly structural priorities with subject area specifications subordinated to them and a broadening of the range of subjects being included in the priorities. Hungary shifted early, in 1993/94, to almost pure structural priorities without listing any specific subjects. The term 'structural priorities' is used here to cover a wide range of priorities on a more general level than priorities relating to a subject area or academic discipline, that is, priorities which might apply to all kinds of subjects (e.g. development of curricula for new academic professions, short-cycle higher education, restructuring of degree courses).

Since the beginning of TEMPUS II, in 1994/95, national priorities have been accorded a more important status insofar as:

- only those applications were selected for support which were in full compliance with national priorities
- more emphasis was put on the identification of the project objective and a precise definition of potential output
- the number of priority areas per CEE partner country was limited and became more focused in order to better contribute to the structural reform processes in each country.

Stricter adherence to priorities than was typical for TEMPUS I, the introduction of additional preferences (e.g. several institutions from one CEE country cooperating within a JEP, preference for projects in which institutions from the CEE country concerned took over coordinator and/or contractor functions, etc.), sometimes even the indication of a proportion of available JEP funding for each of the individual priorities – all these newly emerging aspects contributed to an increased role of national priorities in TEMPUS II. The improvement of links between TEMPUS and Phare was underscored by the list of Phare objectives and priorities preceding the list of national TEMPUS priorities for each CEE partner country in the Guideline for Applicants.

In the second year of TEMPUS II (1995/96), structural priorities have became dominant. Newly emerging emphases are being put on institutional management and overall higher education development, explicit links to Phare objectives and labour market demands including the promotion of short-cycle, practically oriented higher education, and in four CEE countries Mobility JEPs or support for student mobility is named as one of the priorities. In addition, we find in the 1995/96 Guidelines for Applicants the formulation of five overall 'project objectives' introduced by the European Commission on top of the national TEMPUS priorities. Four of the five objectives apply to structural JEPs and one to Mobility JEPs. Each objective has a number of eligible activities sub-ordinated to it and any JEP application must clearly fit into one of these overall objectives apart from being in full compliance with national priorities in order to become eligible for support. The overall objectives were introduced to complement national priorities and serve as an additional structural framework or bracket to achieve the aims of the TEMPUS Programme and emphasise higher education systems development more strongly than before.

The eligible activities listed under the heading of each overall objective are more or less the same activities eligible in the previous years. Insofar as there are changes, the new pattern could be interpreted as a more targeted approach and re-structuring of the typical TEMPUS activities. However, there is one exception. One of the objectives is directed at structural JEPs aiming at a review and improvement of university management. In addition, a new requirement influencing the selection of applications states that all letters of endorsement should be accompanied by a statement from the central level concerning the project's coherence with a development plan of the respective institution or faculty and an account of this plan. This requirement is not only addressed to those JEPs aiming at reforms of the university management and administration but also to other project proposals. Four of the eleven CEE partner countries have introduced institutional management and development into their national priorities in 1995/96.

The national TEMPUS priorities for 1996/97 show that further CEE countries intend to promote institutional development and management by means of TEMPUS support. A general overview of new priorities indicates, however, another trend. TEMPUS funds in a majority of CEE countries will be used to achieve a higher degree of compatibility of national higher education with what is assumed to be a European standard. The instruments or measures to achieve this goal vary from country to country. The following priorities can be found most frequently:

- introduction of quality evaluation systems
- development of European Studies and other inter-disciplinary degree courses
- increase in teaching and learning of modern European languages
- introduction of a European dimension into higher education.

Together with the continued promotion of student mobility including ECTS arrangements, national TEMPUS priorities reflect the trend towards using TEMPUS as an instrument for the preparation of higher education faculties and departments to participate in SOCRATES in many of the CEE countries. However, in all CEE partner countries students still suffer most from serious delays in the transfer of grants so that some kind of regular emergency measure should be found. Students from some CEE partner countries still have difficulties to obtain the necessary visas for their stay in an EU Member State or handling of visa applications is seriously delayed by the respective embassies and consulates (up to three months). Both kinds of delays cause considerable difficulties to carry out arranged mobility plans and often lead to a loss of recognition arrangements because students arrive in their host countries in the middle instead of at the beginning of the term.

In quite a few of those CEE countries in which the trend to promote increased student mobility is clearly visible, a stage of development has been achieved in which the character of TEMPUS as an emergency support programme has lost its importance and the desire to cooperate with Western European partners on equal terms and to be recognised as having achieved a comparable standard in higher education has moved into the foreground of strategic considerations. After six years of TEMPUS activities in cooperation with Western partners, confidence in their own standards and achievements as well as trust in being able to make competitive bids for support from other European and international programmes have increased. Participation in the ERASMUS part of SOCRATES as soon as possible has almost become a matter of ambition and prestige for various institutions and academic staff members in the CEE countries.

It must be pointed out, however, that the number of mobility grants for students from CEE countries continually decreased from a peak of 5,612 in 1992/93 to 3,589 in 1995/96 (also see Table 3.14). The average proportion of Mobility-JEPs among all JEPs was 11 per cent in the first two years of TEMPUS II with a slight increase in the second year. It remains an open question whether in the last two years of TEMPUS II student mobility will really become a more integrated activity. It should also be pointed out that student mobility in TEMPUS does not compare to student mobility in the ERASMUS part of SOCRATES. TEMPUS student mobility is considerably less determined by reciprocity of exchanges and not as highly organised as ERASMUS student mobility and – during TEMPUS I – frequently lacked curricular integration and recognition arrangements. JEP partners in CEE countries have also sometimes reported the impression that their Western partners preferred to host academic staff rather than students.

Impulses for changing foci of national TEMPUS priorities seem to have been generated frequently by the European Commission. Referring to the role of national priorities during TEMPUS I, a key actor in one of the CEE countries stated during one of the interviews that national priorities were there for Western partners to read and make a choice. This has clearly changed in TEMPUS II. The increased strategic approach to the establishment of national priorities together with a more focused selection of structural priority areas and – at least in most of the CEE partner countries – the gradual shift from assistance to partnership in the character of TEMPUS activities and support have also changed to a certain degree the relevance of various elements in the bundle of activities eligible for support. Although the majority of national TEMPUS actors in the CEE countries opt for a continuation of TEMPUS with the same four activities (i.e. structural development including provision of equipment, cooperative educational measures including curriculum development, staff and student mobility) as before, the following changes become visible:

- In some of the CEE partner countries the provision of equipment through TEMPUS grants has become less important, although it is still highly appreciated.
- Structural development has started to be geared more strongly towards reforms of central institutional management and administration.
- Curriculum development and other cooperative educational measures are more frequently specified for subjects with a European dimension and residual disciplines which have not yet participated extensively in TEMPUS.
- Staff mobility and international cooperation of academic staff members are still widely favoured but with a growing stabilisation of contacts which were built up in the framework of TEMPUS activities. Opportunities for mobility and cooperation have increased and are further developed also without TEMPUS support. Grants from other programmes or on the basis of bilateral agreements have become increasingly available and often do not exclude research cooperation.

- Organised student mobility has clearly been accorded a more important role in the framework of TEMPUS activities. It is frequently used as a preparation for participation in SOCRATES and seen as proof of having achieved a 'European standard', especially when it is combined with the introduction of ECTS, or as an instrument to achieve compatibility of standards. Another impact of student mobility becomes visible in the statement of a dean saying that student mobility was good because students would come back and demand better teaching and up-to-date material also from those, frequently older professors who have resented change so far.

Concerning the overall direction of TEMPUS priorities, five developments can be pointed out:

(1) The exclusive focus on subjectrelated priorities at the beginning of TEMPUS I has first been replaced by a mixture of structural and subject-related priorities and then shifted towards a stronger hierarchisation with subject-related priorities sub-ordinated to structural priorities and specifying them.

(2) In the national priorities of the first two years of TEMPUS II a stronger reflection of issues of internationalisation, university management and practically oriented short-cycle higher education including the involvement of enterprises can be found in quite a few CEE countries.

(3) TEMPUS priorities have become increasingly structured and refined. A more targeted identification of national needs becomes visible through specifications of areas within subjects. For example, listings like economics or business studies, etc., have been replaced in some CEE countries by specifications like portfolio management, capital market, investment banking, etc.

(4) Through rotation of subjects and subject areas a broader coverage has been achieved of subjects eligible for TEMPUS support. This is not reflected in an equally proportionate increase in the actual number of JEPs covering new subjects. Engineering and applied sciences as well as economics, business and management studies are still dominantly represented among the subject areas covered by JEPs.

(5) Although the TEMPUS partner countries in Central and Eastern Europe increasingly show a different speed and direction of development and change – the field of higher education included – the amount of overlap in national TEMPUS priorities is still large enough to provide sufficient opportunities for cooperation among the CEE countries themselves. The potential for regional activities (in multi-CEE JEPs)

has been overlooked or given away and thus constitutes a missed opportunity. Multi-CEE JEPs have gradually decreased from 21 per cent of the JEPs starting in TEMPUS I to 1 per cent of the JEPs starting in TEMPUS II (also see Table 3.2). It must remain an open question whether regional cooperation was deliberately given up in favour of cooperation with Western partners alone or whether it was made more difficult or even impossible because Phare regional funds were not available any longer. The option for regional activities in the framework of structural JEPs has been reintroduced in the Guidelines for Applicants for 1996/97. However, it is unclear yet whether a special financial basis for them has been established as well.

Overall, it can be noted that the higher degree of structuring and specification of priorities seems to meet the various needs and demands of the CEE partner countries and in some of them also seems to induce a more pro-active involvement of the respective Ministry of Education and a more targeted approach towards determining the role of TEMPUS for higher education development on the systems level.

7.5   The Character of CME+ and JEP+ Projects and their Role for Strategic Planning

In the first year of TEMPUS II (1994/95) two special types of projects were introduced into the TEMPUS Programme, called CME+ and JEP+ projects. Both project types were designed to give national authorities of the CEE partner countries a means by which to reach practical objectives in accordance with their policy for the development of higher education in the country. Both project types were larger in scope than classical JEP and CME projects and also had a higher level of maximum funding: a maximum support of 600.000 ECU for JEP+ projects and a maximum support of 50.000 ECU for CME+ projects. Co-financing by the national authorities of the respective CEE countries was expected. JEP+ projects were supported for up to three years and CME+ projects for up to one year.

The new project types were intended to complement the existing bottom-up approach of the regular TEMPUS measures by involving national authorities more strongly in the proposals. Thus, the national authorities of the respective CEE countries were not only asked to pre-define objectives and expected outputs and name local partners, but they also had to submit all applications to the European Commission. For each project proposal developed by national authorities under the CME+ or the JEP+ measure a national contact person had to be indicated. The national contact person was frequently a representative of the Ministry of Education or the director of the NTO. Proposals together with the name of the national contact person and in some cases also a list of institutions identified as possible partners (including contractors and/or coordinators) in the project were published in special documents and guidelines for applicants. Other application procedures and regulations were the same as for regular JEP and CME projects.

7.5.1 CME+ projects

In the one year in which CME+ projects were supported (i.e. in 1994/95), Bulgaria, the Czech Republic, Latvia, Romania and the Slovak Republic proposed one CME+ project each. Albania proposed two CME+ projects, Hungary proposed three and Poland proposed four. In principle, each project proposal could be covered by several applications.

Altogether seven CME+ project applications were awarded TEMPUS support by the European Commission. The majority of them were feasibility studies. Some of these studies were concerned with the introduction of assessment, accreditation and quality assurance systems; others looked into possibilities for the establishment of short-cycle higher education, for the integration of research into universities or for a restructuring of postgraduate studies. CME+ projects were clearly directed at the systems level of higher education.

7.5.2 JEP+ projects

In the one year in which JEP+ projects were supported (i.e. in 1994/95), three JEP+ projects were proposed by Poland and one each by Bulgaria, the Czech Republic, Hungary and Romania. In principle, each JEP+ project proposal could be covered by several applications.

Altogether eleven JEP+ project applications were awarded TEMPUS support by the European Commission, most of them coming from Poland. The scope of the projects was directed towards the institutional level of higher education. Standing out are activities related to internationalisation (e.g. development of international cooperation departments, introduction of European Studies) and activities related to the creation of computerised information networks (e.g. for libraries). Other projects were concerned with managerial and administrative issues of the central institutional level.

7.5.3 Strategic planning

CME+ and JEP+ projects were clearly intended to promote and support a more strategic approach towards national and institutional planning of higher education. At the time we conducted our interviews in the CEE partner countries in the framework of the TEMPUS evaluation (i.e. in fall 1995), a strong pro-active involvement of the Ministries of Education in TEMPUS was noted only in a minority of the countries concerned. In several of the CEE partner countries frequent changes of government, including the Minister for Education, had prevented the development of strategic approaches towards higher education reforms on the systems level. Draft proposals for new higher education laws on which future actions seemed to depend had sometimes failed to be passed by parliament. The high degree of autonomy given to higher education institutions and faculties after 1989/90 and being strongly defended by them added to a considerable degree of hesitation among national authorities to initiate strong interventions.

The strategic approach has also seemed to come into conflict with the competitive elements in the application and selection procedures. For CME+ projects a rather detailed pre-selection among institutions wishing to submit an application seems to have been undertaken in some cases by the national contact persons. Instead of being able to select among several applications for each project proposal established by the national authorities, the European Commission received only one application. According to information provided by the ETF TEMPUS Department, this has contributed to the discontinuation of the JEP+ and CME+ project scheme. However, since 1995/96 activities similar to those supported in the framework of JEP+ projects can be supported in the framework of regular JEPs according to the new overall objective concerned with a review and improvement of university management. In 1995/96 CME activities also were redefined and divided into three strands, two of which contain eligible activities similar to those supported in the framework of CME+ and JEP+ projects. This development might indicate that a higher degree of integration of strategic approaches towards TEMPUS into the regular framework of the programme has been achieved.

The role of CME+ and JEP+ projects for strategic educational planning at the national and institutional level is difficult to assess, not least because of the limited number of projects which were awarded support and the discontinuation of the project type after one year. An internal evaluation carried out by the ETF TEMPUS Department in Torino and based on the final reports of the CME+ projects and the interim reports of the JEP+ projects after one year resulted in a better rating of the outcomes and achievements of CME+ projects in comparison to regular CME projects. Most of the JEP+ projects also reached those goals which they had intended to achieve in the first year. Nevertheless, JEP+ projects had to cope with more difficulties than CME+ projects concerning financial matters on the one hand and reservations against some of the project activities on the other (e.g. reservations against transmission of data for the establishment of information networks).

7.6 Support for and Strengthening of Institutional Development

Almost all of the institutions of higher education from CEE countries responding to the 'Survey on the Development and Restructuring of Institutions Participating in TEMPUS' participated not only in TEMPUS I but also in TEMPUS II (about 90 per cent). Answers to the questionnaire therefore could not analytically be divided into those only reflecting TEMPUS I and others only reflecting TEMPUS II. Thus, the results of the institutional survey cover the whole period of TEMPUS. However, as regards various aspects concerning the role of the central level of the institutions in strategic planning, for support of TEMPUS projects, etc., it could be expected that the respondents would refer more strongly to the current situation within the institution (i.e. TEMPUS II) than retrospectively to a certain point in time of TEMPUS I. With the exception of only a few questions which were explicitly related to TEMPUS II, the institutions were asked about their general experiences and assessments since 1990/91.

TEMPUS has supported institutions of higher education in Central and Eastern Europe which underwent substantial change since 1990. According to persons at the central level of the institutions responding to the respective questionnaire, about 40 per cent of the degree programmes provided in 1995 had been newly established, almost 30 per cent had changed substantially during that period and only slightly more than 30 per cent had remained more or less unchanged.

According to those in charge at the central level of higher education institutions, TEMPUS has strongly helped to establish international contacts and substantially contributed to staff exchange. At many institutions the contribution of TEMPUS to the improvement of equipment and to the achievement of various educational targets is remarkable. There is a lesser impact, though, on staff development, reorganisation of course programmes and on university management. Also, the faculties and departments involved in JEPs are frequently seen as more active in change-oriented educational activities than other faculties and departments not involved in TEMPUS JEPs, but not so much more active in administrative rearrangements and university-industry relationships. Altogether half of the respondents concluded that TEMPUS activities have had a strong impact on the changes which took place at their institution.

Although the overall impact of TEMPUS on changes that took place at the higher education institutions was rated relatively cautiously by the respondents to the institutional questionnaire, the educational spin-offs of TEMPUS activities beyond the respective institution of higher education were quite impressive. As many as half of the respondents stated that teaching material developed at their institution in the context of TEMPUS cooperation became a standard in the respective country, and about one-third reported a similar dissemination of course programme developments in JEPs.

Respondents to the institutional survey perceived the role of the central level quite similarly to the role in which central level actors are likely to perceive themselves in Western Europe. At TEMPUS-supported institutions, the central level of the institutions seems to have both formally and in practice a major say in the management structure and the administrative procedures of the institution, in the establishment of faculties and in changes of the degree structures. As one might expect, the faculties and departments dominate the scene as far as the establishment of course programmes, changes of curricula and teaching methods as well as research activities are concerned (see Table 6.11).

The different roles played by the central level and the faculties might be influenced by many factors, among others by the size of the institution and specific institutional cultures of the individual institutions. The most centralised approaches could be observed in the Baltic States, while a strong role of the faculties was most obvious in Poland and Romania.

The central level might play a substantial role in TEMPUS because most international offices and other units specifically in charge of support for international activities tend to be located at this level. About three-quarters of the respondents reported that their institution has established one or more units specifically in charge of international activities. The respondents estimated that the international offices at the central level spend more than a quarter of their time on TEMPUS-related activities. The respective proportion at the international offices at faculty-level is about half of their time.

The majority, though by far not all of the representatives of the institutions surveyed, named various kinds of procedural support for the participation in the TEMPUS Programme, for example, regarding the preparation of applications, administrative assistance and financial administration of TEMPUS money. The central level less frequently provided considerable resources for carrying out TEMPUS-related activities, like the assignment of special staff for the management of TEMPUS activities, financial contributions to TEMPUS activities or a reduction of the teaching load of staff involved in TEMPUS activities.

Some respondents also noted a role of the central level of the institution in supra-institutional contacts and negotiations, for example, the use of institutional prestige and contacts, acting as mediators between JEP partners and higher level authorities, or acquisition of additional funds from external sources. The central level of many of the institutions was also active in providing services linked to specific TEMPUS-related activities. These included, among others, administrative support concerning staff and student exchanges, providing accommodation for incoming staff and students, and organising TEMPUS-related meetings.

With the increase of TEMPUS activities in general and with more and more CEE partners being able to take over coordinator and contractor functions within JEPs the service functions of the central administration for JEPs have increased as well. In some higher education institutions JEP funds are centrally administered (including book-keeping and accounting). In those institutions which have a well functioning office for international relations organisational and administrative tasks for JEPs are frequently taken over by these offices, sometimes even the coordinator and contractor functions themselves. Other service functions have been listed above.

The interviews which were conducted in the framework of this evaluation in the CEE countries have also shown that in many cases these service functions are still supplied by the faculties themselves and not by the central institutional level. Many faculties continue to prefer a high degree of autonomy and independence from the central institutional level and have been able to build up their own support structures. Faculties also frequently reported that the central institutional level is not sufficiently capable of taking over administrative and/or accounting functions for the JEPs because of untrained staff. The perception of the quantity and quality of administrative and service functions being taken over by the central level of the institutions for the JEPs still differs considerably in the view of the central level itself on the one hand and in the view of the faculties and departments on the other.

Most of the institutions claim to undertake strategic planning for the development and restructuring of the higher education institution. The strong importance the institutions of higher education placed on TEM-

PUS-related activities at the central institutional level in this context was clearly expressed in responses to a question related to overall development strategies of the institutions: 45 per cent stated that all TEMPUS projects and 40 per cent reported that some TEMPUS projects were integrated into an overall institutional development strategy. Only at 6 per cent of the institutions did TEMPUS activities not play any role in the institutional development strategy, and 9 per cent stated that they did not have any overall development strategy.

The integration of TEMPUS activities into an institutional development strategy means in practice that at more than half of the institutions of higher education the central level made suggestions regarding the objectives of TEMPUS-related activities. At more than one-third of the institutions the central level initiated applications for TEMPUS projects. At some institutions the central level played a stronger role in the actual TEMPUS activities, for example, the determination of objectives or the refusal to confirm TEMPUS project applications by letters of endorsement (see Table 6.14).

According to the respondents at the central level, TEMPUS-related activities rarely encountered difficulties as far as the decision-making at the central level of the higher education institution is concerned. However, there were some difficulties regarding the adoption of teaching material, new courses or whole course programmes developed in JEPs. A substantial number of the respondents noted difficulties as far as the provision of resources for TEMPUS activities on the part of the higher education institutions were concerned.

An analysis of the relationships between the role played by the central level of the higher education institutions and the impacts of TEMPUS activities calls for some caution. A strong involvement of the central level, strategic planning emphasising TEMPUS and support for the daily affairs of TEMPUS-related activities might be helpful in various respects here and there. On average, however, the perceived success of TEMPUS activities in the faculties and departments does not seem to differ strikingly according to the extent the central institutional level is involved.

In order to get an impression about the current and future development and restructuring of higher education institutions in CEE countries, the persons in charge at the central level of the institutions were asked to provide their views with regard to a list of 18 different items. The ranking of the various topics by their importance for change as stated by the actors on the central level of the higher education institutions shows a clear pattern (see Table 7.1):

(1) Improvement of equipment e.g. computer centres, laboratories, etc., was stated by 78 per cent of the institutions as an area for ongoing substantial changes.

(2) Educational, academic and mobility measures:
- 59 per cent of the institutions mentioned the introduction of new course programmes as an area of substantial changes
- 57 per cent the introduction of new teaching methods
- 57 per cent increase of student exchange
- 56 per cent increase of staff exchange
- 55 per cent increase of international research cooperation
- 54 per cent introduction of further education programmes
- 45 per cent changes of the degree structure
- 38 per cent establishment of new faculties/departments
- 38 reorganisation of academic staff development and continuous education programmes.

(3) Management and administrative structures:
- 37 per cent reorganisation of higher education management
- 36 per cent establishment of technology transfer units
- 34 per cent reorganisation of financial administration
- 32 per cent establishment/reorganisation of cooperation with industry/commerce
- 29 per cent reorganisation of administrative staff training
- 27 per cent establishment of a career advisory unit for students/ graduates
- 25 per cent establishment of an international office/unit
- 25 per cent reorganisation of administrative structures at institutional level.

Although a substantial amount of money has been spent on the improvement of equipment since 1990/91, it is not surprising to note that further improvement in this area is seen as important by about three-quarters of the CEE higher education institutions. On the one hand, not all departments, faculties and central services of the institutions were provided with modern equipment during the last years and, on the other hand, the rapid development of new technologies leads to a continuous necessity for further investments in this area.

More than 80 per cent of the institutions are currently undertaking substantial changes or intending to make them in the future regarding at least a single aspect of improving educational facilities and mobility arrangements for students and staff members. This figure shows clearly that de-

Table 7.1
Use of TEMPUS Support for Current and Future Changes at the Higher Education Institutions of CEE Partner Countries (per cent)

	Degree of current and future changes			Use of TEMPUS support *			
	Substantial	Moderate	Not at all	Already available	Available and applied/aim to apply for	Applied for/ aim to apply for	No use intended
Improvement of equipment e.g. computer centres, laboratories, libraries etc.	78	20	2	39	21	32	8
Introduction of new course programmes	59	37	5	39	11	44	5
Introduction of new teaching methods	57	37	6	36	12	46	6
Increase of student exchange	57	41	2	34	15	42	9
Increase of staff exchange	56	40	5	39	14	36	11
Increase of international research cooperation	55	37	8	21	7	49	23
Introduction of further education programmes	54	33	13	19	5	70	6
Changes of the degree structure	45	32	23	23	7	49	21
Establishment of new faculties/departments	38	42	20	14	7	53	26
Reorganisation of academic staff development and continuous education programmes	38	44	19	17	4	58	21
Reorganisation of higher education management	37	43	20	16	4	49	31

(continued)

(Table 7.1)

	Degree of current and future changes			Use of TEMPUS support *			
	Substantial	Moderate	Not at all	Already available	Available and applied/aim to apply for	Applied for/ aim to apply for	No use intended
Establishment of technology transfer units or centres	36	37	27	12	4	56	28
Reorganisation of the financial administration	34	41	26	15	7	50	28
Establishment/ reorganisation of cooperation with industry/commerce	32	49	19	13	6	51	31
Reorganisation of administrative staff training and re-training	29	48	23	22	4	49	25
Establishment of a career advisory unit for students/graduates	27	33	40	0	0	74	26
Establishment of an international office/unit	25	30	45	17	7	57	20
Reorganisation of administrative structures at institutional level	25	48	27	15	0	54	31

* Per cent of institutions stating current or future changes in the respective area

Source: Survey on the development and restructuring of institutions participating in TEMPUS

velopment and restructuring of higher education institutions in CEE countries in these areas are still going on for various reasons.

Altogether, about three-quarters of the institutions surveyed mentioned at least one of the various aspects concerning the management and administrative structures of the higher education institutions as a matter for substantial changes. Although the individual items were seen as less important than the educational measures or the improvement of equipment, most institutions still see the necessity for an improvement of administrative and management structures.

Almost all of the institutions included in the survey had already applied or aim to apply for TEMPUS II support (90 per cent) at the time the survey was conducted. In this respect it is not surprising, that the more strongly the various aspects are emphasised by the institutions as areas for current and future changes, the more often TEMPUS support is already available for running TEMPUS II JEPs or other measures or the institutions had applied or aimed to apply for support. Only 8 per cent of the institutions of higher education responding to the questionnaire stated that they do not aim to make use of TEMPUS support for the further improvement of their equipment. The respective proportion was about 15 per cent on average as regards one of the aspects of educational and mobility measures and more than one-quarter as regards the improvement of management and administrative structures.

By and large, most of the institutions which intended to continue the development and restructuring in one or the other respect expressed their wish to make use of TEMPUS support. The answers to the questionnaire did not allow us to estimate how far the implementation and the success of further developments depend on the TEMPUS support, but it seems to be a matter of fact that TEMPUS is seen as an important source by the actors at the central level of the institutions.

The new emphasis in TEMPUS II on institutional management and strategic planning seems to indicate a certain re-orientation of TEMPUS. During its first four to five years, TEMPUS clearly followed a 'bottom-up' approach of support addressed to educational activities being carried out in the faculties and departments.

Two aspects seem to have greatly influenced the 'bottom-up' approach of TEMPUS. After almost half a century of 'central planning' by the state, higher education laws which were passed in almost all CEE countries have strongly favoured a decentralised structure of higher education, that is, a high degree of autonomy for faculties and departments and a relatively weak role of the rector and the central administration with regard to educational activities and frequently also financial matters of the faculties. This situation is strongly defended by the faculties. On both sides – central level and faculties – central planning and strategic management is often regarded as a form of control rather than a possibility of support and cooperation. The second aspect is that TEMPUS was created as a support programme for higher education reform and renewal targeted to the level of faculties and departments and explicitly focusing on educational activities. Acquisition of equipment, curriculum development, staff and student mobility are eligible activities which even in Western Europe are not taking place on the central level of the higher education institutions.

Although one could argue that impacts or outcomes of TEMPUS support could be improved if project activities had less of an 'island' character and were more strongly integrated into national and/or institutional development strategies, it seems to be more logical to expect outcomes of educational activities and curriculum development for the same subject at other institutions not involved in TEMPUS than for the management and administrative issues of institutional governance. The interviews carried out at institutions in the CEE partner countries clearly showed that the success or failure of TEMPUS JEPs was not dependent on the fact of whether there was a national and/or institutional development strategy or not.

The promotion of institutional management in the framework of TEMPUS seems to have been strongly favoured by the EU rather than in the CEE countries themselves. Although the development of institutional management is meanwhile reflected in the national priorities of several CEE countries and supported by the introduction of new regulations (i.e. statements about institutional development plans and a match of project proposals to these plans have to accompany the letters of endorsement), it is an open question whether the compliance of the central level with these requirements has any impact on TEMPUS activities in the faculties and departments. Of the respondents to the institutional questionnaire about 90 per cent claimed the existence of an overall development plan for their institution, but only 5 per cent of the TEMPUS JEPs actually had institutional management and administration as an objective. Less than 30 per cent of institutions saw a necessity for further reorganisation of their management and administrative structures. This is no contradiction to the fact that we have also come across a few very positive and successful examples of strategic management integrating TEMPUS activities more or less systematically into a development plan for the institution as a whole. During the first two years of TEMPUS II a review and improvement of university management became the objective of only four per cent of all newly established JEPs (see also Table 3.13). Clearly standing out in this respect is the Czech Republic with 21 per cent of newly established JEPs having institutional management as an objective. However, 77 per cent of CME projects selected for support in the 1995/96 selection round were concerned with institutional development and restructuring (cf. also pp. 85 – 90). In addition, a considerably increased allocation of funds can be noted for CME activities in general as well as for individual CME projects.

If the overall institutional development which has been achieved in the field of higher education in CEE countries is compared to the situation at the beginning of TEMPUS I, some aspects may support the view that prerequisites have been established to move from a bottom-up approach in TEMPUS to a strategic management approach. At the beginning of TEMPUS I it could rightly be assumed that potentials for activities were higher in faculties and departments of the higher education institutions and thus a greater dynamics for the development of TEMPUS could be expected using a bottom-up approach. In the meantime, most institutions have development plans and many have well functioning, sometimes highly professionalised international relations offices. It might therefore suggest itself to provide TEMPUS support for the establishment of institutional infrastructures in which international activities can be coordinated. In the face of a considerable increase in these activities, continuity could be achieved if similar tasks and responsibilities were brought together in one central unit and supported by the institutional administration.

Without predetermining the answer to the question whether a more strategically oriented management of TEMPUS activities presents itself as a feasible opportunity on the level of what has to date been achieved with TEMPUS support, a similarity of this scenario to developments in the ERASMUS part of SOCRATES becomes nevertheless visible, namely a trend towards the promotion of strategic management and an institutional infrastructure.

Chapter 8

Major Achievements and Problems of TEMPUS Activities

8.1 Introduction

This report presents and assesses the major findings of the TEMPUS Evaluation Study carried out between July 1995 and February 1996. Its focus is on the administrative framework, the policy decisions and the TEMPUS supported activities in the period between 1990/91 and 1995/96. An emphasis is put on the experiences of CEE institutions, partners and political as well as administrative actors. The extent of their satisfaction with the outcomes of TEMPUS activities, the impacts and achievements perceived by them and the functioning of processes of policy formation and administration which have been established on the national level for TEMPUS activities form the centre of our study. Perceptions of Western partners as regards the major achievements and problems of TEMPUS activities come into play mainly through their inclusion in our JEP questionnaire. In this survey they represent the majority of respondents.

The focus on the supra-institutional setting on the national level of CEE countries involved in TEMPUS (in the framework of our interviews) and on CEE institutions (in the institutional questionnaire) was adopted as the most appropriate approach for this study, insofar as the TEMPUS Programme itself is targeted to support the restructuring and renewal of the higher education systems in the Central and Eastern European partner countries.

In this chapter we will discuss and assess the major achievements and problems of TEMPUS activities as perceived by the JEP partners cooperating in the framework of TEMPUS as well as by the central level of the CEE institutions which have been involved in TEMPUS activities. The chapter takes up the questions posed in Chapter 1 and presents the answers in the light of what has been achieved with TEMPUS support in the CEE partner countries and what the relevant TEMPUS actors in these countries perceive as impacts and problems. Thus, the most interesting results of our analyses are highlighted. The chapter concludes with some considerations for the future of TEMPUS.

TEMPUS, like the PHARE Programme, was launched as a rapid aid mechanism for the new democracies of Central and Eastern Europe. It was the aim of the TEMPUS Programme to promote reforms of the higher education systems of the CEE partner countries and to effectively support the adjustment of these countries to the needs of a market economy. During the past six years, most higher education institutions in the CEE countries experienced substantial changes. The number of students at TEMPUS-supported institutions (about three-quarters of the higher education institutions in the CEE partner countries) increased by more than 50 per cent. About 40 per cent of the degree programmes existing at TEMPUS-supported institutions of higher education in 1995 had been newly established during the last five years, almost 30 per cent changed substantially during that period and only slightly more than 30 per cent remained unchanged. In general, the contribution of TEMPUS to these changes is rated highly by most actors on the departmental, institutional and national level in the CEE partner countries.

TEMPUS had to keep pace with these dynamics and was in almost every year adapted to the changing needs of reform and renewal activities at the higher education institutions. A number of revisions have been made of the various aspects of the structure and the measures of the TEMPUS Programme but no general reconsideration of the programme as a whole has yet been undertaken. When the second phase of the TEMPUS Programme was implemented in 1994/95 by the European Commission, attempts became more visible to restructure TEMPUS activities and emphasise more strongly certain newly emerging issues like national higher education planning and institutional development. An evaluation of the TEMPUS Programme after six years of operation will therefore have to point out main directions for the future TEMPUS-related decisions which can be found in Chapter 9.

8.2   The Policy Framework and Administration

The TEMPUS Programme was obviously perceived in most of the Central and Eastern European higher education institutions, notably during the first years of the programme, as manna falling from heaven: one could not fully explain why and how it came, but it was a lot (for those who were blessed), and it was available only for the chosen few.

The complex setting of the general rules of the TEMPUS Programme, their annual modifications and specifications by the European Commission, the national priorities revised annually (both their distinct and their vague elements), a multitude of rumours about the 'real' underlying political intentions and selection criteria created initially a considerable degree of irritation. First, complaints were frequent about lack of information, notably during the first years TEMPUS support was provided in the respective country. In the beginning there was a noteworthy proportion of proposals the writers of which obviously had not been aware of the target areas, the national priorities and the publicly stated selection criteria. Second, the harsh watersheds of support, the inclusion of subject area *x* and exclusion of subject area *y*, the rich support for activity *a* and the complete neglect of activity *b*, were regarded as somewhat arbitrary. This still holds true although the initial priority of business studies and engineering has been redressed to a certain extent by the subsequent diversification of subject areas.

Many potential participants from CEE countries perceived it as crucial to find smart, prestigious and powerful partners in the West, even if their insight in terms of the needs of the partners in the CEE partner countries was limited. Many believed that the right connection to the national government or to the various layers of the TEMPUS administration was essential. Given the complexity of the support system and the inexperience concerning the ways to cope with it, and given the 'life and death' relevance of being supported during the first years, one cannot be but surprised by how peacefully the first two years of the TEMPUS were 'survived'.

The major thrusts of TEMPUS support set by the Commission were largely regarded as pre-conditions one could not challenge. In some respects, the donor was perceived as being too almighty to be criticised. However, many of the beneficiaries as well as the losers – in the competition for support considered the immediate needs in terms of equipment and the need for provision of opportunities for first encounters with higher education in the West as more urgent than the pursuit of heroic goals of curriculum development, of faculty restructuring or student exchange. This issue was more salient in countries in which TEMPUS was initially, or even until today, essentially the only source of support for new equipment. Some bowed opportunistically, and many eventually accepted the bundle of activities eligible for support as a reasonable strategy for their development. One area stood out where amazement and criticism continued to prevail even after the initial uncertainties vanished: the Commission's strict emphasis on support for teaching without support for research. Instead of having a separation between the academies of science and other research institutes on the one hand and pure teaching institutions on the other, the major rationale of a university is to ensure a cross-fertilisation between research and teaching. The insistence on not supporting the purchase of equipment which might have considerable value for research or on not supporting mobility that was obviously helpful for research tended to be viewed as a misled superimposition of inner bureaucratic principles of the Commission. It was often seen as an irony that a higher education reform in Central and Eastern Europe that aimed to redress the weakness of the previous regime of separating the research and teaching functions institutionally by creating closer links between teaching and research was provided support from the West under the condition that the award should serve only a single of the two major functions of higher education.

Most of those wishing to be awarded support by TEMPUS did not initially share the view that TEMPUS had a 'bottom up' approach. Instead, they felt very much at the mercy of a superstructure of conditions and constraints, irrespective of whether they were seen as the outgrowth of targeted policies from above or as coincidental barriers and constraints due to inertia. Over the years, however, the beneficiaries in the CEE countries noted that conditions for support were relatively open and allowed for specific thrusts of innovation. With the growing refinement of national TEMPUS priorities in the second half of TEMPUS I balancing mechanisms (e.g. rotation of subject areas eligible for support or formulation of additional preferences) were introduced into the priorities to give those institutions and subject areas an opportunity to participate in TEMPUS projects which had felt excluded before.

There is hardly any generalisation possible about the ways the higher education institutions experienced and perceived national TEMPUS policies on the part of national authorities and governments in the CEE partner countries. National TEMPUS policies were seen as too diverse regarding the extent of their vagueness or refinement, or the extent to which they met or questioned the views held by the various representatives of the higher education institutions and departments. Altogether we note, however, frequent changes of governments and vagueness of national policies were more often criticised in the interviews than very targeted government policies, but we cannot exclude a bias of the interviews in this respect, because the interviews addressed more beneficiaries of TEMPUS support than unsuccessful applicants.

The nervous debates and the frequent policy changes in some countries harmed the continuous support over three years for the JEPs to a much lesser extent than it was feared initially. As already shown before, the proportion of Phare support for TEMPUS was relatively stable in most countries, and shifts of national priorities seldom led to a reduction or cancellation of support for already existing JEPs after the first or the second year of support. In addition, most CEE countries involved representatives of the higher education institutions in policy decisions about national priorities. This has, however, not prevented requests for an improvement of information about and transparency of national priorities.

Policy formulation and policy decisions for TEMPUS on the national level of the CEE partner countries are a major task of the TEMPUS advisory or supervisory boards which have been established in all countries. The composition of board members guarantees the involvement of all key actors in the relevant processes of decision-making. The boards serve to coordinate and balance the various interests of the key actors and to give legitimacy to TEMPUS policy decisions on the national level.

Altogether, we note a high level of trust at the higher education institutions in most CEE countries as far as information, communication, advice and support of the National TEMPUS Offices are concerned. Although some criticism was voiced with regard to the transparency of selection processes and selection decisions, the NTOs were generally considered very supportive in their attitude to departments asking for advice. The later the participants were awarded TEMPUS support for the first time, the more they underscored the role the National TEMPUS Office had played for the application. The offices tend to be seen as a rock in the various policy storms potentially affecting TEMPUS support. The growing competence and professionalisation of the National TEMPUS Offices has also led to their influential though informal role in TEMPUS policy formation.

The TEMPUS-related decision-making processes and administrative procedures which have been established in the CEE partner countries are characterised by complex dynamics because they have to:

- ensure a balance between the Western donors and initiators of the TEMPUS Programme itself as well as of the TEMPUS project activities and policy-makers, partners and participants in the CEE countries
- establish a balance between the autonomous views of the higher education institutions and the economic and social demands of societies in a process of rapid change
- involve a broad range of actors in TEMPUS policy formation
- ensure a smooth coordination of the various stages of decision-making about the programme and the various stages of the award process.

In theory, we observe a clear model of decision-making in which a single key actor is defined for each stage. In practice, however, the inter-relations of the various stages as well as frequent overlaps and some confusion about the actual activities created a centripetal pressure towards a single major decision-making arena and towards a managerial unit serving as moderator and trouble-shooter for most key administrative processes and – by more or less tacit agreement – taking over an informal though influential role for TEMPUS policy formation.

The TEMPUS advisory or supervisory boards in each of the CEE partner countries serve the former and the National TEMPUS Offices serve the latter function.

Although the TEMPUS advisory or supervisory boards as well as the National TEMPUS Offices work amazingly well, some limitations regarding their role should be stated as well. First, we note a smooth functioning and successful activities in the majority but not in all CEE countries. If the NTOs and the boards do not work well, TEMPUS activities as a whole become vulnerable. Second, the mechanisms and procedures which have been created for TEMPUS policy decisions and administration are helpful for the coordination processes within the respective countries, but not necessarily for ensuring good cooperation between the EU and the actors in the CEE countries. Third, the national authorities involved in TEMPUS (i.e. the Phare coordination units and the Ministries of Education) vary considerably in terms of their involvement and their strategic behaviour. Finally, the NTOs might acquire an even more conflicting set of functions as they have currently if the process of decentralisation and transfer of tasks and responsibilities from the ETF TEMPUS Department to the NTOs continues.

The actual involvement of the Ministries of Education in the CEE partner countries in the processes of policy formation and decision-making for TEMPUS on the national level varies considerably. On the whole, a more pro-active involvement of the ministries in TEMPUS could have been expected because TEMPUS is also targeted to achieve impacts on the level of the higher education systems in the CEE partner countries. A coherent and integrated higher education development strategy existed in none of the CEE partner countries during TEMPUS I. Although we found a rather close cooperation between the Ministries and the NTOs, the growing professionalisation of the latter had led in most countries to the tacit agreement that the NTOs could be depended upon when decisions had to be prepared, proposals to be drafted, briefings were needed, or preliminary negotiations had to be conducted. The majority of the NTOs has to report regularly to the Ministry, but this is less understood as a form of bureaucratic control than as a form of keeping the ministry informed about what is going on in TEMPUS on the national level.

The Phare responsibles have a somewhat ambiguous role in the steering of the TEMPUS Programme. On the one hand, TEMPUS is one of Phare's sub-programmes and the TEMPUS budget comes from national Phare resources. On the other hand, the logic of the TEMPUS Programme was structured on the model of incentive programmes like ERASMUS and thus has a somewhat different legal structure and is much more decentralised. Nevertheless, the participation of Phare responsibles in the main domains of policy formation and decision-making is arranged in most CEE countries by their membership in the TEMPUS advisory boards. Phare responsibles have three basic options for their degree of involvement in TEMPUS:

- They could exercise a stronger control of the TEMPUS Programme by using their 'power of the purse'.
- They could exercise a stronger bureaucratic control by making the determination of the TEMPUS budget dependent on the fulfilment of certain conditions.
- They could opt for a bottom-up approach because being a member of the TEMPUS advisory or supervisory board ensures sufficient consideration of their views.

We have found examples of all three options listed above. Because of the difference in the sectors addressed by TEMPUS and by Phare we had, however, assumed more serious conflicts of interests between the key actors. There were only two cases in which one of the actors involved in the relevant policy decisions left the established arena for dialogue and coordination on the national level to lobby with higher level authorities.

The involvement of Phare responsibles in the major policy decisions for TEMPUS on the national level has not led to a very strong integration of actual TEMPUS project activities into the Phare activities. Although Phare responsibles became more and more aware of the possible contributions of TEMPUS for the achievement of Phare objectives, they have tended to avoid overlaps and even complementarity in concrete project activities which would have been possible, for example, in areas like transport, urban planning, energy, waste disposal, geology, or environmental protection. On the project level the dissociation of the two programmes from each other was more visible than on the level of policy formation.

National TEMPUS Offices (NTOs) have been established in all CEE partner countries for the administration of the TEMPUS Programme. The overall technical assistance for the programme and administration of the programme was taken over originally by the EC TEMPUS Office in Brussels and then integrated into a special unit at the European Training Foundation in Torino, the TEMPUS Department.

At the beginning of TEMPUS it was evident that the role of the EC TEMPUS Office was most important for getting the programme established and running as well as helping the countries involved with information and advice. In addition, the EC TEMPUS Office took over the responsibility of training the NTO staff and support them in all their tasks.

The increased routinisation and stabilisation of TEMPUS administration in the CEE partner countries, together with a considerable professionalisation of NTO staff members, has led to a gradual transfer of tasks and responsibilities from 'Brussels' to the NTOs. Frequently, the NTOs have complained about a lack of recognition of this increased professionalisation by the EC TEMPUS Office/ETF TEMPUS Department. In addition, technical problems have made communication and cooperation more difficult after technical assistance was transferred to Torino.

Thus, it does not come as a surprise that the NTOs tend to ask questions about the future role of the ETF TEMPUS Department. NTO Directors have become interested in a new agreement concerning the division of labour among the ETF TEMPUS Department and the NTOs.

8.3   Changes in National Priorities

The annual establishment of national priorities for the award of TEMPUS support in each of the CEE partner countries has become an important procedure of policy formation. In all CEE partner countries, the TEMPUS advisory or supervisory boards are involved in the discussion and proposal of these priorities.

At the beginning of TEMPUS priorities were not highly differentiated although in some countries they tended to function as a substitute for the only embryonic existence of a national policy for the reform of higher education. A second important function of national priorities was and still is to constitute a link between Phare and TEMPUS objectives on the one hand and national as well as institutional reform and renewal activities on the other.

It is therefore not surprising that the rather simple list of subjects and subject areas forming the national priorities at the beginning of TEMPUS quickly became more detailed and refined in most of the CEE partner countries. Notably, the rather thematic approach was complemented by structural priorities. Frequently, both appeared in combination, with thematic priorities subordinated to structural ones.

Parallel to the growing importance of priorities, various national foci became visible, thus reflecting differences in the pace and shape of higher education reform and renewal. This process was supported in TEMPUS II by a growing emphasis on support for higher education planning and strategic management of higher education institutions.

The development and changes in the character of national priorities in the first six years of TEMPUS can be divided into the following three stages:

(1) During the first two years of TEMPUS I the thematic approach dominated, consisting mainly of a list of subjects and subject areas for which TEMPUS support was awarded preferentially. However, applications did not always have to comply strictly with national priorities in order to be accepted. Priorities were also quite similar in most of the CEE partner countries.

(2) During the second half of TEMPUS I national priorities gradually started to diverge and to become more detailed for most of the CEE partner countries. Structural priorities became more important or combinations of structural and thematic priorities were introduced reflecting at the same time various national thrusts of higher education reform and renewal. The assessment of applications was handled more strictly according to the criterion of compliance with national priorities.

(3) At the beginning of TEMPUS II the trend towards divergence continued. Structural priorities tended to dominate and applications had to comply fully with national priorities in order to become eligible for support. In most CEE partner countries additional preferences were introduced for JEP and IMG applications. For the first time, priorities were introduced for CME applications. Finally, all applications had to be endorsed by the rector of the respective higher education institution, who also had to state whether and how each application fitted into the institutional development strategy.

Except for rare occasions, the annual process of establishing national priorities has been without problems. The TEMPUS advisory or supervisory boards in each CEE partner countries serve as an arena in which all key actors involved in TEMPUS are represented and can find a consensus. In principle, this has turned out to be an optimal model. Problems were caused only in those cases in which one of the actors or groups of actors involved tried to influence the decision-making process by addressing a higher level authority or in which priorities were changed without seeking feedback and agreement from the other actors involved.

It is in the nature of making priorities to establish hierarchies and preferences. Therefore it is not surprising that some institutions and some subjects or subject areas always feel excluded from being able to launch a successful application. Together with an emphasis on high quality applications, this tended to exclude weaker institutions and subjects at the beginning of TEMPUS. However, the problem has been redressed to a certain extent by various means:

- a broadening of the range of subjects and subject areas named in the national priorities to include those being under-represented
- an annual rotation of subjects or subject areas
- an emphasis on structural priorities including all subjects or subject areas
- the introduction of a preference for the participation of several institutions from one country within one JEP so that weaker institutions could learn from the stronger ones
- an offer of special help and advice by the NTOs to help weaker institutions with the formulation of an application fulfilling the quality requirements.

There is one issue which has not yet been solved in a satisfactory way, and that is the early conveying of information to potential applicants about national priorities. As a rule, applications are prepared a long time in advance before submitting them. The decision-making processes about the national priorities as well as the consultation process with the European Commission about them lead to a relatively late announcement of national priorities so that applicants often find it difficult to take them properly into account before having to meet the deadline for submission. Usually, the NTOs organise information days for all higher education institutions as soon as the priorities are finalised. However, in the course of our interviews there were some complaints about late arrival of important information.

8.4 Institutions and the Institutional Setting

In the first half of the 1990s, substantial and rapid changes of the higher education systems in the Central and Eastern European countries have occurred. Our survey of institutions participating in TEMPUS showed an increase of full-time student numbers by about 50 per cent. New faculties were established in more than two-thirds of the institutions responding to our survey and new departments in about 90 per cent of the institutions. Forty per cent of the degree programmes offered in 1995 were new and 30 per cent had changed substantially. TEMPUS has considerably contributed to these changes.

Between 1990 and 1995, altogether almost 70 per cent of the higher education institutions in the CEE partner countries participated in TEMPUS and were awarded support for their activities. Although this figure is rather impressive, some imbalances could be noted with regard to different types of higher education institutions participating in TEMPUS activities. During the first two years of TEMPUS I, support tended to concentrate in larger and frequently more prestigious institutions located in the capitals or in other cities with several higher education institutions. Non-university higher education institutions were under-represented, as were smaller and specialised institutions in the provinces. Towards the end of TEMPUS I balancing mechanisms have been introduced into the national priorities to achieve a better coverage of institutions and to broaden the range of subjects eligible for TEMPUS support.

During TEMPUS I a better balance between types and sizes of CEE higher education institutions participating in TEMPUS has gradually been achieved. This has been less the case in terms of the subject balance. A concentration of TEMPUS support remains on business studies and engineering, while other subjects are better represented, their proportion among the JEPs is still very low. Other imbalances concerning JEP participation remain as well. For example, the proportion of the Phare budget allocated to TEMPUS varies considerably among the CEE countries so that the number of JEPs which can proportionally be supported disadvantages some CEE countries in terms of the profits and impacts which can be gained for restructuring and renewal of their higher education systems.

With regard to the involvement of higher education institutions from EU Member States, The Netherlands and the UK are clearly over-represented in TEMPUS activities in comparison to their participation in ERASMUS, and the participation of G24 countries that are not EU Member States might be characterised as negligible.

Concerning the partner configuration within individual JEPs, we note some changes during TEMPUS I. First, there was an increase of the number of partners within the JEPs. This increase was largely due to the growing number of partners from one CEE country as well as of Western partners in a JEP. The number of partners from different CEE countries clearly decreased so that multi-CEE JEPs practically disappeared. The involvement of enterprises in Joint European Projects decreased considerably during TEMPUS I. In 1990/91 the proportion of JEPs with enterprise involvement was 31 per cent and in 1993/94 the respective figure was 20 per cent. Our interviews have conveyed the impression that involvement of enterprises in Joint European Projects was predominantly a passive one and can quite frequently be characterised as a 'sleeping partnership'. Actual enterprise involvement in JEPs consisted mostly in the provision of places for internships. Only very few of the respondents to the institutional questionnaire stated a substantial impact of TEMPUS on links between higher education and industry.

Most persons from faculties and departments involved seem to agree that TEMPUS-supported activities during the first four years of the TEMPUS Programme were more or less a matter of the respective faculties or departments in the eligible countries. The university as an institution did not come into play very much in CEE countries:

- Here and there, the prestige and the political influence of the rector or another top executive of the university was seen as instrumental in influencing national TEMPUS policies or as helpful in other ways of ensuring support for the decision to award grants to the respective JEP and department.

- Resources for administrative support were mostly provided through decisions in the respective departments, and funds to complement the TEMPUS-supported activities were hardly made available at all.

- The university administration was not infrequently viewed as inexperienced in those matters and not very supportive in their attitude. In some countries, however, a change towards more active support of the departments involved in international cooperation has begun in the second half of TEMPUS I.

- TEMPUS support addressed the cooperating departments in an institutional environment prevailing in most CEE countries which was shaped considerably by a traditional and strong formal competence and influence of the faculty.

Approximately two-thirds of the institutions included in the institutional survey had, however, an international office at the central level of the institution typically staffed with two or three professionals and one or two secretaries. It was estimated by those surveyed at the central level that these offices spend more than a quarter of their time on TEMPUS-related activities. At various institutions, a strengthening of the international offices was observed. This tended to be regarded by JEP partners in the faculties and departments as helpful for information and for the improvement of some administrative processes. Few, however, considered this as becoming instrumental to major internationalisation policies of the respective university.

The views conveyed by the JEP partners during our interviews with regard to the role of the central institutional level contrasted to a certain extent to the responses of actors on the central institutional level to our institutional questionnaire. Respondents to this questionnaire have reported a number of further initiatives to provide administrative support to the faculties and departments involved in JEPs. Concerning assistance for administrative tasks of TEMPUS activities provided by the central level of the institutions, the following items were listed most frequently:

- administrative support concerning student and staff exchange was mentioned by almost three-quarters of the respondents
- somewhat less than two-thirds stated the provision of accommodation for incoming staff and students
- general administrative assistance was offered by more than half of the responding institutions
- more than half also stated the financial administration of TEMPUS money
- the organisation of TEMPUS-related meetings was taken over by half of the institutions responding
- more than one-third assigned special staff for managing TEMPUS activities.

These contrasting views about the role of the central level for TEMPUS activities might be linked to the character of central level activities considered supportive for TEMPUS by the central level itself on the one hand and by the faculties and departments carrying out TEMPUS projects on the other. For example, the central level provided less frequently additional resources for carrying out TEMPUS-related activities. For various reasons the administration of TEMPUS funds by the financial department of the institution was often not seen as advantageous and helpful by JEP partners in the faculties and departments.

Apart from support and assistance offered to faculties and departments involved in TEMPUS activities, most institutions claim to undertake strategic planning, but the reality seems to be more moderate than the term 'strategic planning' leads to expect. This is supported by experiences in the course of our interviews. The success of TEMPUS activities in faculties and departments as perceived by representatives of the central institutional level seems to depend less on strategic planning than could be assumed. The extent to which such planning might contribute to an increased impact of TEMPUS on overall structural changes and to changes of the administrative arrangements and institutional management still remains to be seen.

The views of CEE partners in Joined European Projects responding to our JEP questionnaire varied to quite a degree about the question whether a more pro-active role of the university administration should be deplored or hailed, if the central administration should be strengthened or not and if yes, in which direction the institution should head eventually. Many favour a more competent, efficient and service-oriented administration. For example, financial support for the training of the administrators was often named as a valuable investment for the future. But opinions diverge fundamentally, whether a stronger role of the university was desirable. Views are widely supported – not infrequently by rectors as well – that strong faculties serve best the prime goals of the universities and are less vulnerable to inappropriate infringements of academic freedom. In various CEE countries this is also reflected in debates about the question whether the competences of the faculties or those of the central level of the university should be determined and spelled out by higher education legislation. Views also differ as regards the best possible use of TEMPUS support. Some consider the prime utilisation of TEMPUS support by single faculties or smaller units as the best strategy for promoting reforms in higher education, while others favour a wider spread of its utilisation within an institution of higher education.

8.5 Strategic Management

With the beginning of TEMPUS II, the European Commission introduced strategic planning and management activities into the programme to complement the bottom-up approach of educational activities followed in TEMPUS I. In the first year of TEMPUS II, projects to support national higher education planning became eligible in the framework of CMEs (CME+ projects). Projects to support strategic management of higher education institutions became eligible in the framework of JEPs (JEP+ projects). For both types of projects only national higher education authorities in the CEE partner countries were allowed to define objectives and aims and to suggest potential institutions from their own country to tender for and carry out these projects in cooperation with Western partners.

Only very few CME+ and JEP+ projects were eventually awarded support. According to the European Commission, this was due to a lack of competitive tendering and insufficient quality of some of the applications. However, other reasons seem to have played a role as well.

First, there is a considerable degree of resistance from higher education faculties and departments against attempts to re-centralise higher education steering and planning. Higher Education Laws in most of the CEE partner countries gave faculties and departments a rather high degree of autonomy and power to organise their internal affairs.

Second, attempts at national higher education planning are just starting and are still a rather new experience in many CEE countries – this all the more so because such attempts are to be different from planning practices before 1989. In some CEE countries frequent changes of government hindered the establishment of a certain amount of continuity in planning. Widespread characteristics for this problem are, for example, a considerable growth of private higher education without proper accreditation procedures and a large increase in student numbers because of less restricted access. At the same time institutions are being faced with insufficient budgets.

Third, higher education planning and strategic management were and still are impeded by very low budgets for public institutions, covering just the bare necessities for survival in some CEE countries. Whereas brain-drain to Western countries caused by TEMPUS opportunities has not been a serious problem, brain-drain of young researchers and academics to private enterprises is sometimes considerable. This was mentioned frequently by deans of faculties or heads of departments in the course of our interviews.

The CME+ and JEP+ projects of the first TEMPUS II year were integrated in the second TEMPUS II year into the classic TEMPUS activities eligible for support, that is, applications for structural JEPs may look for support to improve institutional management and applications for CME projects may look for support to improve higher education planning. In general, there is a higher degree of awareness for the necessity of more strategic approaches to institutional management. Altogether, about three-quarters of the institutions surveyed mentioned at least one of a list of eight individual items concerning the management and administrative structures of the institution as an object for substantial change.

Thus, the new emphasis in TEMPUS II seems to indicate a certain re-orientation of TEMPUS. However, the number of JEPs which were actually awarded support for activities to improve strategic management in the first two years of TEMPUS II did not reflect this. Only four per cent of all newly established JEPs during this time aimed at a review and improvement of university management.

Some aspects may nevertheless support the view that the prerequisites have been established to move from a bottom-up approach in TEMPUS to a strategic management approach. Most higher education institutions in the CEE partner countries have institutional development plans and many have well functioning, sometimes highly professionalised international relations offices. A further promotion of strategic management will have to be complemented by an institutional infrastructure appropriate for the ensuing tasks.

8.6 Financial Conditions

The majority of JEPs were awarded less funds than they had applied for. In most cases it was left to the partners cooperating within the JEP to decide where to reduce expenses. The average amount of funding per JEP during TEMPUS I increased somewhat; however, there were variations during the years of operation. Funding for JEPs in their first year was lowest and increased with each year of operation. The respondents to our institutional questionnaire claimed, furthermore, that the TEMPUS support covered on average only somewhat more than half of the administrative costs incurred.

Nevertheless, in response to a direct question, the majority of partners in Joint European Projects from CEE countries rated the funds provided to them as 'generous'. However, the proportion of those rating the financial conditions positively was clearly smaller than the proportion of those praising the educational outcomes of JEP activities. Although the sums seem to be impressive, notably in those countries where TEMPUS continues to be the major source of funding for all activities beyond the basic institutional needs, limits always come into the picture as well: more would be helpful. This notwithstanding, the interviews confirm as well that the beneficiaries of TEMPUS tend to appreciate the amount provided rather than emphasis ing the shortages which remain.

It is very clear that concerns regarding financial issues on the part of beneficiaries primarily were expressed as regards the financial administration. Six issues deserve attention:

(1) The delay in the provision of funds by the European Commission was regarded as the most serious drawback. Responses to the JEP questionnaire show that the participants note delays as well caused by the coordinators and contractors of JEPs, banking problems and the university administration in the CEE countries, but delays caused by the Commission were clearly seen as the most deplorable aspect. The de-

lays, of course, had by far more serious effects for the beneficiaries of TEMPUS support than respective delays in the Commission's educational programmes addressing EU Member States because most prospective beneficiaries in the CEE had no means to start activities before funds actually were available. The seriousness of the problem was confirmed by the respondents to our institutional questionnaire. Delays in the transfer of funds was stated as the most frequent source of financial problems, and delays caused by the Commission were named more frequently than delays caused by the contractors of JEPs. An internal problem caused by this for the central level of the institutions was the pre-financing of activities. In most of the CEE countries current institutional budgets are still too low and discretionary funds almost non-existent so that any pre-financing of activities is difficult.

(2) The problems of transfer of funds to CEE countries were serious notably in the first years, but they continued in some countries for an extended period. Frequently, money had to be carried in cash, equipment had to be transported personally, tickets had to be purchased in the West and mailed, etc. This inflated the administrative burden and often led to a reduction of educational activities originally envisaged. The complaint about those issues obviously were moderated by the view that this problem was clearly out of control of the TEMPUS management. Last but not least, improvement in this respect was visible in most CEE countries.

(3) Respondents to our questionnaire addressed to the central level of the institutions frequently stated internal problems concerning the provision of resources in terms of covering costs not borne by TEMPUS funds or simply not taken into account in the original project proposal. For example, some institutions have difficulties in bringing up the costs for the installation of security systems in laboratories or computer centres newly established with TEMPUS support.

(4) Quite a number of participants from the CEE countries were amazed to note that a considerable proportion of the TEMPUS funds eventually ended up in the West. Some criticism was also voiced concerning the proportion of overheads and administrative costs some Western partners claimed for their involvement in JEP activities. Some Western partners on the other hand complained about insufficient financial support for administrative expenses.

(5) Some interview partners criticised the TEMPUS administration for not allowing the use of funds initially earmarked for certain activities to be eventually used for other activities, for example mobility funds to be used for equipment. Even though the deliberate composition of

various activities was appreciated as a targeted strategy of higher education reforms, a bureaucratic control of consistent spending has forced some JEPs to pay back or to use funds in a sub-optimal way even in cases in which the delay of the provision of funds caused by the Commission was instrumental for the incomplete spending of earmarked funds.

(6) Finally, an uncertainty was felt frequently as regards the continuity of funding. In practice, however, the JEPs established in TEMPUS I were provided support for an average period of 2.7 years. The uncertainty was also redressed in TEMPUS II by the introduction of a pluri-annual system of JEP funding.

There is finally the issue of the three-year limit of support. This approach seems reasonable as a support device for reform 'take-offs', but many beneficiaries mentioned drawbacks of this approach. A library support serving, for example, for the purchase of foreign periodicals is regarded as a waste if the subscription has to be cancelled afterwards. Somewhat more than 10 per cent of the respondents to the JEP questionnaire from the CEE countries already observed deficiencies of the laboratory or office equipment. Those deficiencies were possibly gravest in the most ambitious reform projects. For example, curricular innovation aiming to use computer, multimedia, etc., came to a complete halt in a few cases because the equipment failed. Staff exchange might bear fruit, if not limited to a short period. Last but not least, a substantial proportion of the participants in the CEE countries pointed out that the development of teaching material stopped short of its implementation because no funds were available for printing or other means of material production, especially textbook production. A measure to redress this problem to a certain extent has been provided by the introduction of Joint European Networks (JENs). These are greatly appreciated for helping to wrap up project activities, stabilise ongoing cooperation and make future arrangements for the time when TEMPUS support has stopped.

Asked about changes of the TEMPUS Programme they would consider desirable from the point of view of the central administration, respondents to our institutional questionnaire stated three issues pertaining to the financial conditions of TEMPUS activities:

- a continuation of the TEMPUS Programme and an increase of its overall budget
- an increased support of student mobility
- a greater flexibility in the utilisation of funds, especially with regard to an easier transfer between budget items, a pluri-annual use of funds and an extension of deadlines for the utilisation of funds.

Altogether, we note that the TEMPUS support by the end of TEMPUS I played a strikingly different role in the various CEE countries in the total setting of financial support for higher education reforms. While in some countries it was one of a variety of sources to support innovation and renewal, in others it was the key source beyond bare subsistence. Regardless of the level of financial resources being provided to the higher education institutions out of the national budget, it can safely be stated that without TEMPUS support the development of higher education reform and renewal would have been considerably slower in all CEE countries.

8.7 Cooperation within the Networks

Most TEMPUS funds were made available for educational activities undertaken in the framework of networks comprising partners from the CEE partner countries and the West. In most cases, the cooperation within the Joint European Projects was positively assessed by the persons in charge at faculties and departments from CEE institutions participating in TEMPUS.

The initiative for cooperation came frequently from the Western partners. The CEE partners claim that in about half of the cases a joint initiative was taken, whereas a larger proportion of the Western partners observed the first initiatives coming from the West. Also, most participants from CEE countries interviewed emphasised that the Western partners dominated the scene initially. Many participants from the CEE countries were grateful for the initiative, inspiration and effort shown by their Western partners.

However, reservations were expressed not infrequently. There were many cases of high praise but some cases of bitter criticism as well. Reservations were put forward notably in the following directions:

- The Western partners were often seen as having played a too dominant role, particularly at the beginning of the cooperation. Some of the CEE partners underscored that they had accepted reform concepts or proposals for activities uncritically which they later regretted when their knowledge about possible options had expanded. Communication was frequently shaped by a status imbalance, thus not demanding from the Western partners to reflect on their lack of knowledge and understanding of the conditions and needs of their CEE partners. If CEE partners noted a low academic quality of support from the West, they often did not dare to express their concerns or even to drop the respective partner, because they were afraid to lose the financial support.

- As already noted, a considerable number of partners from CEE countries were amazed to note that their Western partners reserved substantial proportions of the TEMPUS support for themselves, though dramatic shortages were obvious on the part of the CEE partners. Obviously, they expected more solidarity as regards the problems of the higher education institutions in the CEE countries.

- In contrast, most of the Western partners claimed that their administrative efforts were reimbursed only partly and the TEMPUS scheme was financially not attractive. It is interesting, however, to note that institutions of higher education from the United Kingdom and from The Netherlands are over-represented among the Western participants of the TEMPUS Programme, that is, from the two European countries in which higher education institutions in the 1990s seem to be most strongly driven by cost and funding-awareness.

- In response to the questionnaire, about one-third each of the CEE participants reported that they were not fully informed about details of financial plans and accounts and that they did not receive copies of the reports sent to the Commission. About one-tenth expressed strong criticism concerning the imbalance of the budget allocation between partners.

- Finally, a considerable proportion of faculties and departments faced problems of attracting partners from the West. Faculties and departments of a lesser prestige, in remote areas or even more or less all institutions of higher education in some relatively poor CEE countries were so desperate in ensuring partnerships that they were ready to please their partners, for example by accepting financial gains of their Western partners or by accepting their dominance, even if they understood their respective weaknesses.

Obviously, there were general dynamics in the cooperation between the partners:

- The minimum configuration of two partners from the EU Member States was not infrequently on paper only. In those cases, one partner from the West was in charge, while the other served as a 'sleeping partner' to fulfil the official requirements.

- The more partners were officially part of the network, the lower was the proportion of partners the participants from CEE countries actively co-operated with.

- In various CEE countries more partners from the same country were taken on board. This was stimulated by some national governments in order to reduce the imbalance of a few winners and many losers in the competition for TEMPUS support and in order to increase the opportunities for less attractive partners.

- The cooperation of departments from different CEE countries was stimulated by TEMPUS only to a limited extent. The proportion of 'regional', that is multi-CEE, JEPs was small from the beginning and was further reduced, although the survey suggests that multi-CEE JEPs were slightly more successful than networks of the same size which only comprised one or more than one partner from a single CEE country. Reasons for this were obviously administrative and political barriers, especially in terms of the decision-making processes and funding modes involved.

- Other partners, that is enterprises or other organisations (for example research institutions), were frequently official partners within JEPs, but most of them neither played any central role in the administration of the JEP nor in its major activities.

These dynamics are so obvious that they call for a reconsideration. Should one Western partner be sufficient? Should cooperation with other partners, that is, other than those who cooperate most closely with each other and other partners like enterprises and organisations, be more strongly encouraged? What are the drawbacks and potentials of regional JEPs?

Overall, the cooperation was frequently unbalanced because many representatives of the West considered themselves not only as donors and carriers of information but also as academically superior partners. Over the years, however, the latter attitude changed somewhat. Cooperation soon led to a recognition of the academic calibre of the CEE partners. The questionnaire survey also shows that both the partners in the West and in the East consider the mobile students they host from their partners as academically slightly superior on average to their home students.

The dynamics in the cooperation between Western partners and partners from CEE countries has become more balanced once partners from CEE countries were able to act as coordinators and in some countries also as contractors in the Joint European Projects. Although not all countries are ready yet to accept contractor functions, the taking over of coordinator functions has been actively encouraged in national policies and was even introduced as a preference into the national priorities in some CEE countries.

8.8   The Administrative Functions in JEP Activities

The management of TEMPUS-related activities in generally is regarded as a very important task in the CEE countries. When it became possible for partners from an increasing number of CEE countries to act as coordinators and later also as contractors of JEPs in the second half of TEMPUS I, TEMPUS actors on the national level encouraged the taking over of such functions by CEE partners. It was expected that being in charge of such functions would lead to a better recognition of the actual needs of faculties and departments in the framework of the JEP activities as well as a better balance of administrative costs. Being in charge of administrative functions was additionally considered to be a valuable process of professionalisation for CEE partners with regard to later participation in other EU programmes and to further strengthen the self-confidence of CEE partners in the dynamic of cooperation with their Western partners.

The importance assigned to administrative functions within the JEPs is indicated by the fact that rectors, deans, vice-deans, heads of departments, their deputies or influential professors tend to be in charge. Partners from CEE countries without a coordinating function report that they spent more than six hours on average per week for administrative functions related to the TEMPUS Programme. Those in charge of coordination spent about twice as much time on average. Some of them saw this function as advancing their academic career whereas others viewed it as a drawback, that is a reduction of their opportunity to be academically active and productive. A gradual transfer of the coordination and contracting function from the Western to the CEE partners was viewed as a matter of course and is actively supported by national policies.

Many participants from CEE countries wanted administrators of their department to be in charge of the administration of TEMPUS rather than those from the central administration of the university. They saw the need to train the administrators and to be closely in touch with them at many instances.

In some cases, respondents even proposed to transfer the routine administration of the JEP funds to the National TEMPUS Offices. This was suggested in small countries getting involved in TEMPUS at a relatively late stage. In those instances, the administration was viewed as very complicated and the university administration as badly prepared for these tasks.

JEP partners and institutional administrators from CEE countries have both complained about the growing bureaucracy involved in the administration of TEMPUS activities. From the number of individual queries in

this regard three issues stand out: the wish for a simplification of application procedures, more flexibility with regard to book-keeping and a better
coordination of reports to be submitted.

8.9 The Educational Activities

In most of the Joint European Projects the partners were officially involved in all of the four major areas of educational activities supported by
TEMPUS – educational reform measures, structural development, staff
mobility and student mobility. Undoubtedly, some considered the concur-
rent involvement in the various activities as a convincing approach to
reform. Some had clear preferences for some of these activities and became involved in the others only in reaction to the support scheme so that
they eventually put an emphasis on the combination of all activities. There
are some participants as well for whom preferences for some activities
remained and the others were pursued only nominally or, if more than
nominally, merely for the sake of being awarded support for what they
conceived to be the core activities.

By and large, TEMPUS-supported activities in faculties and departments of CEE higher education institutions can be called a success story.
Altogether, the extent to which ambitious reform goals were successfully
pursued, but not successfully implemented or rather pretended, varied
substantially. Most observers, however, seem to agree that the proportion
of real success stories is remarkable and that useful changes could be observed in most cases. Eighty per cent of the JEP participants in CEE
countries expressed a high degree of satisfaction with the achievements
eventually reached.

Highly appreciated by CEE partners was the opportunity to establish or
improve contacts and communication with Western European scholars in
their respective fields, the acquisition of a better knowledge of what is
going on internationally and the integration into an international academic
community. Being able to compare their own theoretical level and standards to those of Western scholars and subject areas and seeing that the
outcome of the comparison was good or even better greatly increased self-
confidence in some cases. The proportion of Individual Mobility Grants
was 10 per cent of the overall mobility during TEMPUS I.

Staff development activities and intensive courses were frequently regarded useful as collective exercises of getting to know partners in other
countries, their activities and their ways of thinking. In general, staff development and intensive courses are seen as being useful to a similar ex-

tent as staff mobility. These impacts of getting a basic knowledge and becoming part of international networks of scholars were often regarded as more important and more likely to be achieved than the official purpose stated for the individual measures. Often, 're-training' of staff in a two-week course or individual visits were viewed as unrealistic, and the requirements for being awarded support and making use of the support were often assessed as merely creating an administrative hurdle which could have been prevented by setting more realistic goals from the outset.

Curricular development and teaching material production varied in their intensity. More than half of the respondents to the questionnaire survey claimed that they undertook substantial changes. There was also a considerable number of those who just modified individual courses or produced texts of minor relevance to the respective courses. In a few cases, it was not more than a franchising relationship: the Western partners just transferred their own models and materials to the CEE partners.

New equipment was the pride of the respective departments in the CEE countries, often a cause of envy of the neighbours in the respective university and sometimes even of their partners in the West. While in some cases it was closely linked to the respective educational measures, it was in most cases viewed as an improvement useful anyway, that is for the quality of educational activities in general, for easing future international cooperation, for supporting the research infrastructure, etc. Structural development met the highest consensus as being an important element of support.

Student exchange tended to be viewed as very helpful for those actually going abroad, but altogether less intertwined with the other reform activities. Obviously, there were only a few cases of close links between student exchange and the major thrusts of educational reform. This is also indicated by a relatively low up-take of Mobility-JEPs during TEMPUS I. Only towards the end of TEMPUS I and at the beginning of TEMPUS II have Mobility-JEPs become more important, mainly due to the expectation that participation in SOCRATES will soon be possible for most of the CEE countries. In this context, Mobility-JEPs are regarded as an appropriate preparation. Respondents to our questionnaire addressed to the central institutional level have also emphasised their wish to see an increased support of student mobility by TEMPUS in the future.

In some cases, students or doctoral candidates were supported who were expected to serve as junior academic staff upon return. In this context it is worth noting that the 'brain drain' effect of the TEMPUS Programme to Western countries was generally viewed as small. This was, however, less the case concerning the 'brain drain' effect of young researchers and future academic staff to industry and the private sector in general. TEMPUS support for postgraduate student mobility as well as staff mobility has more and more been used by higher education institutions in CEE countries as an incentive to keep or attract junior academic staff members.

In various JEPs, we observed a sequence of activities during the three years of support. In the first year, equipment was selected, purchased, delivered and implemented. Later in the year, staff got involved in visits and training, for the utilisation of equipment, for the preparation of joint educational activities and for a general up-grading of their knowledge. During the second and third year, the typical sequences of curriculum development, production of teaching material, etc., were pursued.

Altogether, the acquisition of equipment was most highly appreciated, followed by staff mobility. Curricular innovation, staff development and production of material was viewed as a core activity of higher education reforms for some participants, while others placed less emphasis on it or pursued it nominally. Student mobility was least highly appreciated.

8.10   Outcomes and Impacts

The first and most significant outcome of the TEMPUS activities was obviously the integration of the CEE partners into an international community of scholars and in some cases of administrators. They became accustomed to and versatile in this framework, they were integrated into smaller and larger networks, and they received some training to raise their competences and their status. Participation in TEMPUS activities also familiarised them with the general knowledge and skills necessary to successfully handle EU support instruments and programmes.

In addition, the TEMPUS Programme had tremendous socialising impacts. The efforts undertaken for improvement became feasible and worthwhile. Working in the framework of international networks became a promising innovation strategy.

TEMPUS support ensured significant provision of equipment for most of its beneficiaries. In a substantial number of faculties and departments in CEE higher education institutions far-reaching curricular innovations were achieved, and the development of new teaching material of a strategic nature was realised frequently. Curricular development and other educational activities, however, varied substantially in scope and achievement.

The outcomes in the CEE countries depended on many factors. By and large, we note the highest appreciation of results in countries, institutions and departments which were neither relatively rich and prestigious nor very poor and of little attraction to Western participants. Thus, if we compare according to country, it may not come as a surprise to note that our findings suggest the highest assessment of the outcomes of TEMPUS support in Bulgaria.

The outcomes of JEP activities hardly differed according to the year of start. Concerning the length of TEMPUS support awarded to JEPs, the few JEPs which were supported for only one or two years were clearly less successful than those JEPs having been awarded support for the maximum duration of three year. This can be taken as an indicator for successful monitoring.

Compared to ratings of outcomes and impacts, the rationales for supporting certain subject areas and not supporting others could be viewed nowadays as having been somewhat arbitrary. National policies shifted not infrequently, and good reasons could be presented for almost all and against almost all subjects. The rating of achievements of the actual TEMPUS activities varied little according to subject area.

The successes are mostly regarded as achievements on select islands of innovation privileged to be chosen in the framework of the TEMPUS Programme. Spin-offs within the respective institutions remained moderate or mostly marginal. Our findings do not suggest, however, that substantial spin-offs within the respective institution of higher education could be expected. Improvement of institutional resources and management as included in TEMPUS II could have been a possible option, but it is costly and does not directly gain from other activities. In addition, some of its elements are quite controversial. If the major thrust iseducational innovation within subject-area networks, the spin-off within the institution tends to be limited as a matter of course.

Measures to integrate TEMPUS activities strongly into institutional strategies might have been an approach too much inspired by a Western European *zeitgeist* of searching for managerial miracles instead of reforms based on the basic units in charge of teaching and research on the one hand and convincing national policies on the other.

Spin-offs were stated concerning the adoption of new teaching material and course programmes by departments in the same field at other institutions in the country. However, we note an obvious under-utilisation of experiences acquired in JEPs. Spin-offs could have been improved by giving more attention to and providing more support for information about and dissemination of activities, publication of models of good practice and organising exchange of experiences and information among departments from the same subject-areas having been involved and not having been involved in TEMPUS activities. Thus, the potentials already available could have been used more widely.

A substantial proportion of participants actively involved in regional cooperation within the Central and Eastern European countries considered this as a worthwhile and promising experience. Some interview partners criticised that little has been done to spread successful experiences within the subject areas in the respective CEE country. Regional cooperation also could more easily be taken into account a few years after the rapid political change, and could lead to more promising results than might have been possible in the early 1990s.

Chapter 9

Final Assessment and Conclusions

9.1 Research Design, Methods and Procedures

On 7 May, 1990 the TEMPUS Programme was launched by the Council of European Communities. The aims of the programme are to promote reforms of the higher education systems, to contribute to the overall economic and social development and to effectively support the adjustment of those Central and Eastern European (CEE) countries that are TEMPUS partner countries to the needs of a market economy. The collaboration between the CEE partner countries, the EU Member States, as well as other G24 countries in the field of higher education, based on cooperation, knowledge transfer, equipment aid, structural and curricular development, student and staff exchange, was supposed to provide the necessary prerequisites for an education and training system to fit the new requirements.

In April 1993, the Council of the European Community decided to continue the TEMPUS Programme for a second period of four years (TEMPUS II). TEMPUS II began with the academic year 1994/95 and will be in operation until 1997/98.

Just as the Council decision for TEMPUS I, the Council decision for TEMPUS II also contains a final article (Article 11) concerning the monitoring and evaluation arrangements for the programme. In both articles the Commission is requested, among other things, to make arrangements for the external evaluation of the experience acquired in TEMPUS, taking into account its overall and its national objectives. This evaluation study was commissioned to meet the requirements according to Article 11 of the Council decisions about TEMPUS I and TEMPUS II.

To comply with the goals of providing a comprehensive evaluation and an accurate overview, a description and analysis of the programme activities was carried out according to their structure, their administrative support and their actual realisation in the higher education institutions. Additional emphasis was put on the relationship of TEMPUS activities to the structural changes within the higher education institutions. The role of national authorities and other bodies and key actors involved in policy formation for TEMPUS was analysed, focusing on the steering of the programme according to the national needs of the CEE countries on the one hand and on the impacts of the programme's activities for reforms of the national higher education sectors on the other. The study presented here focuses on the following lines of inquiry:

- the policy framework of the TEMPUS Programme
- the administration of the TEMPUS Programme on the national and the supra-national level
- the participating institutions and institutional settings
- the financial conditions of TEMPUS Joint European Projects (JEPs)
- the cooperation within the JEPs
- the administration of the JEPs
- the educational and infrastructural activities
- outcomes and impacts of TEMPUS.

In order to cover the broad range of topics related to the main goals of the evaluation and to ensure a high validity and representativity of results, two different surveys were undertaken. In addition, available statistics were re-analysed, interviews were carried out with key actors for TEMPUS in all CEE partner countries and a broad range of official documents and written material was taken into consideration.

9.2   Final Assessment

9.2.1 Programme policies

(1)   The TEMPUS Programme is characterised by a *complex dynamic of decision-making and administration* which has to (a) ensure a balance between the Western initiators and donors and the CEE partner countries; (b) establish a balance between the autonomous views of the higher education institutions and the economic and social demands of society; (c) involve a broad range of actors; (d) ensure a smooth coordination of the various stages of programme-related decision-making and the selection and award processes. In theory there is a clear model of stages of decisions in which a single key actor is defined for each stage. In practice, however, the inter-relations of the various stages as well as the constant overlaps have created a centripetal pressure towards a single major decision-making arena, and towards a managerial unit serving as a moderator for most key ad-

ministrative processes. The national TEMPUS advisory or supervisory boards serve the former and the National TEMPUS Offices serve the latter function. The establishment of national TEMPUS advisory or supervisory boards in all CEE countries serving as an arena for dialogue and cooperation of all key actors involved in TEMPUS policy decisions has turned out to be a reasonable option for the necessary coordination processes. The functioning of these boards requires the willingness of all actors to cooperate with each other. If this is not the case, the decision-making and operation of the TEMPUS Programme becomes vulnerable on the national level.

(2)   Although the dynamic conditions and aims of the TEMPUS Programme are frequently emphasised, actual *changes in the structure and activities of the programme were rather moderate during TEMPUS I*. There are two reasons which might have contributed to this: (a) Because of existing regulations and arrangements for the financing of JEPs, the leeway for changes became smaller each year. The necessity to provide funding for a growing number of JEPs in their second and third year of operation on the basis of annual renewal applications gradually decreased the available amount of funding for new JEPs. (b) The supra-institutional decisions with regard to the annual revision of priorities and re-definitions of measures and activities in the TEMPUS Programme did not disrupt the structure and logic of the programme to such an extent that institutions were confronted with a discontinuation of existing project activities.

(3)   Although we can state a certain degree of continuity in national policies and budget allocation procedures, the annual re-definition and re-determination of TEMPUS resources and national priorities as well as their rather late announcement led to *some disquiet among applicants and recipients of grants*. Until the last moment they could not be sure whether their applications would match the priorities or whether their activities would still coincide with policy decisions and further support would be granted.

9.2.2 National priorities

(4)   The national TEMPUS priorities and their annual revision do not only reflect the *divergence in the development of the various CEE partner countries* but also determine the balance of participation as regards institutions and subject areas. During TEMPUS I a broader inclusion of various types and sizes of higher education institutions has been achieved. Approximately 70 per cent of all higher education

institutions in the CEE partner countries participated in TEMPUS. Vis-à-vis the pronounced dominance of business studies and engineering in the beginning of TEMPUS, a somewhat *broader coverage of subjects* can be stated for the second half of TEMPUS I. However, certain disciplines and subject areas are still rather underrepresented in TEMPUS which deserve stimulation for reform in the context of socio-economic transformation.

(5) During TEMPUS II the role of *national TEMPUS priorities* is strongly emphasised by the European Commission. Although most of the CEE countries are still lacking an overall strategy for the development of their national higher education system, the annual formulation of national priorities has become more and more sophisticated. In the first year in which national priorities were introduced they consisted merely of a selected number of subject areas. In the meantime, priorities have actually become more structured and refined.

(6) In general, there seems to be a *more strategic approach to the identification of national needs or directions of change.* However, there are still large differences in the degree of formalisation of national priorities between the individual CEE countries. Although some overlaps in national priorities of single CEE countries can be observed in each year of TEMPUS II, most of the areas selected primarily to be supported by TEMPUS were country specific. This distinctly national character of priorities underlines the increasingly strategic use of TEMPUS to serve national needs on the one hand, but must also be seen on the other hand as an obstacle for the cooperation among CEE countries in individual JEPs. The latter is all the more the case in TEMPUS II because strict compliance with national priorities is required for project applications to become eligible for support.

(7) The *higher education institutions are usually represented in the national TEMPUS advisory or supervisory boards.* Thus, they participate in the annual establishment and revision of national TEMPUS priorities and can bring institutional interests and strategies into play. In general, the higher education institutions are quite satisfied with the communication and information activities of the NTOs. There was no serious concern voiced with regard to the functioning of communication structures among higher education institutions, JEP partners and actors on the national level. Furthermore, sufficient feed-back opportunities exist in both directions: from the institutional to the national level and vice versa.

(8) The annual changes in national priorities as well as frequent programme revisions require intensive *information activities*. Although a general improvement in the availability and quality of information about the TEMPUS Programme was stated by actors on the central level of higher education institutions in CEE countries, it has remained a problem to inform potential applicants about changes at a time which gives them sufficient leeway to match their proposals with the national priorities, to take into account other possible changes and still keep the deadline for the submission of the application. More attention to the timing of information may be needed.

9.2.3 Administration

(9) The *distribution of tasks in the management of the TEMPUS Programme* has changed considerably in the second half of TEMPUS I. The gradual political consolidation and the continuing progress concerning the tranformation in the CEE partner countries as well as the increasing professionalisation of the National TEMPUS Offices have led to a transfer of more and more responsibilities and tasks from the EC TEMPUS Office/ETF TEMPUS Department to the NTOs. This has not only influenced the relationship between the ETF TEMPUS Department and the NTOs but the time seems to have come to reconsider the role and responsibilities of the ETF TEMPUS Department. A higher degree of independence of the NTOs might be connected with a different set of tasks for the ETF TEMPUS Department. The focus of its future tasks might be more strongly related to monitoring, controlling, accountability, evaluation and other supra-national aspects of administration of the programme. However, the division of tasks between NTOs, ETF TEMPUS Department and European Commission depends on the further development of the TEMPUS Programme, for example the importance of introducing a stronger European dimension into the canon of TEMPUS objectives.

(10) Although the potentials of NTOs should be employed in the administration of the TEMPUS Programme as far as possible, it has to be examined whether a *further transfer of administrative tasks to the NTOs* might not lead to conflicts between the different tasks, for example a preference of NTOs to promote applications which were prepared with their help, etc. However, so far no significant difficulties have emerged due to the growing power of the NTOs.

9.2.4 Funding modes

(11) Looking at the different state of socio-economic development and the ability of the individual CEE countries to contribute to the reforms of higher education from their own budget, it has to be considered whether the *funding mode of the TEMPUS Programme* should be adjusted to these differences. For example, the TEMPUS support could cover between 50 and 100 per cent of the project costs depending on the socio-economic status of the individual CEE countries. The requirement for CEE countries to cover parts of the costs of TEMPUS activities may also contribute to an increased coherence between objectives of individual projects and national needs.

(12) TEMPUS JEPs can be supported for periods of up to three years. In contrast to the first phase of TEMPUS, it was not necessary for TEMPUS II JEPs to reapply each year for a renewal of their contract because the *duration of the support period* under TEMPUS II is fixed in the initial award decision. The shift towards *multi-annual funding* of JEPs has been highly appreciated in the CEE partner countries. Multi-annual funding of JEPs offers a better planning perspective for all partners involved and allows a certain degree of *flexibility to adapt activities* to the dynamics of ongoing project work. Nevertheless, JEP partners in CEE countries commented quite frequently on the lack of flexibility in the utilisation of project funds. The most serious criticism, however, was voiced with regard to the delays in the transfer of funds for JEPs and mobility grants. The causes for these delays were sometimes attributed to the banks and also to the JEP contractors. Most frequently, however, they were attributed to the transfer arrangements of the EU. Delays in the transfer of funds combined with typical project dynamics aggravate the problem of inflexibility in the utilisation of funds.

(13) In general, the *overall JEP grants were regarded as generous* by most recipients from the CEE countries even though differences might exist among countries in what is considered as generous. Criticism concerning the amount of support awarded to JEPs was rather directed at issues of continuity in support. It was a typical feature in TEMPUS I that support came like 'manna from heaven' and after three years it stopped without offering any solution to smooth the transition from the fat years to the meagre ones. With the introduction of JENs in the last year of TEMPUS I this problem has been somewhat redressed, but any radical take-off solution for TEMPUS award and support policies must be questioned.

9.2.5 *Network cooperation and JEP management*

(14) TEMPUS has contributed to *substantial change at higher education institutions* since 1990. Only slightly more than 30 per cent of the degree programmes at institutions responding to a respective questionnaire remained unchanged. TEMPUS has also helped strongly to establish international contacts and to organise staff exchange. It has had fewer consequences, however, for strategic planning. Overall, the perceived success of TEMPUS activities at the faculties and departments does not differ strikingly according to the extent in which the central institutional level is involved.

(15) Concerning the *cooperation within the networks,* four issues should be pointed out: the relationship between CEE and Western partners, the number of partners within JEPs, the number of institutions from one country and the role of enterprises.

- The relationship between CEE and Western partners is primarily seen as friendly and cooperative. Many CEE partners are grateful for the tremendous amount of support and commitment they received from their Western partners. Cooperation has increased respect for each other. Nevertheless, complaints of CEE partners were not infrequent about a domineering attitude of some Western partners and the very high amount of administrative costs they sometimes claimed were necessary for their efforts. In contrast to this, Western partners frequently stated that TEMPUS support for their administrative costs did not by far cover all the direct and indirect costs incurred.

- Problems concerning the configuration among partners within JEPs varied according to the size of the JEP. The more partners were officially part of the network, the lower was the proportion of partners with whom participants from CEE countries actively cooperated. Cooperation was more intensive in JEPs with a smaller number of partners.

- In some CEE countries national governments stimulated the co-operation of several institutions from the same country within one JEP. This was done in order to reduce the imbalance of a few winners and many losers in the competition for TEMPUS support and provide an opportunity for less successful institutions to participate in TEMPUS and to acquire the necessary know-how for successful applications and JEP management.

- On the whole, enterprises did not play a very strong role in JEP activities. The number of enterprises participating in JEPs decreased during the period of TEMPUS I and did not change very much during the first two years of TEMPUS II. They participated in only about one-third of the TEMPUS II JEPs. Frequently, enterprises were just 'sleeping partners' or were merely involved by offering places for internships. Higher education institutions did not comment much on the importance or influence of enterprise involvement in JEPs and did not state any preferences in this respect either.

(16) JEPs in which partners from different CEE countries cooperated, i.e. multi-CEE or *'regional' JEPs, were quite successful* and offered special opportunities for trans-border cooperation. The combination of decentralisation and nationalisation in TEMPUS promoted the influence of national priorities and did not only reduce the role of multi-CEE cooperation but also made successful applications considerably more difficult because they had to comply with the national priorities of two or more CEE partner countries. This development has reduced a certain potential and quality of cooperation which should be reconsidered.

(17) In TEMPUS II, partners from all CEE countries are eligible for the *coordinating function* of Joint European Projects and Complementary Measures, and partners from most CEE countries have become eligible to take over the *contracting function*. This eligibility for management functions is leading to a shift in the division of management functions between partners from Western and from CEE countries. While most of the networks during TEMPUS I were coordinated and contracted by Western partners, the majority of TEMPUS II JEPs were managed by partners from CEE countries. On the one hand this development shows an increasing ability and self-confidence of CEE partners to cope with the demands of the management functions. On the other hand the development is also promoted by the national priorities in some CEE countries which explicitly state a preference for projects managed by partners from their own country. In extrapolating the current trend we might assume that almost all JEPs will be managed by CEE partners in the near future.

Although there may be good reasons to support this development, it raises the question of whether partners from Western countries will accept their new role as being 'only' partners in the networks. The asymmetry in the relation of Western and CEE countries in the TEMPUS Programme in their roles as donors and receivers seems to be complemented by another asymmetry in which the CEE countries take over the leading functions in JEPs and CMEs and the Western countries plays the role of assistants.

(18) *Issues of administrative cooperation* within the JEP networks and among the partners as well as between the central level of the higher education institutions and the faculties and departments involved in JEP activities are frequently mentioned as a *source of disagreement and differences in perception*. However, a certain focal point on which these differences would concentrate is not discernible and thus a clear direction for change cannot be indicated.

(19) During the whole period of the TEMPUS Programme *changes were introduced in the structure and hierarchy of JEP activities and objectives*, that is, the various educational and structural measures and student and staff mobility, as main topics or as subordinated topics. However, if we ignore the hierarchy in which activities and objectives are related to each other in the annual guidelines for applicants, the only remarkable change in the list of items was the inclusion of support for the review and improvement of the university management in TEMPUS II. Thus, the TEMPUS Programme is characterised by a high stability in areas of support. Additionally, it should be mentioned that no substantial changes in the proportion of support for the different measures can be observed.

9.2.6 Types of JEPs and major areas of support

(20) The *majority of TEMPUS II JEPs was classified as 'Structural JEPs'* (86 per cent), that is, they were awarded support for cooperative measures in the field of teaching and education or for structural development of departments, faculties or institution(s) of higher education. A further 11 per cent of TEMPUS II JEPs were classified as 'Mobility JEPs', that is networks of institutions of higher education, enterprises and other organisations which were awarded TEMPUS support for the organisation of student mobility, and the remaining 3 per cent were JEP+ projects.

With the beginning of TEMPUS II the classification system of JEP activities used in the administration of applications was changed. Thus, a comparison between TEMPUS I JEPs and TEMPUS II JEPs with regard to their proportion of educational and structural activities is not possible. Following the new classification of TEMPUS II JEPs as defined by the European Commission, 56 per cent of the JEPs in the first two years of TEMPUS II were concerned with the introduction or restructuring of course programmes,

15 per cent with the creation or restructuring of departments, faculties or institutions, 11 per cent with the creation of a network for the organisation of student mobility, 8 per cent with the development of universities' capacities in continuing education and retraining schemes for university staff, 7 per cent with the development of universities' capacities to cooperate with industry, and 4 per cent with the review and improvement of university management.

However, the new sub-ordination of each Joint European Projects to only one objective does not show the variety of activities undertaken within the JEPs. It can be assumed that, similar to TEMPUS I, most of the JEPs are concerned with a bundle of activities like curriculum development, staff training, student and staff mobility, development of teaching material, provision of equipment, etc.

(21)   The *major areas of support in JEPs were constructed as a bundle of activities*: structural development, cooperative educational measures, staff and student mobility. The majority of JEPs opted for carrying out all four of these activities, although preferences for the provision of equipment and for staff mobility were clearly visible. The combination of all four activities contributed considerably to the success of curricular reforms. In addition, the bundle of activities in its current combination is also a preferred option for the future. Two deficits stand out, however. First, it was often regretted that a contribution of TEMPUS to research was explicitly excluded. This exclusion was difficult to understand because TEMPUS aims to contribute to structural reforms of higher education in countries in which there was previously an institutional separation of research and teaching and the integration and cross-fertilisation of these tasks is considered to be one of the major targets of reform. Second, student mobility has been least integrated into the bundle of JEP activities. It was considered worthwhile for those who went abroad but less important in the context of the combined impact of the other three activities. The stronger emphasis on student mobility in TEMPUS II has been triggered by the opportunity to participate in the ERASMUS Programme in the near future. This leaves some questions open concerning the combination of activities eligible for support within JEPs.

(22)   The *opportunity to build up personal contacts and to become integrated into an international community* of scholars was certainly one of the most visible as well as *most highly appreciated* impacts of TEMPUS for CEE partners. However, once such contacts and

cooperation are stabilised and have become normal, the TEMPUS Programme will lose its importance as the only or main source of opportunities for international contacts and integration.

(23) Taking into account the number of respective mobility grants, the *mobility of staff members has become more important* in TEMPUS II. Staff mobility in TEMPUS II is also more targeted as regards the requirements of the JEP objectives and less often intended to organise first contacts between possible project partners. In some of the CEE countries strong requirements as regards the age and academic qualification of staff members have been introduced for the award of Individual Mobility Grants.

(24) Impacts of TEMPUS concerning the *modernisation of equipment and the renewal of teaching and learning have been highly rated by faculties and departments* involved in TEMPUS. They were also more direct and visible than impacts in other areas of structural development supported by TEMPUS. It is therefore not surprising that substantial changes in the structure of degree programmes were undertaken less frequently and regarded less as a direct impact of TEMPUS activities in those cases in which such changes had been introduced.

(25) Only towards the end of TEMPUS I has *student mobility become more important* in the perception of faculties and departments involved in TEMPUS activities. This is mainly due to the expectation that participation in SOCRATES will soon be possible for most of the CEE countries. In this context Mobility JEPs are regarded as an appropriate preparation. It must, however, be noted that TEMPUS support for student mobility can not be compared to ERASMUS student mobility. TEMPUS-supported student mobility is not characterised by a reciprocity of exchanges, it is not as highly organised as in ERASMUS and also frequently still lacks curricular integration and recognition arrangements. Student mobility in TEMPUS was, however, successfully used to a certain extent as an instrument in the selection of potential junior academic staff.

In order to avoid future competition between ERASMUS and TEMPUS, whereby TEMPUS would represent the luxury-liner by providing mobility grants which cover the full amount of costs for a stay abroad, and to ensure that more or less the same conditions prevail for students participating in student mobility programmes of the European Union it could be necessary to delete student mobility from the list of eligible TEMPUS activities, at least for those CEE countries participating in SOCRATES.

(26) The *broadening focus of support areas* from almost exclusively academic areas during TEMPUS I to issues of administrative and managerial development in TEMPUS II (i.e the management and infrastructure of universities) was accompanied by the *introduction of new measures* in 1994/95 (JEP+ and CME+) and the restructuring of objectives to be supported in JEPs and CMEs in 1995/96. The new JEP+ and CME+ projects were intended to complement the existing bottom-up approach of the regular TEMPUS measures by involving national authorities more strongly in the proposals. Both project types were larger in scope than classical JEP and CME projects and also had a higher level of funding. The objectives of JEP+ and CME+ projects focused on the level of institutions or the higher education system in the CEE countries. Only 11 JEP+ and 7 CME+ projects were awarded support in 1994/95.

For various reasons the measures of JEP+ and CME+ projects were discontinued in 1995/96, the second year of TEMPUS II. While the objectives supported by these projects were included in the canon of objectives eligible for support in the regular JEP and CME projects, the special top-down approach which enabled the national authorities to make project proposals was no longer followed. This might be due to the fact that in most CEE countries there is still a lack of a consistent higher education policy and the national authorities did not use the possibilities offered to them by TEMPUS JEP+ and CME+ projects to their full extent.

9.2.7 *Spin-offs and dissemination of results*

(27) *Spin-offs of educational and curricular activities* for the same subjects and departments at other higher education institutions in the country *have been achieved* within TEMPUS. A certain extent of dissemination of results and adoption of curricula and teaching material developed in the framework of JEPs can be noted, although it could be improved by increased support for dissemination, publication of material developed within JEPs and increased communication and exchange. The same kind of spin-offs were a potential of the multi-CEE JEPs and could have led to an exchange of special curricular innovations or outstanding material and course programmes among CEE countries. Overall, the dissemination of results of JEP activities was not strongly promoted and supported during TEMPUS. When TEMPUS support for JEPs ended after three years, there was often no funding left over or no additional

funding available to publish developed material or organise the dissemination of results. Spin-offs might also be increased if they were part of the TEMPUS support system and if a more targeted approach towards dissemination of results was adopted. The issue of spin-offs was improved to a certain extent by the introduction of JENs and in general by a higher degree of awareness. It is, however, still sub-optimal.

(28) The *dissemination of results* of activities supported by TEMPUS has remained an exception rather than become the rule during TEMPUS II. Only very recently, a more targeted approach towards dissemination of results can be noted by introducing a new strand of activities eligible for support in the framework of Complementary Measures and by establishing a special outcome unit at the ETF TEMPUS Department. However, it still remains to be seen whether a better dissemination of results becomes visible in the second half of TEMPUS II and what its effect might be.

(29) The *island character of innovation achieved by JEPs* was a frequent and wide-spread argument when JEP participants and actors on the central level of the institutions were asked about possible spin-offs for the institutional setting. This is understandable insofar as subject-related activities do not automatically lead to spin-offs for the governance and administrative structures of the institution as a whole. The island character may, however, also be due to resistance against change from other academic staff members in the same faculty or department and/or to an unwillingness of those involved in the JEP to share innovation and new resources because there is a high degree of competition.

The island character did not change fundamentally during TEMPUS II. As in TEMPUS I, the impacts of JEPs are first seen at departmental level. It seems to be more likely that impacts can be achieved by having spin-offs or beneficial effects for the same subjects and disciplines at other higher education institutions. Evidence for such considerations can be derived by looking at the descriptions of JEP objectives during TEMPUS II: Much more frequently than in TEMPUS I, JEPs are targeted to aspects explicitly stating an importance for further departments of similar disciplinary orientation at other educational establishments.

9.2.8 Strategic management and the role of the central level

(30)   There are *different perceptions* of the JEP participants on the one
hand and the central institutional level on the other *about the service function of the central level for the JEP activities* and the integration of JEP activities into an institutional development strategy.
JEP participants perceive the support of activities through services
offered by the central level of their institution as considerably lower
than the central level itself. Various styles of institutional management do not seem to influence the success of JEP activities in any
direct way. The validity of the different perceptions is hard to determine apart from the fact that both sides tend to direct their attention to new developments (i.e. in the framework of TEMPUS II)
and base it less on an assessment of previous developments.

(31)   In a considerable number of higher education institutions in the
CEE Countries an *improvement* can be noted *of central administrative services* and the development or restructuring of service units
located at the central level can be reported. In about 64% of institutions included in our survey, international relation offices that exist
at the central level are spending about one-quarter of their time on
TEMPUS-related activities. As regards the findings of our institutional survey, key persons at the central level of the higher education institutions in the CEE countries show an increasing interest
for TEMPUS projects to be carried out in their respective faculties
or departments. More than 50 per cent of the respondents stated that
they provided *institutional support for the preparation of TEMPUS
applications*. More than 50 per cent each also provided administrative and other forms of assistance for running projects. Although
the analysis of such findings calls for some caution, a trend towards
a higher commitment of central institutional level to TEMPUS
projects is obvious.

(32)   As a new objective for JEPs, the *review and improvement of the
university management* was introduced during TEMPUS II. The
new objective covers the development of financial management
structures, library management, inter-faculty cooperation, creation
of international offices, etc. As compared to the number of TEM-
PUS II JEPs established in this area (4 per cent), the improvement
of the administration and infrastructure at the central level of higher
education institutions was at the bottom of the agenda for actual
JEP activities during the first two years of TEMPUS II. In looking
at the needs of higher education institutions for further TEMPUS
support which were expressed in our survey, the dominance of JEPs

concerned with academic matters is justified. However, the proportion of JEPs actually organising a review and improvement of the university management can be considered as surprisingly low when compared to the proportion of higher education institutions in CEE countries intending future changes in this area (about three-quarters).

(33) About 90 per cent of higher education institutions in CEE Countries answering our questionnaire had established an *institutional development plan*. Many institutions initiated TEMPUS projects, undertook a pre-selection of project applications submitted by their institution or used project results for overall reform strategies. Between 40 and 45 per cent of the respondents claimed that all or at least some of the TEMPUS projects were in line with the overall institutional development plan.

(34) A *strong involvement in TEMPUS activities by the central level* of the institution is *not widely appreciated* by the faculties, departments and JEP partners. On the one hand, such an involvement was frequently regarded as an intervention into the autonomy of faculties and departments. On the other hand, JEP partners as well as faculties and departments did not see many advantages in a strong involvement of the central level. In many cases they preferred to be responsible themselves for all administrative and organisational matters of TEMPUS activities. Looking at the quality and success of TEMPUS projects, we could not find any striking differences caused by a more or less pro-active involvement of the central level.

9.3 Conclusions and Considerations for the Future of TEMPUS

TEMPUS, like the Phare Programme, was launched as a rapid aid mechanism for the new democracies of Central and Eastern Europe. It was the aim of the TEMPUS Programme to promote reforms of the higher education systems of the CEE partner countries and to effectively support the adjustment of these countries to the needs of a market economy. *During the past six years, most higher education institutions in the CEE countries experienced substantial changes.* The number of students at TEMPUS-supported institutions (about three-quarters of the higher education institutions in the CEE partner countries) increased by more than 50 per cent. About 40 per cent of the degree programmes existing at TEMPUS-supported institutions of higher education in 1995 had been newly established during the last five years, almost 30 per cent changed substantially during that period and only slightly more than 30 per cent remained un-changed. In general, *the contribution of TEMPUS to these changes is rated highly by most actors on the departmental, institutional and national level in the CEE partner countries.* However, the process of transformation is characterised by high dynamics and shaped by various national and international thrusts.

TEMPUS had to keep pace with these dynamics and was adapted to the changing needs of reform and renewal activities at the higher education institutions in almost every year. A number of revisions have been made of the various aspects of the structure and the measures of the TEMPUS Programme but *no general reconsideration of the programme as a whole has yet been undertaken.* When the second phase of the TEMPUS Programme was implemented in 1994/95 by the European Commission, attempts became more visible to restructure TEMPUS activities and emphasize more strongly certain newly emerging issues like national higher education planning and institutional development.

In contrast to other European programmes, TEMPUS is bound to be unstable because of its logic. The reasons for this are:

• The more successful TEMPUS is, the more the role diminishes of its support provided to the CEE partner countries.

• As a consequence of political and economic stabilisation as well as of growing professionalisation and self-confidence in international settings, the role of the CEE countries vis-à-vis the European Union will become more determined and influential in the relevant decision-making processes.

• Similarly, the role of the National TEMPUS Offices seems to be growing vis-à-vis the TEMPUS Department in the ETF.

At the end of an evaluation study covering six years of TEMPUS operations it seems reasonable to point out a number of general areas of tension which have emerged in the programme. After a short characterisation, each of these areas will be followed by a number of questions arising from them and pointing to basic issues for consideration. Finally, some of the main directions for future TEMPUS-related decisions will be indicated which seem to suggest themselves on the basis of our findings and the respective assessment.

Looking at the rather fast pace of the general transition processes which most of the CEE partner countries have undergone since 1990, it is obvious that the TEMPUS Programme must be flexible and dynamic enough to keep up with this pace. Thus, the questions for the future direction of TEMPUS cannot necessarily be extrapolated from taking stock of experiences gained up to now. Nevertheless, six basic areas of tensions as well as issues for consideration concerning decisions about the future of TEMPUS can be identified.

(1) The bottom-up approach of support for activities being carried out in the faculties and departments of CEE higher education institutions was largely applied during TEMPUS I. It is currently complemented by a trend towards a top-down approach taking national policies more strongly into account and strengthening the central level of the higher education institutions.

Who will be the generators of new ideas for the shape of the TEMPUS Programme and its activities? Which role will be played by national policies, by the central level of the institutions and by the faculties and departments? Have innovations become less significant which are produced in the framework of project activities carried out in the faculties and departments?

(2) The growing professionalisation in the administration of the TEMPUS Programme and increasing skills in managing TEMPUS activities by key actors and TEMPUS project partners in the CEE partner countries has shifted the responsibility for a number of tasks and policy decisions from the West to the East and changed the original distribution of tasks and responsibilities.

Does the fast pace of transformation and the organisational and administrative maturity which can be noted in the majority of CEE partner countries trigger a growing 'nationalisation' of the TEMPUS Programme, or will some overall issues remain to function as a bracket for TEMPUS activities and to shape cooperation between the EU Member States and the CEE countries? What will be the future role of the ETF TEMPUS Department? What will be the future role of Western partners within TEMPUS projects?

(3) There is a growing tension between the areas of TEMPUS support according to the overall objectives for TEMPUS activities and the subject areas and disciplines being actually supported in the framework of TEMPUS projects. The time might have come to reconsider the adequacy of TEMPUS objectives.

Next to issues of teaching and learning, questions related to the organisation and management of higher education institutions have become quite prominent in TEMPUS II. Will the role of the central institutional level be one of support for activities in the faculties and departments, or have issues of curriculum development lost their significance in the framework of TEMPUS?

(4)   Concerning the national and/or institutional policies in the framework of which the various TEMPUS support measures are being
used as part of a dynamic process of reform, change and development, student mobility stands out as a measure which suggests a possible re-allocation.

Has the relationship among the various areas of TEMPUS support
(e.g. upgrading of facilities, cooperative educational measures, student and staff mobility, university management, etc.) shifted because
of the ongoing transformation processes so that a new determination
of their individual relevance might become necessary?

(5)   There are three aspects in the financial modalities of TEMPUS con-
stituting a certain amount of tension: (a) Because of differences in
the speed and level of progress among the various CEE countries,
TEMPUS support is not equally significant for all of them any
longer. (b) Some higher education institutions have profited considerably from TEMPUS support; others have not yet participated in
projects at all. (c) The level of funding for the various measures and
activities supported in TEMPUS has to be reconsidered according to
their possible change in relevance.

Who should be and who will be the main beneficiaries of TEMPUS support in the future as regards the participation of countries, of institutions
and of subject areas or academic disciplines in TEMPUS? Will the TEM-
PUS Programme in general acquire a different significance in the CEE
partner countries?

It seems that with these questions a number of important issues for
TEMPUS-related decision-making have been raised which might change
the overall profile of TEMPUS.

The instability inherent in the logic of the TEMPUS Programme is also
reflected on the level of the JEPs. Most JEPs were active in all four major
areas for which TEMPUS support was granted, although – as already
stated – individual activities tended to be pursued to varying degrees.
Nevertheless, the bundle of activities created an incentive to be more active in educational innovation than initially intended by the JEP partners
in the CEE countries so that the creation of such a bundle can be considered as relatively successful. The time has come now to reconsider this
bundle as emphases and targets of reform and renewal start to shift in
CEE partner countries:

• After four to six years aims and objectives will have to take into account how the take-off and emergency character of TEMPUS has
changed.

- The national dimension of the programme is gradually complemented by a European dimension in the CEE partner countries.
- Individual areas might still need support without, however, being integrated into a bundle of activities.
- New tasks and activities might acquire new importance.

TEMPUS has successfully contributed to a considerable amount of development and change in the higher education institutions of the CEE partner countries. In the face of growing political consolidation and progress in social and economic transformation, TEMPUS has lost its original character as an emergency aid programme for the majority of the CEE partner countries. This implies that the time has come for new basic decisions concerning the direction in which the TEMPUS Programme should develop. For these decisions the successes and achievements of the TEMPUS Programme up to now have to be taken into consideration just as much as the remaining problems and changed conditions in the CEE partner countries. As a result of our findings and in summarising them, four major directions for TEMPUS emerge as possible issues for further considerations about the future of the programme.

(1) The TEMPUS Programme will tend towards 'Socratisation' in which East-West cooperation is substituted by a shift towards cooperation in SOCRATES (especially the ERASMUS part) within a network of equal players. This scenario matches widespread ambitions of some CEE countries, although many educational activities supported in TEMPUS are not strongly represented in SOCRATES. Those CEE countries with ambitions in this direction might not yet be able to provide the complementary resources required for participation in SOCRATES, but it is frequently a matter of prestige and a feeling of being on a par with higher education institutions in the EU Member States which comes into play as a decisive factor.

(2) The TEMPUS Programme will develop more strongly towards 'decentralisation' so that policy formation, administration, monitoring and controlling will become more and more nationalised by the CEE partner countries. The trend towards a transfer of TEMPUS-related responsibilities and tasks to the CEE partner countries continues. This does not only suit the various degrees of stability and economic development which have been reached in the CEE countries but also the various foci in terms of TEMPUS activities. As a consequence, TEMPUS would be bound to become very heterogeneous. The potential for regional spin-offs and cooperation among CEE countries would be further reduced and the European dimension of activities would remain weak or become even weaker.

(3) The TEMPUS Programme will be characterised by 'residualisation', meaning a more selective and targeted continuation of the classic TEMPUS approach addressed to those countries, institutions and subject areas which have not yet participated in TEMPUS. This means that some CEE countries would move towards participation in SOCRATES (and LEONARDO) as is currently already visible, and the remaining CEE countries would form the rest of CEE partner countries in TEMPUS.

(4) The TEMPUS Programme will move towards 'Europeanisation', supporting only those activities and approaches by which a further European integration of the CEE countries and a European dimension in teaching and learning will be achieved. This development might be combined with a restructuring of tasks and of the administration of the programme. The EU might take the lead in stimulating activities which have a strong European dimension and at least a medium-term life-cycle while allowing the individual CEE countries to take care of other remaining take-off support which is short-term in its orientation and national in its approach. This could lead to a higher degree of permanence in the TEMPUS Programme, although it would probably require additional financial support not made available by national Phare funds and not yet taken into account in the national decision-making processes established for the allocation of Phare funds for the TEMPUS Programme.

9.4 General Conclusions

The TEMPUS Programme is highly appreciated and well accepted in the CEE partner countries. Although the overall quality of applications has continuously increased, the majority of applications could not be supported because of the limited TEMPUS budget.

The projects supported by TEMPUS can be considered by and large as successful and important for the development of higher education in the CEE partner countries. Nevertheless, not all potentials and possibilities were used to foster dissemination of results and spin-offs of project activities beyond the 'islands' of innovation in individual departments or faculties supported.

The policy formation for the TEMPUS Programme in the CEE partner countries has gradually become more targeted to the needs of the individual countries. This development underlines the increasing awareness of all actors concerned with higher education on the national level in terms of the potentials of the TEMPUS Programme.

The administration of the TEMPUS Programme in the CEE partner countries can be considered as efficient and appropriate in the face of the complexity and necessity for continuous adaptation of the programme, the number of institutions and subject areas included in the programme and the range of measures of support within the programme.

Although a substantial contribution of TEMPUS to the development of higher education in the CEE partner countries can be observed, further efforts will be necessary at least in some of the CEE partner countries to reach a level of achievement and progress in higher education renewal and restructuring which utilises the potentials of the TEMPUS Programme to a fuller extent in order to reach the aims and objectives of the programme.

Chapter 10

Bibliography

10.1 Official Documents

Commission of the European Communities, Task Force Human Resources, Education, Training and Youth (1990 ff.) *TEMPUS Compendium.* Produced for the Commission of the European Communities by the EC TEMPUS Office. Brussels: EC TEMPUS Office

Commission of the European Communities, Directorate General XXII – Education, Training and Youth (1990 ff.) *Guide for Applicants (Vademecum) TEMPUS-Phare.* Brussels

Commission of the European Communities, Directorate General XXII – Education, Training and Youth (1994) *General Information on CME+ Projects.* Working Document. Supplement to Guide for Applicants 1994/95. Priorities. Brussels

Commission of the European Communities, Directorate General XXII – Education, Training and Youth (1994) *General Information on JEP+ Projects.* Working Document. Supplement to Guide for Applicants 1994/95. Priorities. Brussels

Commission of the European Communities, Task Force Human Resources, Education, Training, Youth (1992) *Annual Report TEMPUS Phare, 7 May 1990 – 31 July 1991.* Brussels, February 1992 (SEC(92) 226 final)

Commission of the European Communities, Task Force Human Resources, Education, Training, Youth (1992) *Annual Report TEMPUS Phare, 1 August 1991 – 31 July 1992.* Luxembourg: Office for Official Publications of the European Communities

Commission of the European Communities, Directorate General XXII – Education, Training and Youth (1994) *Annual Report TEMPUS Phare, 1 August 1992 – 31 July 1993.* Brussels, April 1994 (COM(94) 142 final)

Commission of the European Communities, Directorate General XXII –
Education, Training and Youth (1995) *Annual Report TEMPUS Phare
and Tacis, 1 August 1993 – 31 July 1993*. Luxembourg: Office for Official Publications of the European Communities

Commission of the European Communities (1996) *Evaluation of TEM
PUS Achievements to Date and Views on Partner Countries' Remaining Needs*. Report from the Commission to the Council. Brussels, 8
May 1996 (COM(96) 197 final)

Commission of the European Communities, Task Force Human Resources, Education, Training, Youth (1993) *Directory of Higher Education Institutions in Central and Eastern Europe 1992*. Luxembourg:
Office for Official Publications of the European Communities

Coopers & Lybrand Europe (1992) *Evaluation of TEMPUS*. London, May

Council Decision of 7 May 1990 establishing a trans-European mobility
scheme for university students (TEMPUS). *Official Journal of the
European Communities* L 131, 23 May 1990, pp. 21 – 26

Council Decision of 29 April 1993 adopting the second phase of the trans-
European cooperation scheme for higher education (TEMPUS II)
(1994 – 1998). *Official Journal of the European Communities* L 112, 6
May 1993, pp. 34 – 39

EC TEMPUS Office (1992) *TEMPUS Site Visit Programme. Guidelines
for Monitoring*. Brussels: EC TEMPUS Office

EC TEMPUS Office (1994) *Site Visit Programme TEMPUS Phare. Annual Report Academic Year 1992/93*. Luxembourg: Office for Official
Publications of the European Communities

EC TEMPUS Office (1994) *TEMPUS (Phare) Flagship Joint European
Projects in 1992/93*. Brussels: EC TEMPUS Office, August

EC TEMPUS Office *TEMPUS Joint European Project Management
Handbook*. Edited by M.H. Dominiczak in collaboration with the EC
TEMPUS Office. Brussels

European Commission, Phare Information Office (1995) *Phare Address
Book, May 1995*. Brussels: Phare Information Office

European Commission, Phare Information Office (1994) *What is Phare?*
Brussels: Phare Information Office, June

European Commission, Phare Information Office (1994) *How to Work
with Phare*. Brussels: Phare Information Office, August

European Commission, Phare Information Office (1995) *Phare Operational Programmes 1994.* Update No. 5. Brussels: Phare Information Office, January

European Commission, Phare Information Office (1995) *Phare Infocontract No. 5/1994.* Brussels: Phare Information Office, January

European Commission, Phare Information Office (1995) *Info Phare,* No. 6, February; No.7, April; No. 8, July

Kehm, B., Maiworm, F., Over, A., Reisz, R., Steube, W., Teichler, U. (1996) *Evaluation of the First Phase of TEMPUS 1990 – 1994.* Working Document of the European Commission, XXII/182/96-EN. Brussels: European Commission

Kehm, B.M., Maiworm, F., Over, A., Reisz, R., Steube, W., Teichler, U.(1996) *Evaluation of the First Phase of TEMPUS 1990/91 – 1993/94. Summary.* Report from the Commission to the Council, the European Parliament, the Economic and Social Committee and the Committee of the Regions. Brussels, 20. 09. 1996 COM(96) 428 final

Kehm, B.M., Maiworm, F., Over, A., Reisz, R., Steube, W., Teichler, U. (1996) *Evaluation of the First Two Years of TEMPUS II 1994 – 1996.* Working Document of the European Commission, XXII/183/96-EN. Brussels: European Commission

Kommission der Europäischen Gemeinschaften, Task Force Humanressourcen, allgemeine und berufliche Bildung, Jugend (1992) *TEMPUS-Konferenz: Die Rolle des Hochschulwesens im Rahmen des Reformprozesses in Mittel- und Osteuropa.* Conference report. Brssels, 1 and 2 October

10.2 Documents from/about TEMPUS Partner Countries

Bulgarian TEMPUS Office, National Science Fund, Ministry of Science and Higher Education (1991) *Education in Bulgaria.* Sofia

Centre for Higher Education Studies (1995) *Higher Education in the Czech Republic.* Guide for Foreign Students. Prague

Czech TEMPUS Office (1995) *Joint European Projects 1990 – 1994.* Prague

Czech TEMPUS Office (1995) *TEMPUS Info 1.* Prague

Czech TEMPUS Office (1993) *The First Czech TEMPUS Workshop.* 3 – 4 May 1993, Prague

DAAD (1992) *Zwischenbericht über die Anlaufphase des Projekts: Intensivierung der grenzüberschreitenden Zusammenarbeit deutscher Hochschulen im Rahmen von EG-Programmen TEMPUS/ ERASMUS/LINGUA (Aktion 2)*. Presented by Dep. 314 of the DAAD. Bonn

DAAD (1993) *Erfahrungen aus der Beteiligung deutscher Hochschulen, Organisationen und Unternehmen am TEMPUS-Programm der Europäischen Gemeinschaften. Ein Zwischenbericht über die Programmphase I (1990/91 1993/94) aus der Sicht des Deutschen Akademischen Austauschdienstes*, prepared by B. Wächter and W. Trenn. Bonn

Estonian TEMPUS Office (1991) *Education in Estonia*. Mimeographed paper. Tallinn

European Training Foundation (1996) *TEMPUS Output Promotion Project. Draft report "University Management in TEMPUS"*, prepared by the Association of European Universities (CRE). Geneva: CRE, June

European Training Foundation (1996) *TEMPUS Output Promotion Project. Draft report "Impact of the Changes in Higher education on the National Reform"*, prepared by M. Arrouays, TEMPUS National Contact Point France. Paris: National TEMPUS Contact Point, June

European Training Foundation (1996) *TEMPUS Output Promotion Project. Draft report "From Aid Towards Reciprocity. Mutual Benefits of TEMPUS Project Partnerships"*, prepared by L. Musner and H.A. Winter. Vienna, June

European Training Foundation (1996) *TEMPUS Output Promotion Project. Draft report "TEMPUS Student Mobility"*, prepared by the Bulgarian TEMPUS Office, Nuffic and the National Agency for Higher Education Stockholm. Sofia, The Hague, Stockholm, June

European Training Foundation (1996) *TEMPUS Output Promotion Project. Draft report "University-Enterprise Co-operation"*, prepared by the Slovak TEMPUS Office and the European Centre for Strategic Management of Universities. Bratislava, Brussels, June

Gwyn, R. (1994): *TEMPUS Country Monograph No. 1: The Slovak Republic*. Prepared for the European Commission Directorate-General XXII. Luxembourg: Office for Official Publications of the European Communities

Gwyn, R. (1996) *TEMPUS Country Monograph No. 2: The Czech Republic*. Prepared for the European Commission Directorate-General XXII. Luxembourg: Office for Official Publications of the European Communities

Gwyn, R. (1996) *TEMPUS Country Monograph No. 3: Romania*. Prepared for the European Commission Directorate-General XXII. Luxembourg: Office for Official Publications of the European Communities

Gwyn, R. (1996) *TEMPUS Country Monograph No. 4: Bulgaria*. Prepared for the European Commission Directorate-General XXII. Luxembourg: Office for Official Publications of the European Communities

Gwyn, R. (1996) *TEMPUS Country Monograph No. 5: Hungary*. Prepared for the European Commission Directorate-General XXII. Luxembourg: Office for Official Publications of the European Communities

Gwyn, R. (1996) *TEMPUS Country Monograph No. 6: Slovenia*. Prepared for the European Commission Directorate-General XXII. Luxembourg: Office for Official Publications of the European Communities

Gwyn, R. (1996) *TEMPUS Country Monograph No. 7: Poland*. Prepared for the European Commission Directorate-General XXII. Luxembourg: Office for Official Publications of the European Communities

Hungarian Accreditation Committee (1995) *About the Hungarian Accreditation Committee and its Work in 1994*. Accreditation in Hungary No. 2. Budapest

Hungarian TEMPUS Office (1994) *Evaluation of the Hungarian Experience of the TEMPUS Programme of the European Union 1990 – 1993/94/94. Brief Summary*. Budapest

Ivic, I. (1991) *Education in Former Yugoslavia. Le système de l'enseignement supérieur en Yougoslavie*. Belgrade

Komiteti I Shkences Dhe I Teknologjise, Albanian TEMPUS Office (1996) *TEMPUS Buletin informativ 1*. Tirana

Latvian TEMPUS Office (1991) *Latvia*. Riga

Ministry of Culture and Education of the Republic of Lithuania (1991) *Education in Lithuania*. Vilnius: Publishing Centre of the Ministry

Ministry of Education Romania, National Council for University Research (1995) *Newsletter No. 1*. Bucharest

Ministry of Education, Youth and Sports of the Czech Republic (1994) *National Report on the Development of Education in the Czech Republic 1992 – 1994*. Prague

Ministry of National Education Poland (1994) *Poland: Education in a Changing Society. Background Report for the OECD Review (Short Version)*. Warsaw, October

Ministry of Science and Education, National TEMPUS Office Bulgaria (1994) *TEMPUS I: Review and Analysis of the Bulgarian Participation (1991 – 1993)*. Sophia, September

OECD (1995) *Education in a Federal System*. Documentation of a Seminar held in Moscow, 24 – 25 October 1994. Paris

OECD, European Commission (1996) *Secondary Education Systems in Phare Countries: Survey and Project Proposals*. Pilot-Project on Regional Co-operation in Reforming Higher Education. Paris

OECD, European Commission (1995) *Seminar I: Quality Assurance and Accreditation in Higher Education*. Ljubljana, 9 – 11 March 1994. Pilot-Project on Regional Co-operation in Reforming Higher Education. Paris

OECD, European Commission (1994) *Seminar II: Mobility in Higher Education*. Tallinn, 26 – 28 April 1994. Pilot-Project on Regional Co-operation in Reforming Higher Education. Paris

OECD, European Commission (1995) *Seminar III: Research in Pedagogy*. Costinesti, 18 – 20 May 1994. Pilot-Project on Regional Co-operation in Reforming Higher Education. Paris

OECD, European Commission (1995) *Seminar IV: Professional and Social Competence*. Warsaw, 14 – 16 June 1994. Pilot-Project on Regional Co-operation in Reforming Higher Education. Paris

OECD, European Commission (1995) *Seminar V: Higher Education Policy for Economies in Transition. National Strategies and Future Dimensions for Regional Co-operation*. Bratislava, 7 – 9 September 1994. Pilot-Project on Regional Co-operation in Reforming Higher Education. Paris

OECD (1996) *Reviews of National Policies for Education: Czech Republic*. Paris

OECD (1996) *Reviews of National Policies for Education: Poland*. Paris

Polish Ministry of National Education (1994) *Poland: Education in a Changing Society*. Background Report for the OECD Review. A Short Version. Warsaw

Polish Ministry of National Education, Office for International Programmes (1991) *Higher Education in Poland. TEMPUS Activities*. Warsaw

Polish TEMPUS Office (1994) *Report on the Implementation of the TEMPUS Programme/Phare in the Years 1990/91 – 1993/94*. Warsaw, April

Polish TEMPUS Office (1993) *TEMPUS Joint European Projects, 1990/91 – 1992/93*. Warsaw

Polish TEMPUS Office (1995) *TEMPUS II Joint European Projects*. Warsaw

Romanian TEMPUS Office (1995) *TEMPUS II. Buletin Informativ* No. 4, February

Romanian TEMPUS Office (1994) *Compendium Anul Academic 1993/94 TEMPUS/Phare*. Bucharest

Slovak Ministry of Education, Youth and Sports (1991) *Education in Czecho-Slovakia*. Bratislava

TEMPUS France Bureau National d'Information (1994) *Evaluation du Programme TEMPUS. Les partenariats avec la France*. Paris

10.3 Literature

Amsterdamski, S. and Rhodes, A. (1993) 'Perceptions of Dilemmas of Reform: Remarks and Interpretations Concerning a Study by the Vienna Institute of Human Sciences'. *European Journal of Education* 28, 4, pp. 379 – 402

Bremer, L. (NUFFIC) in cooperation with HIER, TSC, HRTI (1996) *Impact of the TEMPUS Programme on Hungarian Students*. Budapest, The Hague: NUFFIC, HIER, TSC, HRTI September

Centre for Higher Education Studies (1993) *Higher Education in the Czech Republic*. Prague: CHES

Centre for Science Policy and Higher Education, East-West Science Center (1994) *Changes in Higher Education in Central European Countries*. Warsaw, Kassel: Centre for Science Policy and Higher Education, East-West Science Center

Cerych, L. (1993) 'Implementation of Higher Education Reforms in Central/Eastern Europe: Factors of Success and Failure'. Paper presented to the European Cooperation Fund *Workshop on Implementation of Higher Education Reforms in Central/Eastern Europe: Factors of Success and Failure*, Brussels, 29 – 30 April

Cerych, L. and Hendrichová, J. (eds.) (1994) 'Higher Education Reforms in Central and Eastern Europe'. *European Journal of Education* 29, 1

Council of Europe, 'Standing Conference on University Problems (ed.) (1990) East-West Academic Mobility'. Report by Prof. D. Kallen presented at the *European Conference on Our Common Cultural Heritage: A Challenge for East-West University Cooperation*, Hamburg, 3 – 5 October 1990 (DECS/ESR (90) 50)

Council of Europe, Standing Conference on University Problems (ed.) (1992) 'Current Initiatives for East-West Cooperation'. Information and discussion document for the *European Conference Universities and Democratisation*, Warsaw, 29 – 31 January 1992. Council of Europe DECS-HE 92/14

Council of Europe (1995) *Access for Under-Represented Groups. Volume I: Report on Central and Eastern Europe*, prepared by M. Woodrow and D. Crosier. Strasbourg: Council of Europe

Deutscher Akademischer Austauschdienst (1994) *Reader der TEMPUS-Jahrestagung des DAAD an der Universität Gesamthochschule Kassel*, 21./22. Oktober 1993. Bonn, Januar

Deutscher Akademischer Austauschdienst (1992) *Organisation und Verwaltung von Gemeinsamen Europäischen TEMPUS-Projekten*. Tagungsmaterialien. Bonn, May

Finocchietti, G. (1990) Progretti per L'Est. *Universitas* 36, 2, pp. 32 – 36

Hochschulrektorenkonferenz (1994) *Stand und Perspektiven der Zusammenarbeit mit Hochschulen und Wissenschaftseinrichtungen in Estland, Lettland und Litauen*. Materialien zur Hochschulkooperation 1/1994. Bonn, May

Holenda, J. (1994) 'Higher Education Reform in the Czech Republic'. *Higher Education in Europe* XIX, 4, pp. 94 – 99

Hüfner, K. (ed.) (1995) *Higher Education Reform Processes in Central and Eastern Europe*. Frankfurt/M.: Peter Lang

Institut für vergleichende Bildungs- und Hochschulforschung (1995) *Mittel- und Osteuropäische Bildungssysteme. Kurzdarstellungen.* Wien

Institut für vergleichende Bildungs- und Hochschulforschung (1995) *C.E.U.S. Central and East European Education and University Systems*. Informationsbulletin No. 2, Vienna

Institute for Human Sciences (1994) *Issues in Transition 1994*. TERC, Vol. 7, Vienna, October

Institute for Human Sciences (1995) *Western Paradigms and Eastern Agenda: A Reassessment*. TERC, Vol. 8, Vienna, January

Institute for Informatics in Education (1994) *Education in the Czech Republic*. Prague

Institute of International Education (1991) *Raising the Curtain. A Report with Recommendations on Academic Exchanges with East Central Europe and the USSR.* East Central Europe Information Exchange/ Report 1. New York

Kallen, D. (1991) 'Academic Exchange between Central/Eastern and Western Europe – Towards a New Era of Cooperation.' *Higher Education Policy* 4, 3, pp. 52 – 62

Kallen D. (1991) *Workshop on the Development of Higher Education in Central/Eastern Europe and Priorities for Western Assistance*, May 1991. Summary of Discussions

Kehm, B. (1996) 'Schritte in die Selbständigkeit'. *DUZ* 52, 24, pp. 24 – 25

Kovác, L. (1991) *Toward Re-establishment of the Unity of Education and Research in Post-Socialist Countries*. Mimeographed paper, Prague

Koucky, J. (1990) *Czechoslovak Higher Education at the Cross-Roads*. Mimeographed paper, Prague

Kozma, T. (1992) *The Invisible Curtain. Academic Mobility in Central and Eastern Europe*. Paper presented at the ISA Sociology of Education Mid-Term Conference, Amsterdam, 21 – 25 July (mimeo)

Kozma, T. (1990) 'Higher Education in Hungary: Facing the Political transition'. *European Journal of Education* 25, 4, pp. 379 – 390

Kwiatkowski, St. (1990) *Survival through Excellence. On the Polish University Perspectives*. Mimeographed paper, Warsaw, August

Lajos, T. (1990) *On Some Practical Problems of the External Aid for Central and Eastern European Countries*. Mimeographed paper, Budapest, December

Mihailescu, I. and Vlasceanu, L. (1994) 'Higher Education Structures in Romania'. *Higher Education in Europe* XIX, 4, pp. 79 – 93

Reisz, R. D. (1994) Curricular Patterns Before and After the Romanian Revolution. *European Journal of Education* 29, 3, pp. 281 – 290

Roth, O. (1993) *Problems of Contemporary Higher Education Policy in the Czech Republic*. Mimeographed paper, Prague, May

Vereinigung für Internationale Zusammenarbeit (ed.) (1995) *Die neue Dimension. Kulturelle und wissenschaftliche Zusammenarbeit mit Mittel- und Osteuropa*. Bonn

Wilson, L. (1993) 'TEMPUS as an Instrument of Reform'. *European Journal of Education* 28, 4, pp. 429 – 436

Wilson, L. (1993) 'Case Study TEMPUS: One Instrument of External Assistance'. Mimeographed Paper, Brussels

Zalai, E. (1991) 'Universities and Research Institutes under the Academy of Sciences: Current Situation and Perspectives in Hungary'. Mimeographed paper, April